Introduction to the Personal Software Process^{SM}

Watts S. Humphrey
CARNEGIE MELLON UNIVERSITY

▲▲ ADDISON-WESLEY

An imprint of Addison Wesley Longman, Inc.

Reading, Massachusetts • Harlow, England • Menlo Park, California
Berkeley, California • Don Mills, Ontario • Sydney
Bonn • Amsterdam • Tokyo • Mexico City

 **Software Engineering Institute**

The SEI Series in Software Engineering

The Personal Software Process and PSP are service marks of Carnegie Mellon University.

Library of Congress Cataloging–in–Publication Data

Humphrey, Watts S., 1927–
    Introduction to the personal software process / by Watts S.
Humphrey.
        p.   cm. — (SEI series in software engineering)
    Includes bibliographical references and index.
    ISBN 0–201–54809–7
    1. Software engineering.   I. Title. II. Series.
QA76.758.H858 1997
005.1'068'4—dc20   96–31726
                                                CIP

The programs and applications presented in this book have been included for their instructional value. They have been tested with care but are not guaranteed for any particular purpose. The publisher does not offer any warranties or representations, nor does it accept any liabilities with respect to the programs or applications.

Many of the designations used by manufacturers and sellers to distinguish their products are claimed as trademarks. Where those designations appear in this book, and Addison-Wesley was aware of the trademark claim, the designations have been printed in caps or initial caps.

Access the latest information about Addison-Wesley books from our World Wide Web page: http://www.awl.com/cseng

1 2 3 4 5 6 7 8 9 10-CRW-0099989796

FOR BARBARA

My love, my life, my wife

FACULTY FOREWORD

We used a draft version of this book to teach process principles in the first year Computer Science program at Embry-Riddle Aeronautical University. The book provides a subset of the Personal Software Process (PSP)^{SM} elements and activities that a freshman can easily assimilate with the more traditional first-year programming topics. The book also provides the motivation and a structure for introducing students to disciplined personal practices. We have enjoyed using this book and feel it is helping our students to become competent software professionals.

For some years we have been trying to provide our students with realistic software engineering experiences. We have had moderate success with introducing software engineering theory and practice early in the curriculum and adding team projects to some upper division courses. Unfortunately, we have found that when students work on these projects, they do not understand time management, scheduling, and quality management. As industry has found, the ability of engineering teams to develop quality software products efficiently and effectively greatly depends on the ability of the individual engineers. On reflection, the students' problems with time and quality management are not surprising since we had not provided courses that show students how to plan and manage their work. We thus decided to try introducing process concepts at the beginning of the undergraduate curriculum.

We felt that beginning college students could best learn and benefit from time management practices, so we started by introducing this book's Chapter 1 through Chapter 10 materials in CS1. Although all students entering our CS1 course had

^{SM}Personal Software Process and PSP are service marks of Carnegie Mellon University.

some programming experience, they were not yet ready for a formally defined software development process. They first needed exposure to the problems of modern software development before they could truly comprehend the roles and practices of software engineers.

After finishing CS1 and completing their first college semester, students were ready for a more disciplined way to develop programs. We then introduced the PSP process in CS2, using the materials in Chapters 11 thorough 20. Here, the students planned each of their programming projects. Following the defined PSP practices, they used their own historical data to estimate size, effort, and quality (defect projection). They also collected and recorded actual data for each project on a summary report form.

After a year of experience, we have found that the approach of introducing process activities to beginning computer science students can work. What we mean by "can work" is that students can learn how to use the process outlined in the book. They do, eventually, see the value of recording effort, size, and quality data, and they can use these data in planning projects and analyzing their personal effectiveness. Collecting data on their own work gives them a quantitative basis for estimating. They regularly perform structured reviews and they learn to follow defined development phases in their work (e.g., planning, design, coding, compiling, testing, and postmortem). We also feel that delaying the introduction of PSP for another semester (or year) would allow sloppy and undisciplined programming practices to become more entrenched and would make the students more resistant to change.

The PSP has helped the students understand the importance of a disciplined approach to developing software. It also provides a more rigorous foundation for later introducing more advanced individual and team topics. For the most part, student data are accurate, but one must be careful to analyze and reject suspicious data. Unfortunately, the students did not become better at scheduling their work. Many still put off assignments until near their due date—a perennial beginning programmer problem.

Not surprisingly, we discovered that the success of the PSP approach was highly dependent upon our ability to motivate students to learn and practice these concepts. We used the ideas and arguments in this book to encourage a positive view of process methods. We found that providing the class with regular feedback and analysis of class data stimulated students' interest in looking more closely at their personal data. Inviting industry professionals to discuss their process experiences with the class was also very helpful.

There were some problems at first in teaching the new courses. Initially, we did not sufficiently integrate the PSP materials with the rest of the CS1 and CS2 courses. The students thus had trouble relating the time management activities to their programming work. We also failed to provide sufficient feedback of class aggregate data.

An interesting and beneficial side effect of the PSP is the large supply of data available to the teacher. In CS1 we get weekly activity reports on how students spend their time in the course. In CS2 we get a PSP summary on each programming project that provides size, effort, and defect data. These data often provoke discussion about the methods taught in the course and how they affect programmer productivity and program quality. The PSP provides a quantitative basis for detailed analysis and discussion of such questions.

We are continuing to teach the PSP in the freshman year of our program. We also require students who have completed CS1 and CS2 to use the PSP in the Data Structures and Algorithms course that follows CS2. We believe this will better prepare them for the more complex team projects they will face in their junior and senior years. We also plan to guide students in extending and enhancing the PSP for their subsequent courses.

We have found this book helpful in introducing our students to professional software disciplines and hope that other students and teachers using this book will experience similar benefits.

Thomas B. Hilburn, Aboalfazl Salimi, Massood Towhidnejad
Embry-Riddle Aeronautical University

STUDENT FOREWORD

After we finished the PSP course in our freshman year, a couple of the faculty at Embry-Riddle Aeronautical University asked if we would like to collaborate on writing a foreword to the finished textbook. We agreed. Since we were not sure how to write a foreword, they suggested that we merely answer some questions. Here are the questions and our answers:

1. What type of tasks did you do in the PSP course?

   We kept track of all the time we spent on programming assignments and projects. There was a lot of paperwork to keep track of. We also kept track of program size and defects and used the data we collected to estimate time, size, and defects on future projects.

2. How did it work? How did this material fit with the material in the other freshman courses?

   It fit well into the course work, and having an estimate helped provide confidence in what you were doing.

   At the beginning it looks like the PSP work is a hindrance to the other course work, but once you get to the end of the course, you realize that these activities actually help you complete your work. You go through the course and keep asking yourself, "Why am I doing this?," but later you start to see that having an estimate of what it is going to take you to complete a program actually helps you.

   It is very important not to fudge the data (times) because then the data you collect are not as helpful.

3. What did you learn?

In addition to what we have already talked about, you learn how you can use your time more efficiently and do some work before you get to the computer. You end up doing a lot of work on paper before you get to the computer.

You also learn about your mistakes and other people's mistakes (through examples and discussions). It also helps you keep your programming organized (since you do work on paper before you get to the computer). The PSP is also something that can be used in other activities (not only in software development), although the forms need to be modified.

4. What would you recommend to other students who will use the PSP in the future?

Do it right. Don't fudge it. Follow instructions. Try to understand the big picture and understand the concepts. Don't let the paperwork get to you; it will pay off.

Ben Bishop, Andrew Henderson, Michael Patrick
Embry-Riddle Aeronautical University

PREFACE

If you are studying to be a software engineer, this book is designed for you. It describes the methods many experienced engineers use to do competent work and it provides exercises to help you learn these methods. Each chapter describes a single topic in which you will become skilled as you practice the homework exercises. Completed examples of each exercise will help you to check your work.

Why I Wrote This Book

Developing software products involves more than just stringing programming instructions together and getting them to run on a computer. It requires meeting customer requirements at an agreed cost and schedule. To be successful, software engineers need to consistently produce high-quality programs on schedule and at their planned costs. This book shows you how to do this. It introduces the Personal Software Process (PSP), which is a guide to using disciplined personal practices to do superior software engineering.

The PSP will show you how to plan and track your work and how to consistently produce high-quality software. Using PSP will also give you data that show the effectiveness of your work and identify your strengths and weaknesses. This tool is like the stop-watch and distance measures you need to test yourself on joining a track team and deciding which events to try for. To make an intelligent decision, you would need such measures to know where you excel and where you need to improve. Like a track team, software engineering has many specialties, and engineers have widely varying skills and talents. To have a successful and rewarding career, you need to know your skills and abilities, strive to improve them, and capitalize on your unique talents in the work you do. The PSP will help you do this.

Using the PSP

By using the PSP, you will be practicing the skills and methods professional software engineers have developed through many years of trial and error. Building on the experiences of your predecessors will help you to learn more quickly and avoid repeating their errors. The essence of being a professional is understanding what others have done before you and building on their experiences.

How Students Will Benefit

While the PSP is now generally introduced in graduate software engineering programs, its principles can be learned and practiced by beginning students. This book is designed to introduce the PSP methods in gradual steps as you do your other course work. As you read each chapter, do the exercises at the end. These show how to manage your time, how to plan and track your work, and how to consistently produce high-quality programs.

Since it takes time to develop effective skills and habits, you should practice the PSP methods with every software assignment. If you do this, you will have learned, practiced, and perfected these skills before you need them in software engineering work.

How Working Engineers Can Use This Book

Practicing software engineers can also use this book to learn the rudiments of the PSP. I suggest that you work through the exercises from the beginning of the book to the end, using them as guides for improving the way you do your regular work. Practice each exercise until it feels natural, then read the next chapter and add its methods. Again, practice both the new and the already learned methods before advancing to the next step. The key is to take the time to master one method before progressing to the next.

With some dedication and discipline, you should have no trouble mastering this material by yourself. Success is more likely, however, if you do this work in a class or with a group of co-workers with whom you can exchange experiences and share ideas. In any case, plan to spend about an hour or two each week studying the textbook, recording and analyzing your PSP data, and adapting the PSP methods to your work. Although the time you need to learn the PSP will depend on your current habits and practices, once you have completed this material, you will have a sound foundation for continued professional development. Note, however, that the key to learning the PSP is to look at and think about the data on your work and what these data tell you about your personal performance.

Some Suggestions for Instructors

This book is designed as a companion text for traditional two-semester computer science or software engineering courses. It makes no assumptions beyond a college preparatory education. The book presents the PSP in steps that students can use with their regular course work. The exercises in the first ten chapters are quite general and can be used with programming or nonprogramming work. The exercises in the final ten chapters are designed for use with about six to eight or more small programming exercises.

Although some students first learn to program in college, many now learn basic programming in high school. This material is thus designed for use in either a first programming course or a more advanced course. Whether the students already know how to program or are just learning, they should readily understand the material and find it immediately helpful.

This material is an introduction to the PSP and not a replacement for it. The book does not, for instance, cover the statistical techniques needed for accurate estimating or data analysis. It also does not cover the methods for scaling up the PSP for larger projects or the process definition and improvement techniques used in applying the PSP to tasks other than writing small programs. The full PSP should thus be taught at a later point in the student's educational program.[1]

As you lead students through the material of this book and they complete the assignments, they will learn to track and monitor their work, to manage their time, and to make plans. In the second semester, they will learn about program quality and ways to do reviews and use various quality measurement and management methods. They will also learn about defects, their causes, and the engineers' personal responsibility for the quality of the products they produce. At the end of the two-semester course, the students will have learned the rudiments of the PSP. To build on this foundation and to give them added experience with

---

[1]The PSP and the PSP course are described in more detail in my textbook *A Discipline for Software Engineering* (Reading, MA: Addison-Wesley, 1995). The textbook support materials include an instructor's guide and an instructor's diskette with lecture overheads and assignment materials.

these methods, later courses should require the students to continue using the PSP.

A Teaching Strategy

Since this book is meant to be used in conjunction with a two-semester introductory computer science or software engineering course, its material is divided into a first semester that covers time management (10 chapters) and a second semester that covers quality. Teaching this material takes about six lecture hours spread over the two semesters. Since the students use PSP methods while doing their currently required course work, this material does not add significantly to student workload. Any additional time students spend learning these methods is very likely compensated for by the efficiency they gain.

As you progress through the textbook, assign the exercises at the back of each chapter. Experience has shown that it is best to cover the first 10 chapters in the first few weeks of the first semester. The students then have the rest of the semester to practice the methods introduced. The second semester should follow the same strategy of introducing the PSP topics in the first few semester weeks and then using these methods during the balance of the semester.

It is crucial to present this material as an integral part of the course. Explain that these are essential software engineering methods that the students must learn and practice to satisfactorily complete the course. As you assign each exercise, explain that the students' grades will depend both on the quality of their work and on how well they apply the PSP methods. They must do each PSP exercise and then continue to use each PSP method after it is first introduced. The course strategy, suggested lecture contents, and assignment kits are included in the instructor's guide and support materials described on the last page of this text.

Instructor Preparation

In teaching this course, you will find it helpful to have used these methods yourself. You could, for example, use the planning and time management methods to prepare the class lectures or grade homework. After you have personally used the PSP, you will better appreciate the personal discipline required. This background will help you explain the PSP to the students and guide them in its use. When they find that you have used the PSP, they are more likely to use it themselves.

Acknowledgments

In writing this book I am especially indebted to the Computer Science faculty of Embry-Riddle Aeronautical University. They encouraged me to develop this textbook and they kindly reviewed the manuscript. Because they have both taught several freshman classes and used the PSP methods themselves, they made many helpful suggestions. For their support and encouragement, I particularly thank professors Tom Hilburn, Iraj Hirmanpour, Aboalfazl Salimi, Davie Srachet, and Massood Towhidnejad. I also thank three of their students, Ben Bishop, Guillermo José Hernandez, and Richard Rickert, for sharing their course data and class experiences with me. In addition, I thank Ben Bishop, Andrew Henderson, and Michael Patrick for very kindly describing their experiences with this material in the Student Foreword.

Several friends and associates at the SEI and elsewhere have kindly reviewed the manuscript and offered helpful suggestions and comments. I am grateful to Steve Burke, Howie Dow, John Eikenberry, Andy Huber, Julia Mullaney, Glenn Rosander, Marie Silverthorn, and Bob Stoddard. My secretary Marlene MacDonald has been a great help in reading and commenting on parts of the manuscript and in helping with manuscript distribution and review. I also thank Peter Gordon, Helen Goldstein, and the professional staff at Addison-Wesley for their helpful support in getting this book into print.

Finally, I am blessed with a wonderful wife. Barbara has provided much needed help and encouragement through yet another book. As she has with all my other books, she has read the final manuscript before I submitted it for publication. In spite of all this help and support, I am certain that neither Barbara nor my many helpful associates could have found all my oversights and mistakes. The remaining errors are entirely my own.

Watts S. Humphrey   *Sarasota, Florida*

CONTENTS

1

The Software Engineer's Job

Besides describing the software engineering job and some of its key activities, this chapter also gives an overview of this book's strategy to help you develop and improve your software engineering skills. The chapter concludes with an assignment to list the principal tasks you will be doing as you work through this book.

1.1   What Is Software Engineering?

The job of a software engineer is to deliver high-quality software products at agreed cost and schedule. There are thus three aspects to doing an effective software engineering job: producing quality products, doing the work for the expected costs, and completing the work on the agreed schedule. Through years of sometimes painful experience, many software engineers have learned that, to do an effective job, they need to:

1. plan their work,
2. do their work according to this plan,
3. and strive to produce the highest quality products.

The principal objective of this book is to show you how to do this.

1.2   Why Is Good Engineering Important?

Historically, few software organizations have reliably met their cost and schedule commitments. This poor record has not only given software engineering a bad name, it has also caused serious business problems. There are many examples of business failures, contract disputes, lawsuits, and customer inconvenience. A multi-billion-dollar FAA air traffic control project more than doubled in cost and was repeatedly delayed largely due to software problems. Ashton Tate, a major software firm, went out of business because of poor quality software. Defective software has even killed people [Leveson].

Computer software is now critical to many businesses. It runs most modern factories, handles the daily international transfer of trillions of dollars, and is a key element in just about every product and service modern human beings use. As the business significance of software increases, the effectiveness of software engineering groups becomes progressively more important. In consequence, your most important single asset as a working engineer will be your ability to consistently meet your commitments with quality products.

1.3   The Personal Software Process

The Personal Software Process (PSP)^{SM} was designed to help software engineers do good work. It shows them how to apply advanced engineering methods to their daily tasks. It provides detailed estimating and planning methods, shows engineers how to track their performance against these plans, and explains how defined processes can guide their work.

The full Personal Software Process is taught with a 15-lecture graduate university course in which students practice the PSP methods while they complete 10 programming exercises as well as 5 analysis exercises. These help them understand how the PSP works for them. The PSP has been taught in a large number of universities and is being introduced by many industrial organizations. Course data on thousands of PSP class programs show that the PSP is effective in improving engineers' planning performance and the quality of the products they produce.

The PSP is also effective in industrial software work. In one case, before learning the PSP, a group of three engineers took an average of five times longer than they had estimated to develop three components of a software system. After PSP training, the same engineers completed the next six components of the same product in 10.4% less time than they had planned. When measured in customer-

[SM]The Personal Software Process and PSP are service marks of Carnegie Mellon University.

found defects, the quality of the components they finished after PSP training was five times better than the quality of the earlier program components.

Each chapter of this book introduces a PSP method you should apply in your subsequent work. Using it will show you how the method works and give you practice in applying it.

It takes considerable effort and perseverance to consistently apply PSP methods, but that is the only way to learn them. The course lectures and textbook are important, but the principal learning vehicle is the data you gather on your own work as you complete each PSP exercise. It is important to keep these data so you can later see how the PSP has improved your performance.

1.4   The Discipline of High-Quality Work

Discipline is defined as an activity or exercise that develops or improves skill. Contrary to the popular view of discipline as an onerous constraint, it is a framework for learning and personal improvement. The discipline of the PSP provides a structured framework for developing the personal skills and methods you will need as a software engineer. The question is not whether you need personal skills but how long it takes you to develop them and how consistently you use them. The discipline of the PSP will accelerate your learning.

Professionals in many other fields learn and practice the skills and methods of their professions during their formal education. Chemists learn to handle laboratory equipment and to make precise analyses. Before they can practice surgery, medical interns observe and practice under experienced surgeons. No one would dream of having them learn about hygiene, infection, or operating-room procedures on the job. Airline pilots are highly qualified before their first commercial flights, and musicians spend years in training before their debuts. Thus, in other fields, professionals demonstrate basic competence before they are permitted to do even the simplest procedures, while in software, engineers without PSP training must learn the skills they need on the job. This is not only expensive and time consuming, but increasingly risky.

1.5   The Importance of High-Quality Work

As a practicing software engineer, you will likely develop parts of large products or systems. No matter how small your piece of the overall product or how seemingly unimportant, any defects in it could potentially damage the entire system. Not only is the quality of a software system generally governed by the quality of its parts, but even trivial mistakes in support programs can have devastating consequences.

Modern computing systems can execute millions of instructions per second. Thus an unusual defect that might happen only once in a billion times can occur several times a day. With software, unusual conditions come up all the time; seemingly impossible conditions take a little longer. Defects in even minor elements of large systems can cause unpredictable and occasionally severe problems. If you make a trivial mistake that leaves a defect in the product, the result can be major user inconvenience or even physical damage.

To produce quality software systems, every engineer must learn to do quality work. If you do learn to consistently produce high-quality programs, you and your products will be highly valued by your employers and by your customers.

1.6   How to Improve the Quality of Your Work

When I was in the U.S. Navy I had to learn to shoot a machine gun. Training started with shotguns and clay pigeons. My scores were terrible and they didn't improve, even with practice. After watching me for a while, the instructor suggested that I try shooting left-handed. Being right-handed, I found this unnatural at first, but after a few trial shots, I consistently got near-perfect scores.

There are several parts to this example. First, measurements are needed to diagnose a problem. By knowing how many clay pigeons I hit and missed, the instructor and I could easily see that I had to do something differently. Next, we had to use these measurements in some kind of objective analysis. By watching me, the instructor could analyze the process I used to shoot the shotgun—the steps I followed in loading, positioning, tracking, aiming, and firing the gun. The instructor's objective was to discover which steps were the source of my problem. He quickly zeroed in on aim and suggested that I make a change.

Finally, and most important, came the change itself. Process improvement is difficult because people are reluctant to try new things. Their current habits seem so natural they can't believe the change would help. I had always been right-handed and it never occurred to me to shoot with the left. Once I made the suggested change, however, my scores improved.

Defining measures is not always easy, but it is almost always possible. This book defines several software process measures. Once you have defined measures for your work, you must gather and analyze data. If you need to improve, you next analyze the process to see where to make changes. Finally, to improve, you must actually change what you do.

If I hadn't changed my process, I could have kept score for years without becoming a better shot. Measuring alone will not produce improvement, and neither will trying harder. How you work largely determines the results you get. If you continue working the same old way, you will continue producing the same old results.

1.7   The Improvement Process

The steps needed to change the way you work are the same as the steps I followed in learning to shoot clay pigeons. They are not complicated. The improvement process is charted in Figure 1.1.

☐ Define the quality goal. Obviously, my objective was to hit the target as often as I could, 100% being the ultimate goal.

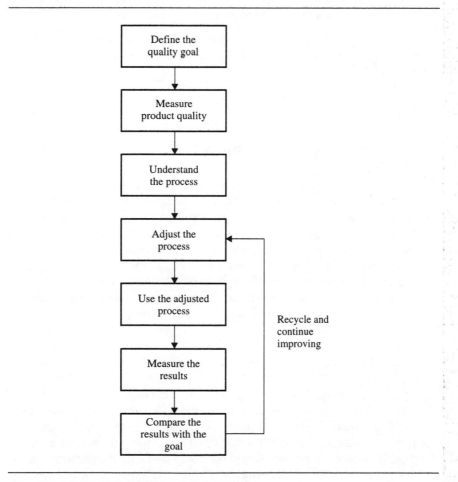

FIGURE 1.1 THE IMPROVEMENT PROCESS

□ Measure product quality. The instructor and I could see that my scores were terrible and that something had to be done.

□ Understand the process. The instructor observed what I did to see what I should change.

□ Adjust the process. He suggested that I shoot left-handed.

□ Use the adjusted process. I next shot several more rounds, but this time I shot left-handed.

□ Measure the results. We counted the number of pigeons I hit and missed.

□ Compare the results with the goal. From these data, we could see that my scores were dramatically better.

□ Recycle and continue improving. Because learning to shoot clay pigeons was simple, continuous process improvement was not needed.

With more complex processes, several cycles are generally required. With a sophisticated process like software development, the improvement cycles should never end.

1.8   The Strategy of This Book

This book introduces some key software engineering methods, one at a time. These methods are all important, but they must be taught in some order. It is a little like explaining to someone how to swim. You may talk about breathing, kicking, floating, and arm strokes as individual activities, but you have to put them all together to actually swim. You will generally teach breathing first, but the order in which you explain the rest doesn't make much difference. You must, however, cover them all. In any event, until you do them all, you cannot swim. With this book, we are more fortunate. Most of these methods can be used independently and they will each help you in some way. They do, however, reinforce each other. Therefore until you use them all, you will not get the full benefit of a disciplined software engineering process. Just as you must first learn to breathe in the water before you can swim, in disciplined software engineering you must start by gathering data.

The strategy of this book is to introduce you to the improvement process steps shown in Figure 1.1. While the order is not critical, I have chosen to present this material in two parts. The book's first 10 chapters deal with planning and time management—the planning process. The last 10 chapters deal with product quality—the defect-management process. It is important to deal with the planning process first because it provides a solid foundation for the defect-management process.

1.9   Summary

Software engineers should plan their work, then do it according to that plan. The result will be high-quality products within budget and on time. The Personal Software Process (PSP) is a framework designed to teach software engineers to do better work. It shows you how to estimate and plan your work, how to track your performance against these plans, and how to improve the quality of the programs you produce.

Quality methods take time to learn and practice, but they will help you in your engineering career. To consistently improve the quality of your work, you must establish goals, measure product quality, understand the process, change and reuse the process, measure and analyze the results, and finally recycle and continue improving.

The strategy in this book is to show you how to schedule and plan your work and how to manage the quality of the programs you produce. The first steps in understanding your process are to identify the tasks you do, estimate how much time you will spend on each task, and measure the time you spend.

1.10   Assignment 1

The first step in understanding your process is to identify the tasks you do. For example, as a student, you will attend classes, write programs, read the textbook, and do various other homework tasks. At some point, you will need to study for exams. As part of doing your homework, you will also write programs. One way to de-

TABLE 1.1 EXAMPLE COURSE TASKS

Engineer _____ Student X _____ Date   _9/9/96_

Task	Frequency	Time (minutes)
Attend classes	M, W, F	180/week
Read textbook	Weekly	180/week
Homework	Weekly	420/week
Write programs	Weekly	420/week
Prepare for exams	Once a semester	300/semester
Review notes	During homework, study	Included in other times

scribe these tasks would be in the tabular format in Table 1.1. Here, Student X expected to spend about 1200 minutes on his weekly tasks and another 300 minutes once in the semester studying for exams. This is a total of 20 hours each week and another 5 hours studying for exams.

For the first assignment, define your principal activities for this course and list them on a form like those in Table 1.1. After you have made this listing, estimate the frequency of these tasks and how much time you expect to spend on each. For weekly tasks, estimate the time you will spend each week. and for the monthly or semester tasks, estimate the monthly or semester times. This assignment does not require that you measure these times. An estimate is adequate. Make and keep a copy of this listing before you turn in your homework. Also, be sure to put your name and date on the form.

Reference

[Leveson] Leveson, Nancy G. *Safeware, System Safety and Computers.* Reading, MA: Addison-Wesley, 1995.

2

Time Management

This chapter shows you how to manage your time and explains why it is important to do so. It also describes how and why to use an engineering notebook. For the chapter assignment, you will make an engineering notebook to use in your work.

2.1 The Logic of Time Management

The logical basis for time management is as follows.

You will likely spend your time this week much the way you spent time last week. In general, the way you spent your time last week provides a fair approximation of the way you will spend time in future weeks. There are, however, many exceptions. During exam week, for example, you may not attend the same classes and you will probably spend more time studying and less time doing homework.

To make realistic plans, you have to track the way you spend time. While you may think you know how you spent time last week, you would probably be surprised by actual data. People remember some things and forget others. For example, the time spent doing homework is probably much less than estimated, while the time at meals or relaxing with friends is often much more than expected. Our memories tend to minimize the time we spend on things that seem to move quickly because we enjoy doing them. Conversely, slow-paced, boring, or difficult activities seem to take much longer than the reality. Therefore, to know where your time goes, you need to keep an accurate record.

To check the accuracy of your time estimates and plans, you must document them and later compare them with what you actually do. While this will not be a serious problem in school, it is critically important for working engineers. Planning is a skill that few people have mastered. There are, however, known planning methods that can be learned and practiced. The first step in learning to make *good* plans is to make plans. Then write down your plan so you will later have something to compare with your actual data.

To make more accurate plans, determine where your previous plans were in error and what you could have done better. When you do the planned job, record the time you spend. These time data will be most useful if noted in some detail. For example, when doing course work, separately record the time you spend attending class, reading the textbook, writing programs, and studying for exams. When writing larger programs, you will similarly find it helpful to record the time for various parts of the job—designing the program, writing code, compiling, and testing. While this level of detail is not needed for very short tasks, it can be helpful when working on projects that take several hours or more.

When you have a documented copy of your plan and have recorded the actual time you spent, you can easily compare the actual results with the original plan. You will then see where the plan was in error and how your planning process can be improved. The key to accurate planning is to consistently make plans and compare them each time with subsequent actual results. You will then see how to make better plans.

To manage your time, plan your time and then follow the plan. Figuring out what you could do to produce better plans is the easy part. Actually doing it is far more difficult. The world is full of resolutions that are never fulfilled, like sticking with a diet or quitting smoking.

Initially, following a plan is likely to be difficult. While there are many possible reasons, the most common is that the plan was not very good. Until you try to follow it, you probably will not know that. By working to the plan, you gain the first of two benefits: You learn where the plan was in error, which will help you better plan the next project.

The second benefit of working to the plan is that you will do the job the way you planned to. While this may not seem terribly important, it is. Many of the

problems in software engineering are caused by ill-considered shortcuts, careless-
ness, and inattention to detail. In most cases, the proper methods were known and
specified but just not followed. Learning to establish usable plans is thus important, but learning to follow these plans is absolutely crucial.

Another and more subtle benefit of working to a plan is that it actually changes
your behavior. With a plan, you are less likely to waste time deciding what to do
next. The plan also helps you focus on what you are doing. You are less likely to be
distracted and more likely to be efficient.

2.2   Understanding How You Spend Time

To practice time management, the first step is to understand how you now spend
time. This calls for several steps:

Categorize your major activities.   When you start tracking time, you will probably find that most of the time is spent on relatively few activities. This is normal.
To accomplish anything, we must focus on the few things that are most important.
If you break your time into too many categories, it will be hard to make sense of
the data. Three to five categories should be enough for tracking time for one
course. If you later need more detail, break the more general categories into subcategories.

Record the time spent on each major activity.   It takes a fair amount of personal
discipline to consistently record time. To keep an accurate record, record the time
at the start and end of every major work category. At first you will often forget to
do this, but after some practice it will become second nature. Chapter 3 discusses
recording time in more detail.

Record time in a standard way.   Standardizing your time log is necessary because
the volume of time data will grow very quickly. If you don't record and carefully
store these data, they will get lost or disorganized. Messy or confused data are also
hard to find or interpret. If you don't intend to handle the data properly, you might
as well not gather the data at all. Chapter 3 describes the standard Time Recording Log used for gathering PSP time data.

Keep the time data in a convenient place.   Because you will need to keep the time
recording log with you whenever working on this course, keep it in a convenient
place. This is one of the principal uses for the engineering notebook.

2.3   The Engineering Notebook

In this course, you will use an engineering notebook to track time. You will also use it for other things such as recording assignments, tracking commitments, making class notes, and as a workbook for design ideas and calculations.

As a software professional, you will also have many uses for an engineering notebook, such as keeping a time log, entering calculations, and making design notes. You could even use it as evidence that you followed sound engineering practices, important evidence for the defense of your organization if it ever has to defend a product liability lawsuit. When injured parties sue a company, their principal objective is to show that the supplier was negligent. For the company, the best defense is evidence that the engineers followed sound engineering practices. For this reason keeping an engineering notebook is a good habit.

An additional use for engineering notebooks is in protecting your employer's intellectual assets, for example by recording patentable ideas. Once, in a design meeting, my colleagues and I came up with what we thought would be a patentable idea. We wrote the idea out in my engineering notebook and all signed every page. The patent attorney told us this would be helpful in establishing the invention date. We were, in fact, later issued a U.S. patent on the invention. The company also gave us each a cash award.

While these issues will not likely concern you as a student, this course is about learning the methods and establishing the habits that you will need as a practicing engineer. That is why you should make your own engineering notebook now and get in the habit of using it.

2.4   The Notebook Design

The particular notebook design is not critical, but general industrial practice is to use spiral binders. If you number every page, the spiral design will both keep the pages in order and provide a legally useful record of your work. The disadvantages, of course, are that you will have to record your notes in chronological order and you cannot easily insert and remove pages.

A suggested layout for the cover of your engineering notebook is shown in Table 2.1. At the top, you should label the notebook with a notebook number. After you have kept engineering notebooks for a few years, you will accumulate quite a few of them. Numbering the notebooks will make it convenient to store them in chronological order. Also, label each notebook with your name and phone number

TABLE 2.1 ENGINEERING NOTEBOOK SAMPLE COVER

<table>
<tr><td style="text-align:right" colspan="2">Notebook Number: __1__</td></tr>
<tr><td colspan="2" style="text-align:center">

Engineering Notebook
Company or University Name

</td></tr>
<tr><td>Engineer's Name</td><td>_____<u>Jane Doe</u>_____</td></tr>
<tr><td>Phone/e-mail</td><td>_____<u>jd@db.xyz.edu</u>_____</td></tr>
<tr><td>First Date <u>9/9/96</u></td><td>Last Date _____</td></tr>
</table>

or e-mail address. Next, list the first date when you made an entry in the notebook and, when you have completely filled the notebook, enter the date of the last entry.

Inside the notebook, number each page, setting aside the first two notebook pages for a brief table of contents. In the contents, list any special items you may later wish to find, such as course assignments. This will save you the trouble of searching through the entire notebook. There is no need to record the contents for pages you don't expect to reference in the future.

2.5   Engineering Notebook Examples

A sample engineering notebook contents page is shown in Table 2.2. For material you think might be needed in the future, list on the left the notebook page number followed by a brief description of the subject. For example, the student recorded on page 3 all the CS1 assignments for two weeks. The contents also show that the assignment listing continued on page 11. A partial example notebook page 3 is shown in Table 2.3.

The contents also show that between 9/9 and 9/13, the student took class notes on pages 4, 5, 6, and 7. She then continued taking notes on page 10. Whenever you have to skip some pages because of other entries, it is a good idea to note on the bottom of the page where that topic is continued. See, for example, the last line on Table 2.3.

2.6   Summary

To manage your time effectively, you need to plan your time and then follow the plan. To make realistic plans you will first have to track the way you spend time. Then you must document your plans and compare them with what you actually do. To improve planning accuracy, determine where the previous plan was in error and what you could have done to make a better plan.

The first step in planning and managing time is to understand how you spend time now. To do this, you need to classify your activities into major categories; then, in a standard way, record the time spent doing each activity. To keep these data in a convenient place, use an engineering notebook. In this course you will also use this notebook for recording assignments and taking notes and also as a workbook for design ideas and miscellaneous calculations.

TABLE 2.2 ENGINEERING NOTEBOOK SAMPLE CONTENTS PAGE

Engineering Notebook Contents		1
Page	**Subject**	**Dates**
3	CS1 assignments	9/9–16
4	CS1 notes, lectures 1, 2, 3, 4	9/9–13
8	Design notes, 1st program	9/11
9	Phone calls, etc.	9/11
10	CS1 notes (cont.), lectures 4,	9/13–
11	CS1 assignments (continued)	9/23–

TABLE 2.3 AN EXAMPLE ENGINEERING NOTEBOOK PAGE

Date	3
9/9	CS1 assignment, due 9/16
	make an engineering notebook
	reference, page 206, textbook
	read programming text, chapter 1
9/11	CS1 assignment, due 9/20
	do programming exercises, chapter 1
9/13	CS1 assignment due 9/23
	read programming text chapter 2
	review the exercises in chapter 2 and prepare for quiz
9/16	CS1 assignment, due 9/23
	complete a time log on time
	use the Time Recording Log
	put log pages at back of engineering notebook
	see textbook chapter 3 for examples
	(assignments continued on page 11)

2.7   Assignment 2

Make an engineering notebook for the work you will do in this course. The cover should include the items described in Section 2.4, and its table of contents should include at least one entry for the course assignments or work commitments for the current week. Show the notebook to the instructor at the next lecture. Thereafter, the instructor may occasionally ask you to turn in the engineering notebook for review. Note that this is an optional assignment. You need not do it unless requested to by your instructor.

3

Tracking Time

This chapter describes a procedure and a form for tracking and recording the way you spend time. It also gives examples of the kinds of time records to keep. For the assignment, you will establish and use a Time Recording Log.

3.1 Why Track Time?

As described in Chapter 1, the way to improve the quality of your work is to start by understanding what you currently do. This means you have to know the tasks you do, how you do them, and the results you get. The first step in this process is to define the tasks and find out how much time you spend on each. To do this, you must actually measure the time. This chapter describes how to measure time and it introduces a form to help you do it.

My experience writing an earlier book demonstrates what this can do for you. In planning to write *A Discipline for Software Engineering,* I had reviewed my data on previous books and found I had spent an average of 26 hours per week on writing. This seemed like a lot of time because I was working a full schedule and could only spend evenings and weekends on writing. I thus decided to plan on 20 hours a week when writing the new book. At this rate, I would finish the manuscript the following January.

After working on the new book for about a month, I found that the job was much more difficult than I had anticipated. On reviewing my data, I found each chapter was taking more time than planned. Also, instead of 20 hours per week, I was actually spending more than 30 hours. Even though the job was bigger than I had expected, my time log data enabled me to project that I would finish the manuscript four months ahead of the original plan. That is when I actually did finish.

Even if you don't expect to write many books, you will find it much easier to control the amount of time you spend on any project than to increase your productivity. When people say they are working harder, they really mean they are working more hours. Unless you know how much time you are actually spending, you will not be able to manage the way you spend it.

3.2   Recording Time Data

When recording time, remember that the objective is to obtain data on how you actually work. The format and procedure used to gather the data are not important as long as the data are accurate and complete. I personally use the method described in this chapter and have taught it in courses with many students. I have also taught this approach to many working engineers who have used the methods with considerable success. After they get over their natural resistance to using forms and procedures, most engineers find the methods both simple and convenient. You probably will as well.

As you work through this book, use the methods described in this chapter for recording time. You may wonder: "Why should I use this form? Why not design my own form?" The answers are:

□ In a class, it would be impractical to have each student use a different form or method.

□ Without prior data-gathering experience, it would be difficult for you to devise a workable personal form and procedure.

□ After completing this course, you will have the knowledge and experience to modify the forms and procedures to suit yourself.

In other words, use the methods described here. Then, after you have tried using these methods in this course, feel free to change them or design something entirely new. No matter what form you use, however, if you want to manage your time you must continue to track it.

___

3.3 Tracking Your Time

When people talk generally about what they do, they often use hours as the measure. This, it turns out, is not very useful. The reason is that you will rarely do anything for a full hour. For example, Figure 3.1 shows a summary of times Student 7 took in a recent course to write some relatively small programming exercises. These exercises took an average of four to six hours each, and the students were required to track when they started and stopped their work. As you can see, about 90% of Student 7's work periods were less than an hour long.

The typical amount of uninterrupted time engineers spend on tasks is generally less than an hour. Measuring work in units of hours thus will not provide the detail needed to later plan and manage your work. It is also much easier to track time in minutes than in fractions of an hour. Consider, for example, what the time records would look like if you used fractions of an hour. The entries would have numbers like 0.38 hours or 1.27 hours. While units of hours might be more useful in weekly or monthly summaries, these fractional amounts are both difficult to calculate and hard to interpret. Instead of 0.38 hours, for example, 23 minutes is eas-

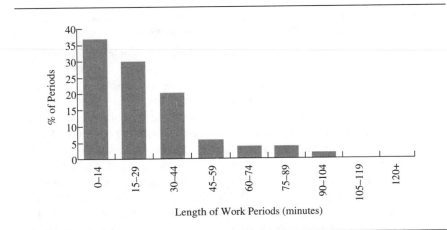

FIGURE 3.1 STUDENT WORK PERIODS

ier to understand and to record. Once you decide to track time, it is no more difficult to track it in minutes than in hours.

3.4   Use a Standard Time Recording Log

The form used for recording time is shown in Table 3.1. The top of the form is
called the header and it has spaces for your name, the date you complete the
header information, the instructor's name, and the class name or number. The
columns in the body of the form are for recording the time data. Each time period
is entered on one line of the form as follows:

□ Date. The date you did some activity, like attending a lecture or writing a program.

□ Start. The time you started the activity.

□ Stop. The time you stopped the activity.

□ Interruption. Any time lost due to interruptions (see next section).

□ Delta time. The time spent on the activity, in minutes, between the start and
stop times, less any interruption time.

□ Activity. A descriptive name for the task.

□ Comments. A more complete note on what you were doing, the type of interruption, or anything else that would be helpful when you later analyze the
time data. Again, see the next section on interruptions.

□ C (Completed): Check this column when you complete a task, like reading a
textbook chapter or writing a program (Section 3.6).

□ U (Units). The number of units in a task when you complete it (Section 3.6).

An example of how the Time Recording Log is completed is shown in
Table 3.2. Here, Student Y first entered her name and the date she started to fill
in the form. She also entered the instructor's name and the course name or number. When she started to keep time records on September 9, she recorded that
date on the top line in the body of the form and made the first entry at the left.
Her first activity was to attend a CS1 class lecture at 9:00 A.M. The class lasted
until 9:50, or a total of 50 minutes. The student then entered 9:00 in the Start column, 9:50 in the Stop column, and the 50 minutes duration in the Delta Time
column. At right, she entered the name of the activity in the column labeled Activity. Finally, in the Comments column, she noted what she was doing. As Student Y continued through the day, she noted her other activities for the CS1
course in the time log.

TABLE 3.1 TIME RECORDING LOG

Student ——————————————————   Date ————————————————

Instructor ——————————————————   Class ——————————————

Date	Start	Stop	Interruption Time	Delta Time	Activity	Comments	C	U

TABLE 3.2 TIME RECORDING LOG EXAMPLE

Student _Student Y_ _____   Date _9/9/96_ _____

Instructor _Mr. Z_ _____   Class _____ _CS1_ _____

Date	Start	Stop	Interruption Time	Delta Time	Activity	Comments	C	U
9/9	9:00	9:50		50	Class	Lecture		
	12:40	1:18		38	Prog.	Assignment 1		
	2:45	3:53	10	58	Prog.	Assignment 1		
	6:25	7:45		80	Text	Read text - Ch 1&2	X	2
9/10	11:06	12:19	6+5	62	Prog.	Assignment 1, break, chat	X	1
9/11	9:00	9:50		50	Class	Lecture		
	1:15	2:35	3+8	69	Prog.	Assignment 2, break, phone	X	1
	4:18	5:11	25	28	Text	Text Ch 3, Chat with Mary	X	1
9/12	6:42	9:04	10+6+12	114	Prog.	Assignment 3	X	1
9/13	9:00	9:50		50	Class	Lecture		
	12:38	1:16		38	Text	Text Ch 4		
9/14	9:15	11:59	5+3+22	134	Review	Quiz prep, break, phone, chat		

Recording time in this way means you will have to keep track of the time. If you don't have a watch, you would be wise to get one.

3.5 Handling Interruptions

One common problem with tracking time is interruptions. It is surprising how often we are interrupted by phone calls, people wanting to chat, occasional annoyances, or the need to take a break. The way interruptions are handled with the Time Recording Log is to note them in the column labeled Interruption Time. As shown in Table 3.2, for example, Student Y started her homework at 11:06 on the 10th and stopped at 12:19. During this period, she was interrupted twice, once for 6 minutes and once for 5. The net time she spent on her homework is thus 73 minutes less 11 minutes of interruption time, or a total of 62 minutes. Student Y not only noted these times in the Time Recording Log; she also briefly described the interruptions in the comments column.

One trick that I have found useful is to use a stopwatch for tracking interruptions. When I am interrupted, I start the stopwatch, and when I am ready to resume work, I stop it. Before I start working again, I note the interruption time in the log and reset the stopwatch. I find this more convenient than writing down the start time of each interruption. It is also more accurate than guessing. One chess-playing engineer told me that he found a chess clock ideally suited for tracking interruption time. The technique you use is not important as long as it works for you.

Since interruption time is not productive job time, you must track interruptions. If the amount of this time was constant, it would not make much difference how you handled it. Interruption time, however, is highly variable. If you don't measure it, you would essentially be adding a random number to all of the time data. This would make it far more difficult to use these data to plan and manage your time.

Time log data can also be used to understand how often your work is interrupted. Interruptions not only waste time, but they break your train of thought, leading to inefficiency and error. Understanding how much you are interrupted could therefore help to improve the quality and efficiency of your work. Some engineers have told me that learning to control the number and duration of interruptions was one of the most important benefits of tracking their time.

3.6 Tracking Completed Tasks

To keep track of how you spend time, you also need to track the results produced. For attending classes or meetings, for example, a simple record of the time would be adequate. When developing programs, reading book chapters, or writing reports, however, you will need to know how much work was accomplished. You could then calculate the task productivity. An example would be how long it took to read a textbook chapter or to write a program. With this knowledge, you will be better able to make plans for future work.

The C and U columns on the right of the Time Recording Log stand for Completed (C) and Units (U). These columns help quickly identify the time spent on various tasks and what was accomplished. You will use this information in subsequent chapters in this textbook, starting with Chapter 4.

Here, a unit is a unit of work. When you have read a chapter, you have completed one unit of work. A completed program is another unit of work. In Chapter 6, we introduce more detailed measures of work units, like pages of text or lines of program source code. Then, an 11-page chapter would be 11 units of work. While you can count units in any way that is useful, more detailed units like lines of code or text pages are generally more useful than the larger units of chapters or programs. For now, however, we will use these larger units and defer discussion of more detailed unit measures until Chapter 6.

To fill in the C column, check it when you have completed a task. In Table 3.2, for example, Student Y read the textbook from 6:25 to 7:45 on September 9. During this time, she completed reading two chapters. She thus checked the C (Completed) column for that row. To note the units of work completed, she also entered a 2 in the U (Units) column. Later, when she summarized her work for the week, she could quickly scan down these columns to find the completed items. She could also determine how many units of work she accomplished and how much time they took. On Table 3.2, for example, there are three entries for Text but only two of them have checks in the C column. In these two rows, Student Y spent a total of 80 + 28 = 108 minutes reading a total of 2 + 1 = 3 textbook chapters. Using these data, Student Y could see that, on average, she read a textbook chapter in 36 minutes.

To keep accurate time records, it is important to complete the C and U columns every time you finish a task that has measurable results. If you forget to do this, you can usually find the information, but it is much easier to fill it in at the time you finish a task. The Time Recording Log Instructions are repeated in Table 3.3 for ease of reference; review them before you first use the log and check back later to make sure you are recording time properly.

3.7   Keeping Time Logs in the Engineering Notebook

To keep complete time records, you must have a copy of the time log handy when you spend time on this course. The engineering notebook turns out to be a convenient place to keep Time Recording Logs. I record my time in the back of my en-

TABLE 3.3 TIME RECORDING LOG INSTRUCTIONS

Purpose	This form is for recording time spent on this course. Use the pages at the back of the engineering notebook for the Time Recording Log.
General	Record all the time spent on this course. Record the time in minutes. Be as accurate as possible.
Header	Enter the following: Your name and today's date. The instructor's name and the course name or number. Make sure your name is on any Time Recording Log copies you turn in with your homework.
Date	Enter the date when the entry is made.
Example	9/14/96
Start	Enter the time when you start working on a task.
Example	9:15
Stop	Enter the time when you stop working on that task.
Example	11:59
Interruption Time	Record any interruption time that was not spent on the task and the reason for the interruption. If you have several interruptions, enter their total time.
Example	5 + 3 + 22, break, phone, chat
Delta Time	Enter the clock time you spent working on the task, less the interruption time.
Example	From 9:15 to 11:59, less 30 minutes or 134 minutes.
Activity	Enter the name or other designation of the task or activity being worked on.
Example	Review
Comments	Enter any other pertinent comments that might later remind you of any unusual circumstances regarding this activity.
Example	Quiz prep
C (Completed)	When a task is completed, check this box.
Example	At 7:45 on 9/9, you completed reading one or more chapters, so check this box.
U (Units)	Enter the number of units of work you completed.
Example	From 6:25 to 7:45 on 9/9 you read two chapters, so enter 2.
Important	Record all your time for this course. If you forget to record a time, promptly enter your best estimate. If you forget your Time Recording Log, note the times and copy them in your log as soon as you can.

gineering notebook because I frequently work on several different projects at the same time. Since I start and finish projects all the time, I have found it easier to keep track of one engineering notebook than to locate multiple time sheets.

The method I have found most convenient is to enter the time log on the last notebook page and work forward a page at a time. When I fill one page, I move forward to the next. I keep doing this until the material from the front of the notebook meets the time log from the back. When this happens, I start a new notebook.

There are, however, reasons why you might want to keep a separate time log for each project. When you only do one project at a time, it is often more convenient to use separate pages. Also, in a course, your instructor may want you to record time on separate time log sheets because they are then easier to turn in and to grade. As long as you record your time, however, the particular approach you select does not make much difference.

3.8   Hints on Logging Your Time

Tracking time is simple in concept. A few tricks, however, can help you to do it more consistently and accurately.

□ *Keep the engineering notebook with you at all times.* This seems obvious, but in the beginning you will occasionally forget it. When you do, note the time information on a separate piece of paper and copy it into the log as soon as you can. Also, if you use the notebook for keeping track of other important items like class notes, assignments, and appointments, you will more likely remember to bring it along.

□ *When you occasionally forget to record the start time, stop time, or interrupt duration, make an estimate as soon as you remember.* This will not be as accurate as recording the exact time but it is the best you can do. It will generally be pretty close to the actual time.

□ *You may use a stopwatch to track interruptions.* This may seem overly precise, but it is easier than recording the starting and stopping times of every interruption.

□ *Summarize your time promptly.* You will use a Weekly Activity Record to summarize your weekly time in this course. How and why to do this is discussed in Chapter 4.

Another approach is to record the time data on a computer. I have tried this and found that it took more time and was less convenient than making notes on paper. Computing systems should be ideal for this purpose, but suitable application support would be needed. Until such support is developed, your choices are either to write the support yourself, use a manual time recording system, or not track your time.

3.9 Summary

This chapter describes how to track your time. Track time in minutes using the Time Recording Log, which you should keep at the back of your engineering notebook. Keep the notebook with you when doing tasks for the course. If you forget the notebook, you can still record the time for a task by making note of it and then copying the time into the notebook as soon as you can. Consider using a stopwatch to track interruptions.

3.10 Assignment 3

Use the time log to track the time you spend on the various activities for this course. As part of this assignment, examine the activities list you established for Assignment 1 and adjust it as needed. Turn in a copy of your time log for the next week. You will be required to turn in a copy of the time log every week from now until the end of the course.

4

Period and Product Planning

This chapter describes period and product planning and shows how they relate to your personal work. You will learn how to complete a Weekly Activity Summary for the Time Recording Log data you have recorded so far in this course.

4.1   Period and Product Plans

There are two kinds of planning. The first is based on a period of time, any calendar segment—a day, week, month, or year. A period plan concerns the way you plan to spend time during this period. The second kind of plan is based on an activity, like developing a program or writing a report. The products may be tangibles like programs or reports or intangibles like the knowledge you get from reading a textbook or the service you provide when working in an office.

To see the difference between period and product planning, consider the activity of reading this textbook. To plan this work, you would first estimate the time for the total job. For example, you might expect to take 20 hours to read the 20 chapters in the entire book. For the product plan, you would then schedule the time to do the reading, say one hour a week. The product plan for this task would then be the objective of reading the book chapters in 20 hours. The period plan would be the way you allocate reading time in one-hour weekly increments.

The Relationship Between Period and Product Plans

We all use both period and product plans in our daily lives. In business, for example, the two are related as shown in simplified form in Figure 4.1. The left half of the figure deals with the product-based tasks and the right half with the period-based tasks. These two are related as follows.

   Corporate management provides funds for engineering and manufacturing to develop and produce products. Engineering develops products and releases them to manufacturing. Through the marketing group, manufacturing delivers these products to the customers, who pay for them. Engineering and manufacturing also provide product plans to finance and administration, who use the product plans to produce period plans for quarterly and annual revenue and expense. Finance and administration give their plans to corporate management. They also give pricing and forecast information to engineering and manufacturing so they know how many products to build each month and what to charge the customers for them. Corporate management decides what dividends and interest to pay the investors and how much new investment they need. When they know how much money they

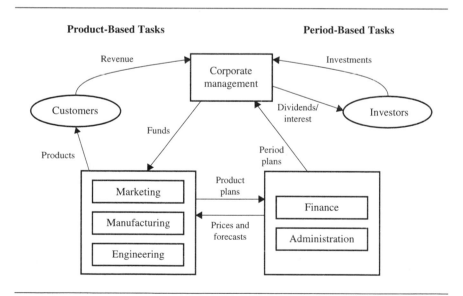

FIGURE 4.1 PERIOD AND PRODUCT PLAN

will have in the future, corporate management can then decide on the funds to provide engineering for future product development and manufacturing, completing the cycle.

The Importance of Period and Product Plans

In businesses, product plans are important because they tell marketing when they can expect new products to sell to customers. They also tell finance what development and manufacturing will cost. Finance can then determine the prices they need to charge and provide accurate period plans to corporate management. Management can then allot the money engineering and manufacturing will need. If the product plans are not accurate, the period plans will also be inaccurate. Management, marketing, the investors, and even the customers will be misinformed. This in turn could mean that the necessary funds would not be available to engineering and manufacturing when they are needed. Without adequate funds, engineering and manufacturing might have to cut back their plans. When they cut back their plans, *you* could be laid off.

While this planning cycle may sound theoretical and may take several years, the threat is real. The key to job security in any business is the financial health of the organization. And a key to business financial health is accurate period and product plans. It is therefore important that engineers know how to make sound period and product plans.

While period and product plans must be related, they are different. Your work schedule, your income, and your other daily activities are governed by time periods. That is, you sleep, eat, work, and rest during certain periods of the day or week. Your expenses and income are governed by weekly, monthly, and annual schedules. You thus live in a world with period activities, rules, and constraints. The principal purpose of your work, however, is to produce products and services of value to others. The cost, schedule, and quality of these goods or services are thus important. Since your work will be on products and your life will be in periods, both period and product plans are important to you. You cannot make a competent plan for either one without also planning the other. This chapter focuses on period planning; the next chapter discusses product planning.

4.2 The Weekly Activity Summary

To do period planning, it is important to understand how you spend time. Step 1 is to track your time using the Time Recording Log introduced in Chapter 3. After gathering a week or two of time data, you will begin to see how you spend time. Since the time logs are far too detailed for planning purposes, you need to summarize the data in a more useful form. The Weekly Activity Summary shown in Table 4.1 formats time data so they are more convenient for period planning.

Lines 1 through 10 of the Weekly Activity Summary provide a record of the time you spent on each principal activity during each day of the previous week. Right below this, on lines 13 to 16, are the average, maximum, and minimum times you spent on each task category during the earlier weeks of the semester.

TABLE 4.1 WEEKLY ACTIVITY SUMMARY

Name   **Date**

1	Task									Total
2	Date									
3	S									
4	M									
5	T									
6	W									
7	T									
8	F									
9	S									
10	Totals									

11   Period Times and Rates   Number of Weeks (prior number +1): _____

12   Previous Week's Times

13	Total								
14	Avg.								
15	Max.								
16	Min.								

17   Current Week's Times

18	Total								
19	Avg.								
20	Max.								
21	Min.								

Lines 18 to 21 show the total, average, maximum, and minimum times you spent in each work category for the entire semester so far, including the latest week.

When you wish to make a period plan for the next week, start with the latest Weekly Activity Summary. Based on the time previously spent on each task, you can judge how much time you will spend on these tasks in the next week. The simplest way to make such a plan would be to assume you will spend the same amount of time in the future as the average you have spent in the past. A more sophisticated approach would be to consider the work to be done in the next week and judge where it might fall between the maximum and minimum times of previous weeks. This will often result in a more accurate plan. The following sections describe how to complete the Weekly Activity Summary.

4.3 Summarizing Weekly Times

An example of a partially completed Weekly Activity Summary is shown in Table 4.2. These calculations use data from the Time Recording Log shown in Table 4.3. Complete the form in the following way:

1. Enter your name and the date.
2. List the work categories as column headings. In the example in Table 4.2, the work categories are Class, Write Prog., Quiz Prep., and Read Text.
3. Enter the date in the Date column by the Sunday of the first week (row 3).
4. For each day, total the minutes for each work category on the time log and enter it in the work column. For example, in Table 4.2 the first task category is Class. In the Time Recording Log in Table 4.3, Student Y spent the 50 minutes, from 9:00 to 9:50 A.M. on 9/9, in class. Thus, she entered 50 in row 4 in the Class column for 9/9 in Table 4.2. The Write Prog. amount is found by noting there are two Prog. entries for this day: 38 and 58 minutes, for a total of 96 minutes. She thus entered 96 under Write Prog. in row 4 in Table 4.2.
5. After completing all the entries for each day, total these numbers across and put the sum in the total column for that day. For example, the totals for row 4 of Table 4.2 are 50 + 96 + 80 = 226.
6. Repeat this process for each day of the week (rows 5–9).
7. Calculate the weekly totals for each task category in row 10. For example under Write Prog., you would get 96 + 62 + 69 + 114 = 341.
8. Next, total across row 10 to get the total time spent that week on all activities. In this case, this total is 150 + 341 + 134 + 146 = 771.

TABLE 4.2 EXAMPLE WEEKLY ACTIVITY SUMMARY

Name Student Y   **Date** 9/16/96

	Task	Class	Write	Quiz	Read					Total
1	Task	Class	Write	Quiz	Read					Total
2	Date		Prog.	Prep.	Text					
3	S 9/8									
4	M	50	96		80					226
5	T		62							62
6	W	50	69		28					147
7	T		114							114
8	F	50			38					88
9	S			134						134
10	Totals	150	341	134	146					771

11   Period Times and Rates   Number of Weeks (prior number +1): ___1___

12   Previous Week's Times

13	Total									
14	Avg.									
15	Max.									
16	Min.									

17   Current Week's Times

18	Total	150	341	134	146					771
19	Avg.	150	341	134	146					771
20	Max.	150	341	134	146					771
21	Min.	150	341	134	146					771

9. Finally, total the daily totals to check that you get the same result. In this case, 226 + 62 + 147 +114 + 88 +134 = 771, so there is no error. If these numbers differed, you would have to retotal across the days and down the tasks to find the addition error.

10. The Current Week's Time summary is completed as explained in Section 4.2.

   A good way to minimize errors when you add a column of figures is to always add twice: down from the top and up from the bottom to make sure you get the

TABLE 4.3 FIRST WEEK'S TIME RECORDING LOG EXAMPLE

Student _Student Y_   Date _9/9/96_
Instructor _Mr. Z_   Class _CS1_

Date	Start	Stop	Interruption Time	Delta Time	Activity	Comments	C	U
9/9	9:00	9:50		50	Class	Lecture		
	12:40	1:18		38	Prog.	Assignment 1		
	2:45	3:53	10	58	Prog.	Assignment 1		
	6:25	7:45		80	Text	Read text - Ch 1&2	X	2
9/10	11:06	12:19	6+5	62	Prog.	Assignment 1, break, chat	X	1
9/11	9:00	9:50		50	Class	Lecture		
	1:15	2:35	3+8	69	Prog.	Assignment 2, break, phone	X	1
	4:18	5:11	25	28	Text	Text Ch 3, Chat with Mary	X	1
9/12	6:42	9:04	10+6+12	114	Prog.	Assignment 3	X	1
9/13	9:00	9:50		50	Class	Lecture		
	12:38	1:16		38	Text	Text Ch 4		
9/14	9:15	11:59	5+3+22	134	Review	Quiz prep, break, phone, chat		

same total. Another way to minimize calculation errors would be to use the EXCEL spreadsheet provided with the support materials available for this textbook.[1]

4.4 Calculating Period Times and Rates

A simple summary of your weekly times would be adequate if you only had to worry about one week, but you are actually interested in the average, maximum, and minimum times spent on these tasks over a semester or even an entire year. To show how these data are obtained, we next complete the Weekly Activity Summary shown in Table 4.4. This uses Student Y's Weekly Activity Summary for week 1, shown in Table 4.2. Using these data, the Period Times and Rates section of Table 4.4 are completed as follows:

1. Enter the total weeks elapsed. Check row 11 of the prior week's activity summary to see how many weeks were covered. Since Table 4.2 has a 1 in the space on line 11, enter $1 + 1 = 2$ in the Number of Weeks space on Table 4.4.

2. In rows 13–16 of the current week's table (Table 4.4), copy all the entries from rows 18–21 of the previous week's table (Table 4.2).

3. Sum the times spent on each task in the current week. For each column of row 18 of Table 4.4, enter the sums of row 13 and row 10. For the first column, Class, this is $150 + 150 = 300$. For the second column, Write Prog., it is $339 + 341 = 680$. Make similar entries for the other columns. Each column of row 18 now shows the total time spent on each task in the first two weeks of this semester.

4. Calculate the average time spent each week on each task during this semester. For row 19 in Table 4.4, divide the number in each column of row 18 by the Number of Weeks. The first Avg. entry is $300/2 = 150$ and the second entry is $680/2 = 340$. Repeat this calculation for the remaining columns.

5. To find the greatest amount of time you have spent on a task in a week, you calculate the maximum time. Calculate the Max. entries in row 20 by comparing each column of row 15 with the same column of row 10. Enter the larger number in row 20. For the Read Text column, the previous Max. entry was 146 in row 15 and the current week's value is 224 in row 10. Since 224 is greater, enter it in row 20.

6. To understand how little time you have spent on a task in a week, you calculate the minimum time. Calculate the Min. entries in row 21 by comparing

[1]Descriptions of the support materials and instructions for obtaining them are given on the last page of this textbook.

TABLE 4.4 PERIOD TIMES AND RATES, SECOND WEEK

	Name Student Y							**Date** 9/23/96	
1	Task	Class	Write	Quiz	Read			Other	Total
2	Date		Prog.	Prep.	Text				
3	S 9/15								
4	M	50	93		80				223
5	T		95						95
6	W	50			71				121
7	T		77						77
8	F	50	74		40				164
9	S				33				33
10	Totals	150	339		224				713

| 11 | Period Times and Rates | Number of Weeks (prior number +1): __2__ |

12   Previous Week's Times

13	Total	150	341	134	146				771
14	Avg.	150	341	134	146				771
15	Max.	150	341	134	146				771
16	Min.	150	341	134	146				771

17   Current Week's Times

18	Total	300	680	134	370				1484
19	Avg.	150	340	67	185				742
20	Max.	150	341	134	224				771
21	Min.	150	339	134	146				713

each column of row 16 with the same column of row 10. Enter the smaller number in row 21. For the Read Text column, the previous Min. entry was 146 in row 16 and the current week's value is 224 in row 10. Since 146 is smaller, enter it in row 21. Row 21 now gives the minimum time spent each week on each task. Note that you ignore 0 entries in calculating the minimum times.

7. Note that, except for the first week, the Max. and Min. of the Total time will not usually be the same as the total of the Max. and Min. times.

The Quiz Prep. column gives an example of why you should ignore 0 entries in calculating the minimum times. Since no time was spent on this activity this week, the average time is only 67 minutes. That is, Student Y spent 134 minutes one week and 0 the next, for an average of 67 minutes. The Max. value is calculated as before, but for the Min. value zero would not be a useful number. The reason is that for this activity you already know that you will spend no time studying for quizzes during most weeks of the semester. Thus a zero value for Min. adds no new information. It might be interesting, however, to know that, when you did review for quizzes, the minimum time you spent was 134 minutes. Since you only want to know what the minimum amount of time is when you do this task, only replace the minimum in row 16 with a smaller nonzero value in row 10.

The directions for completing the Weekly Activity Summary are listed in Tables 4.5 and 4.6.

4.5   Using the Weekly Activity Summary

By completing this form this way every week, you will have a running tally of the average, maximum, and minimum times you have spent in each activity each week. While this form may appear a little complicated, after a little practice it will seem straightforward. You will then find that this is a simple way to organize and retain a large amount of time data. If you use a spreadsheet to do these calculations, it will be easier still.

The data in the Weekly Activity Summary will help you understand where you spend time. With this information, for example, you could judge that a large task will likely take nearly the maximum time and a simple task close to the minimum. You can then use these data to plan subsequent weeks. Planning is discussed further in the following chapters.

While you will initially learn a great deal from the Weekly Activity Summary, it will soon add relatively little new information each week. When you reach this point, preparing a Weekly Activity Summary once every month or so to check the current time distribution will be adequate. Also, once you start gathering project data in Chapter 5 and later, you will know how much time you spend on projects and can readily summarize this in a Weekly Activity Summary when you need to.

The practice I have evolved is to use a Monthly Activity Summary to track time I've spent on two principal activities: writing books and doing other projects. Since I write books on my personal time and do projects on company time, it is important to know how much personal and how much project time I can expect to have available during any week or month. This helps me to make accurate plans

TABLE 4.5 WEEKLY ACTIVITY SUMMARY INSTRUCTIONS:
(1) SUMMARIZING WEEKLY TIME

Purpose	This form is used for tracking and analyzing the time spent on this course. These data are summarized from the Time Recording Log.
General	Summarize the data from the Time Recording Log at the end of each week. If the task categories are not appropriate, change them. If you do not have enough columns for all the tasks, use additional copies of the form.
Header	Enter the following: Your name Today's date
Task	Enter the names of the principal tasks on which you spent time for this course.
Example	Class, Write Prog., Quiz Prep., Read Text, etc.
Date	By S (for Sunday), enter the date for that day.
Example	9/8
Columns	For each day of the week, find the total time spent on each task type from the Time Recording Log. Enter this number in the appropriate column for that day.
Example	For Monday, 9/9, the Write Prog. times on the Time Recording Log were 38 and 58 minutes. Enter the sum, or 96 minutes under Write Prog. in row 4 for Monday 9/9.
Week Totals (row 10)	Total the numbers for each task for the entire week and enter them on row 10.
Example	96 + 62 + 69 + 114 = 341 for row 10 under Write Prog.
Totals	For each row, total the task times to give the daily total in the rightmost column. If you use several forms, put the total for all the columns from all the forms in the rightmost column of the first form.
Example	50 + 96 + 80 = 226 for the Total for Monday 9/9.
First Check	Total the total numbers to get the total time spent for the week and enter it in the Total column and Total row for that week.
Example	226 + 62 + 147 + 114 + 88 + 134 = 771 is the total for the week.
Final Check	150 + 341 + 134 + 146 = 771 for the task totals in row 10. Since this equals the total of the right column, there is no addition error.

TABLE 4.6 WEEKLY ACTIVITY SUMMARY INSTRUCTIONS:
(2) SUMMARIZING PERIOD TIMES AND RATES

Purpose	This form is used for tracking and analyzing the time spent on this course. These data are summarized from the Time Recording Log.
General	These instructions are a continuation of those given in Weekly Activity Summary Instructions (1). For header and other information, consult those instructions.
Number of Weeks (row 11)	This is the number of weeks covered by the summary data. Consult the Number of Weeks entry on row 11 of the prior week's summary. Add 1 to that number, and enter the total here.
To Date Times (rows 13–16)	For rows 13 to 16, copy, column by column, the data from rows 18 to 21 of the previous week's summary. Include the Total, Avg., Max., and Min. rows for every column, including the total column.
Current Times Total (row 18)	To calculate the values in row 18, add the numbers in row 10 and row 13. Do this for every column of this table.
Example	On Table 4.4, the Write Prog. column value for row 18 is calculated as 339 + 341 = 680.
Current Times Avg. (row 19)	The Avg. value is calculated by dividing the row 18 entry in each column by the Number of Weeks in row 11.
Example	In Table 4.4, the Write Prog. Avg. entry is 680/2 = 340.
Current Times Max. (row 20)	The row 20 values are found by comparing row 15 to row 10. Enter the larger of the two numbers. Do this for every column, including the Total column.
Example	From Table 4.4 and for Write Prog., the Max. value was 341 and the value for this week is 339 so the new Max. value is still 341.
Another Example	From Table 4.4 and for Read Text, the Max. value was 146 and the value for this week is 224 so the new Max. value is 224.
Current Times Min. (row 21)	The row 21 values are found by comparing row 16 to row 10. Enter the smaller nonzero number. Do this for every column, including the Total column.
Example	From Table 4.4 and for Write Prog., the Min. value was 341 and the value for row 10 is 339 so the new Min. value is 339.
Another Example	From Table 4.4 and for Read Text, the Min. value was 146 and the value for row 10 is 224 so the new Min. value remains 146.
A Further Example	From Table 4.4 and for Quiz Prep., the Min. value was 134 and the value for row 10 is 0, so the new Min. value remains 134.

and to consistently meet commitments. For this purpose, a monthly track is sufficient. I do find it helpful, however, to summarize my time each month.

4.6 Summary

This chapter shows how period and product planning relate and describes period planning. The first step in period planning is to understand your time data. Start with the basic time data from the Time Recording Log, and produce a Weekly Activity Summary every week. The Weekly Activity Summary provides a record of the time spent by activity and the average, maximum, and minimum weekly times spent on each activity during the semester. Eventually you can stop summarizing time every week and just make a summary when your time distribution changes or you may ultimately find it adequate to summarize time on a monthly basis.

4.7 Assignment 4

Complete and submit a Weekly Activity Summary for each of the previous two weeks. Use the daily time logs to complete these forms. Also, submit a copy of those time log pages you have not previously submitted.

5

Product Planning

This chapter describes how to use time log data to make product plans. A new form, the Job Number Log, is introduced to help you track historical product data and an example shows you how to complete the form. For the assignment, you will complete the new Job Number Log for the productlike tasks you have completed so far with this course.

5.1 The Need for Product Plans

Some years ago while at IBM, I was put in charge of a large software development department with many projects. Most of the projects were seriously late and senior management was very upset. My job was to straighten out the mess. The first thing I did was to review the major projects. To my surprise, none of them had any documented plans. I immediately insisted the engineers produce plans for all their projects. Never having prepared formal plans before, it took them a couple of months to do it. We even set up a special class on project planning. After they had made plans, however, they could establish realistic schedules for their work.

The act of making plans had a dramatic effect. This development group had never before delivered a product on time. Starting with their new plans, however, they did not miss a single date for the next two and a half years. And they have been planning their work ever since. Planning is a critical part of a software engineer's job, and to be an effective engineer, you need to know how to make plans. The key is practice, so to get the most practice, start making plans now and continue to do so for all your future projects.

5.2   Why Product Plans Are Helpful

In this book, I suggest that you develop product plans for all your projects or major tasks: writing a program, reading a textbook, or preparing a report. The product plan will help you judge how much time the work will take and when you will finish. Plans also help you track progress while doing the work.

When engineers work on development teams, they need to plan their personal work. Planning provides a sound basis for committing to completion dates, and it allows engineers to coordinate their work on joint products. Their individual product plans enable them to commit dates to each other for their interdependent tasks and to consistently meet those commitments.

Businesses use product plans for the same reasons you will: to plan and manage their work. A well-made plan includes a project cost estimate. Estimates are essential for development contracts because customers often need to know the price in advance. Estimates are also necessary when developing products. Project cost is a major part of product price and must be kept low enough for the price to be competitive in the marketplace.

Engineers also use product plans to understand project status. With reasonably detailed and accurate plans they can judge where a project stands against the plan. They can see if they are late and need help or if they will have to delay the schedule. They may even be ahead of schedule and be able to help their teammates or deliver early. When engineers make plans, they can better organize their time and avoid last minute crises. They are then less likely to make mistakes and will generally produce better products.

Because plans are so important, you need to know how to make accurate plans. You also need to know how to compare these plans with actual results so you can learn to make better plans.

5.3   What Is a Product Plan?

The first step in producing a product plan is to get a clear definition of the product you plan to produce. While this seems obvious, it is surprising how often people dive into the mechanics of developing a product before they define what they are trying to do. Only after you know what you want to do, should you start thinking about how to do it. That is when to start planning.

A properly produced product plan includes three things:

☐ the size and important features of the product to be produced,

☐ an estimate of the time required to do the work,

☐ a projection of the schedule.

The product could be a working program, a program design, or a test plan. A product plan thus identifies the product to be produced and contains estimates of the product size, the hours to do the work, and the schedule. More complex products require more sophisticated planning and many kinds of information such as responsibility assignments, staffing plans, product or process specifications, dependencies on other groups, or special testing or quality provisions. In this book, however, we will only deal with the three basic plan elements: size estimates, projected hours, and the schedule.

5.4 Product Planning in This Book

Product planning is a skill that can be improved with practice. By starting now to make plans, you will develop your planning skills. Then, when you need to produce a plan for an important project, you will know how to do it. Starting with this chapter, you should produce a plan for every major task. Then, starting in Chapter 10, you will make more comprehensive plans for developing programs.

In this book, we start by planning small jobs because that is a good way to learn how to plan. After all, if you can't plan a small task how could you possible plan a large project? Working engineers do many small tasks as parts of every big job. Thus, if you plan each of these small tasks, you will have more opportunities to develop your planning skills. For larger jobs, you can combine these many small plans into one larger plan for the entire job. This, it turns out, is the most effective way to make accurate plans for larger jobs.

5.5 Planning Small Jobs

It is important to produce a plan that is appropriate for the magnitude and complexity of the work to be done. It would make little sense, for example, to produce a sophisticated plan for a task that will only take an hour or two. Conversely, with a task that could take several weeks, a more substantial plan is warranted.

The most basic product plan would consist of only the estimate of time needed to do a task or job. Once you can accurately estimate the time to do a job, all the other planning questions can usually be handled rather easily.

By gathering data on how long various tasks have taken in the past, you can predict how long similar tasks will likely take in the future. This approach can be applied to almost any product-related task that takes from a few hours to a few days. The key data needed are how long it has previously taken to do similar work. For example, if you plan to read a textbook chapter, it would be helpful to know how long it took to read several previous chapters. With data on the average, the maximum, and the minimum reading times, you can better predict your likely reading time for the new chapter.

5.6   Some Definitions

Before proceeding, we need to define some terms:

- □ A **product** is something you produce for a co-worker, an employer, or a customer.
- □ A **project** typically produces a product.
- □ A **task** is a defined element of work.
- □ A **process** defines the way to do projects. Chapter 11 deals more fully with processes.
- □ **Plans** describe the way a specific project is to be done: how, when, and at what cost? You can also plan individual tasks.
- □ A **job** is something you do, either a project or a task.

5.7   The Job Number Log

The Job Number Log shown in Table 5.1 is designed to record estimated and actual time data. Note that this log is a product planning document since it deals with product data. Conversely, the Time Recording Log and Weekly Activity Summary contain data on weekly periods. They are thus period planning documents.

The entries in the Job Number Log are completed as shown in Table 5.2. This example uses data from Student Y's Time Recording Log in Table 5.3. The Job Number Log instructions are also summarized in Table 5.4. Note that in the log, Student Y tracked two general activities: attending class and reviewing for exams.

TABLE 5.1 JOB NUMBER LOG

Name: _____   Date: _____

Job #	Date	Pro-cess	Estimated		Actual			To Date				
			Time	Units	Time	Units	Rate	Time	Units	Rate	Max	Min
		Description:										
		Description:										
		Description:										
		Description:										
		Description:										
		Description:										
		Description:										
		Description:										
		Description:										
		Description:										
		Description:										
		Description:										
		Description:										
		Description:										
		Description:										
		Description:										
		Description:										
		Description:										

TABLE 5.2 A JOB NUMBER LOG EXAMPLE

Name: _____ Student Y _____   Date: _____ 9/9/96 _____

Job #	Date	Process	Estimated		Actual			To Date				
			Time	Units	Time	Units	Rate	Time	Units	Rate	Max	Min
1	9/9	Prog	100	1	158	1	158	158	1	158	158	158
Description: Write program 1 (minutes per program)												
2	9/9	Text	50	2	80	2	40	80	2	40	40	40
Description: Read textbook Chapters 1 and 2 (minutes per chapter)												
3	9/11	Prog	158	1	69	1	69	227	2	113.5	158	69
Description: Write program 2												
4	9/11	Text	40	1	28	1	28	108	3	36	40	28
Description: Read textbook Chapter 3												
5	9/12	Prog	114	1	114	1	114	341	3	113.7	158	69
Description: Write program 3												
6	9/13	Text	60	1	118	1	118	226	4	56.5	118	28
Description: Read textbook Chapter 4												
7	9/16	Prog	114	1	93	1	93	434	4	108.5	158	69
Description: Wrote program 4												
8	9/17	Prog	109	1	95	1	95	529	5	105.8	158	69
Description: Write program 5												
9	9/18	Text	57	1	71	1	71	297	5	59.4	118	28
Description: Read textbook Chapter 5												
10	9/19	Prog	106	1	151	1	151	680	6	113.3	158	69
Description: Write program 6												
11	9/20	Text	59	1	40	1	40	337	6	56.2	118	28
Description: Read textbook Chapter 6												
12	9/21	Text	56	1								
Description: Read textbook Chapter 7												
Description:												
Description:												
Description:												
Description:												
Description:												
Description:												
Description:												

TABLE 5.3 A TIME LOG EXAMPLE

Student __Student Y__   Date ___9/9/96___

Instructor __Mr. Z__   Class ___CS1___

Date	Start	Stop	Interruption Time	Delta Time	Job #	Comments	C	U
9/9	9:00	9:50		50	Class	Lecture		
	12:40	1:18		38	1	Assignment 1		
	2:45	3:53	10	58	1	Assignment 1		
	6:25	7:45		80	2	Read text - Ch 1&2	X	2
9/10	11:06	12:19	6 + 5	62	1	Assignment 1, break, chat	X	1
9/11	9:00	9:50		50	Class	Lecture		
	1:15	2:35	3 + 8	69	3	Assignment 2, break, phone	X	1
	4:18	5:11	25	28	4	Text Ch 3, Chat with Mary	X	1
9/12	6:42	9:04	10 + 6 + 12	114	5	Assignment 3	X	1
9/13	9:00	9:50		50	Class	Lecture		
	12:38	1:16		38	6	Text Ch 4		
9/14	9:15	11:59	5 + 3 + 22	134	Review	Quiz prep, break, phone, chat		
9/16	9:00	9:50		50	Class	Lecture		
	2:10	4:06	4 + 19	93	7	Assignment 4, break, phone	X	1
	7:18	8:49	11	80	6	Read text - Ch 4, chat	X	1
9/17	9:26	11:27	4 + 22	95	8	Assignment 5, break, phone	X	1
9/18	9:00	9:50		50	Class	Lecture		
	4:21	5:43	11	71	9	Text Ch 5, break	X	1
9/19	6:51	9:21	51 + 16 + 6	77	10	Assignment 6		
9/20	9:00	9:50		50	Class	Lecture		
	12:33	1:18	5	40	11	Text Ch 6, break	X	1
	1:24	2:38		74	10	Assignment 6	X	1
9/21	11:18	11:51		33	12	Text Ch 7		

TABLE 5.4 JOB NUMBER LOG INSTRUCTIONS

Purpose	This form is used to track the job numbers for each project. It also records key information on each project. A project is any activity that you wish to track such as developing a program or writing a paper.
General	When starting a project, enter the new job number in this log. Assign sequential numbers starting with 1.
Header	Enter your name. Enter the date this Job Number Log page is started.
Job #	Enter the job number you selected.
Date	Enter the date you start the job.
Process	Enter the type of task. For example, for a technical paper use *Paper,* for developing a program, use *Prog.,* etc.
Estimated Time	Enter the total time in minutes the job was estimated to take. Use the To Date Rate, Max, and Min values as guides. If these rates seem unreasonable, use your judgment.
Estimate Units	Enter the estimated units for the finished job. When you do one task, enter 1 for the units.
Actual Time	Enter the final actual total time the job took.
Actual Units	Enter the final actual number of total units. Again, enter 1 unit for each completed job.
Actual Rate	Enter the Actual Time divided by the Actual Units.
To Date Time	Find the most recent previously completed job of this type. Add the To Date time from that job to the actual time for this most recent job. Enter this total in the To Date Time space for the new job.
To Date Units	Find the most recent previously completed job of this type. Add the To Date units from that job to the actual units for this most recent job. Enter this total in the To Date Units space for the new job.
To Date Rate	Divide the To Date Time by the To Date Units to get the minutes per unit for all the jobs completed to date. Enter this number in the To Date Rate space for this job.
Max	Enter the maximum rate for all jobs completed of each type.
Min	Enter the minimum rate for all jobs completed of each type.
Description	Enter a description of the job to be done. Be sufficiently clear so the job content can be easily identified. The first time data on a task type are recorded, describe the unit of measure.

She also tracked two projectlike activities: writing programs and reading textbook chapters. The entries in Table 5.2 are completed as follows:

1. Job #   When planning an activity, assign a job number, starting with 1.

2. Date   Enter the date you start working on the job.

3. Process   Enter the type of task, such as reading the textbook, writing a program, or preparing a report.

4. Estimated Time   Estimate the time this task will take and enter it under Estimated Time. In making this estimate, examine the data on previous similar projects and use these data in making the estimate. Note that in estimating program 6 (job 10), Student Y used the average time for programs 1–5. She found this to be 105.8 minutes by looking at the previous program's To Date Rate (job 8).

5. Estimated Units   For single units of work, enter a 1 under Estimated Units. The next chapter introduces more refined size measures.

6. Actual Time   At the end of the job, enter the time the job took. For job 10, this time was 151 minutes.

7. Actual Units   Also, when done, record the actual units. Here, this would be 1 for each job. In the next chapter, you use a product size measure for the job units.

8. Actual Rate   The Actual Rate is the Actual Time divided by Actual Units. For program 6 (job 10) the Actual Rate is $151/1 = 151$ minutes per program.

9. To Date Time   At the end of the job, calculate and enter the To Date Time for all the tasks done to date of the same process type. For example, with 151 minutes Actual Time for program 6 and the To Date Time for programs 1 through 5 as 529 (see job 8), the To Date Time for program 6 is $151 + 529 = 680$ minutes.

10. To Date Units   Enter the To Date Units for all the tasks completed of each type. Again, with program 6, add the Actual Units for this job to the To Date Units for the most recent preceding job of this type (again, job 8): $5 + 1 = 6$.

11. To Date Rate   The To Date Rate is the To Date Time divided by To Date Units, or $680/6 = 113.3$ minutes/program. This is the average time it has taken you to do a job of this type.

12. To Date Max   To find the maximum rate for any task of this type so far, compare the Actual Rate on the most recent job with the

To Date Max on the previous job of this same type and enter the larger number. For program 6, the To Date Max for program 5 (job 8) is 158 minutes per unit, which is greater than the Actual Rate of 151 minutes per unit for program 6, so enter 158 for program 6 To Date Max.

13. To Date Min   The To Date Min value is the minimum rate for any task of this type so far. Find this value by comparing the current job Actual Rate with the To Date Min of the most recent previous job of this type and entering the smaller number. For program 6, for example, the Actual Rate of 151 minutes per unit is more than the 69 minutes per unit for the To Date Min of program 5 (job 8), so the program 6 To Date Min is still 69.

    With these data, you can readily look up the average rate for any given task type as well as the maximum and minimum rates. The principal advantage of the Job Number Log is that it provides a compact way to record and access a large amount of historical project data. This, you will find, is the key to making accurate estimates. Accurate estimates, in turn, are the key to good planning.

5.8   Some Suggestions on Using the Job Number Log

The following practices should help you make effective use of the Job Number Log:
    For the first jobs of a given type, Student Y had no prior data to guide her estimates. She thus had to guess. Guessing the first time is OK as long as you start gathering data so you don't have to keep guessing.
    Generally, in estimating the time for a new job, you will want to use the To Date Rate for the most recent prior job of the same type. Student Y generally did this. For Job 6, Student Y did not use the To Date Rate of 36 minutes per chapter. Presumably, she thought Chapter 4 would take longer to read than the average of the previous chapters. While she was right, she still took much longer than expected. It is important to remember that the data in the Job Number Log are to help make plans. Think about the numbers, however, and if you think a larger or smaller estimate would be more accurate, use your judgment.
    To quickly find all the Time Recording Log entries for a given job number, it is helpful to add the Job # in the Activity column in the Time Recording Log, as shown in Table 5.3. In fact, you will find it most convenient to drop the activity type all together and just refer to the activities by their job numbers. We follow this practice in the examples in the rest of this book.
    After you learn how to use the Job Number Log, you will probably find it more convenient to use a spreadsheet to make the calculations. An example

spreadsheet of this type is included in the available support for this textbook. Instructions for obtaining these support materials are given on the last page of this textbook.

5.9 Using Product Times and Rates Data

Suppose you had the data in Table 5.2 and wanted to plan your time for the next week. You might, for example, plan to write two programs and read four chapters. You also might know that one of the two programs is more complex than any you have written and the other seems about average.

To estimate the times to write these two programs, look in Table 5.2 at Job 10. Here, the average time to write the first six programs is shown as 113.3 minutes, or a little under 2 hours. The maximum time has been 158 minutes, or about 2 1/2 hours. The average program will then likely take about 2 hours and the more complex one would likely take at least 158 minutes and possibly more. To be on the safe side, you assume that the complex program will take 3 1/2 hours, or 210 minutes. This gives a total of 330 minutes of programming for the next week.

For the book chapters, you expect that two chapters will be about average and the other two will take quite a bit more time. From the data for Job 11, the average times to read chapters have been 56.2 minutes. You thus assume that you can read the two average chapters in about an hour each. The more complex chapters, however, will likely take near the maximum times of 118 minutes, or about 2 hours each.

In total, you now expect to spend about 5 1/2 hours writing programs and 6 hours reading the textbook during the next week. With this information, you can better plan for this work.

As you will soon see, the times for small tasks will vary considerably around your estimates. This is normal. The key to good estimating, however, is to learn to make balanced estimates. A balanced set of estimates has about as many overestimates as underestimates. In the example in Table 5.2, 5 of the 11 estimates were low, 5 were high, and Job 5 was right on. The low estimates were Jobs 1, 2, 6, 9, and 10; the other five estimates were high. Student Y had thus learned to make balanced estimates. She did this by generally using her prior average rates when estimating a new job. As long as you consistently do this and as long as your jobs are reasonably similar, you will soon make balanced estimates.

The advantage of having balanced estimates is that on average your jobs will take about as long as you estimated. That is, when one job takes longer, it will be compensated by another that takes less time. When estimating large jobs as collections of many small jobs, you are then more likely to come in reasonably close to the overall plan.

5.10 Summary

Product plans help you to summarize and manage time data for the products you plan to produce—a program you develop, reports you write, a textbook chapter you read, and exams you study for. The Job Number Log is a tool for tracking the time spent on each product task. The Job Number Log's calculations use the time data from the Time Recording Log.

When completed, the Job Number Log provides the average, maximum, and minimum times taken to complete each of your projects so far. You can use this information to plan work for the next week or to formulate more sophisticated plans required in later chapters.

5.11 Assignment 5

Complete and submit a Job Number Log for the work you have completed so far in the course. Where you have estimated data, enter it; otherwise leave the estimated spaces blank. Use the daily time logs to complete these forms. Continue to complete the entries in the Job Number Log for each project. Make an estimate of the time and units before starting each job, and then record the actual and To Date data when finished.

6

Product Size

Thus far we have considered large units of work like programs or book chapters. To make product plans, however, you need to use more precise measures. This chapter describes how to measure and estimate product size. For the chapter assignment, you will measure the sizes of the jobs you have done for the prior assignments with this textbook and calculate your productivity rates for that work.

6.1 The Product Planning Process

Product planning is not an exact process. While you should make the best plans you can, also recognize that these plans will likely be inaccurate. Planning is a skill that can be developed and improved. You do this by making plans for each job you do. Then, for each finished job, compare the plan with what you actually did. You will then better understand the errors in these plans and learn how to make better plans.

In making a product plan, compare what you plan to do with what you have done before. Start with data on similar jobs and compare the new task with these prior jobs. Look for previous jobs that produced about the same sized result as the

---

planned job. Then, based on how long these previous jobs took, estimate how long the new job will take.

The principal reason for gathering data on the work in this course is to learn how much time you take to do various tasks. If, for example, you judge that a new task is most like two previous tasks that took 3 and 4.2 hours respectively, you would likely conclude that the new task would take about the same average amount of time, or about 3.6 hours. This crude estimate would likely be better than an estimate made without any historical data.

6.2   Size Measurement

Since tasks often vary considerably in size and complexity, it would be helpful to have a way to compare their sizes. Consider reading textbook chapters. With data on how long it took to read five chapters, you could estimate the time to read a sixth chapter. One way would be to pick an average of the prior chapter reading times. While this would be better than nothing, it would not distinguish between long and short chapters. It would presumably take less time to read a short chapter than a long one. You should thus consider measuring the chapter reading times in minutes per page rather than in minutes per chapter.

Consider now Student Y's data in Table 6.1 on times to read textbook chapters. The times to read chapters range from 28 to 118 minutes. The ratio from the longest to the shortest times is more than 4. When measured in minutes per page, the range is from 2.33 minutes per page for Chapter 3 to 7.38 minutes per page for

TABLE 6.1 STUDENT Y CHAPTER READING TIMES

Student _Student Y_   Date _9/30/96_
Instructor _Mr. Z_   Class _CS1_

Chapter	Reading Time	Pages	Minutes/page
1 & 2	80	20	4.00
3	28	12	2.33
4	118	16	7.38
5	71	17	4.18
6	40	12	3.33
Totals	337	77	
Averages	56.17	12.83	4.38

Chapter 4. This is still a wide range, but it is only about 3 to 1. While there will likely be considerable variation, it looks as if you could better estimate the times to read textbook chapters if you based the estimate on the size of the chapter and the historical average reading rate in minutes per page. To calculate the average reading rate, add all the reading times and divide this total by the total of the chapter pages. Thus:

$$\text{Average rate} = (80 + 28 + 118 + 71 + 40)/(20 + 12 + 16 + 17 + 12) = 337/77$$
$$= 4.38 \text{ minutes per page.}$$

6.3   Some Cautions on Using Size Measures

While this use of size measures seems simple enough, there are some complications. First, some documents are much more difficult to read than others. This means you should consider the type of work involved, not just its size.

Also, there is a question of prior exposure. Suppose, for example, you were preparing for an examination. Your times for rereading previously studied chapters would presumably be less than your original reading times. Similarly, even for rereading a document that you have written, reading times could vary dramatically, depending on intent. For an initial edit of a draft document, you might take 15 or 20 minutes per page. A quick skim of a completed document, however, could take a minute or less per page.

Similar issues arise in planning program development. Productivities for different kinds of work, such as reusing previously developed programs, modifying an existing program, or developing new programs, will be quite different. To handle such issues, you should keep separate size and time records for the different kinds of work you do.

6.4   Program Size

When estimating the time required to write a program, base the estimates on the times previously taken to write similar programs. As shown in Table 6.2, Student Y's times to write programs ranged from a low of 69 minutes to a high of 158 minutes. While this is only a range of a little over two times, it will widen in the future as student Y writes larger programs. Here again, it is a good idea to base time estimates on program size.

The measure we use for program size is the lines of text in the source program. That is, if the program listing takes 16 lines of print, the program has 16

TABLE 6.2 STUDENT Y PROGRAM DEVELOPMENT TIMES

Student ___Student Y_____ Date ____9/30/96____
Instructor___Mr. Z_____ Class _____CS1_____

Program	Development Time	LOC	Minutes/LOC
1	158	20	7.90
2	69	11	6.27
3	114	14	8.14
4	93	10	9.30
5	95	14	6.79
6	151	18	8.39
Totals	680	87	
Averages	110.0	14.5	7.82

lines of code (LOC). In counting LOC, it is conventional not to count blank lines or lines of comments. A line with both a comment and a program statement is counted as a LOC. Although you could choose almost any consistent standard, in this book we will count lines of code without counting either blank lines or lines with only comments. Thus, the following Ada program fragment would have five LOC.

Example 1

```
-- comment describing the program's function
If (X_Average >= 100) then
            Size := X_Average;
        else
            Size := X_Average/2;
end if;
```

Similarly, if you wrote this same program fragment without comments and in a more compressed format, it would only have three LOC:

Example 2

```
If (X_Average >= 100) then
        Size := X_Average;
        else Size := X_Average/2; end if;
```

While these are identical programs and their development times would likely be the same, their sizes are different by this counting method. As long as you are consistent in the way you write programs, these counting variations are not important. To ensure that size counts are consistent, however, I suggest you adopt a standard format for writing programs. While you should follow the format called for by your professor, I personally prefer the more open format shown in Example 1.

The LOC measure is generally applicable to most programming languages. For example, the same program fragment in C++ would look like the following:

Example 3

```
// comment describing the program's function
if (X_Average >= 100)
        Size = X_Average;
else
        Size = X_Average/2;
```

When written this way, this C++ code fragment would have four LOC. The following slightly larger C++ code fragment would have 12 LOC:

Example 4

```
while (n > 0)
{
        push (n);
        cout << "Enter a positive integer. \n";
        cout << "Enter 0 to stop. \n";
        cin >> n:
}
// read out the stack
while (stack_pointer != NULL)
{
        cout.width(8);
        cout << pop ();
}
```

Using this LOC counting approach, the sizes of Student Y's six programs are shown in Table 6.2. The range of minutes per LOC is from 6.27 for program 2 to 9.3 for program 4. Since your times in minutes per LOC will change significantly with experience, you should track the minutes per LOC rate and base estimates on the rates achieved with your most recent 5 to 10 programs.

6.5   Other Size Measures

Although we do not use them in this book, there are many other potential software size measures. For example, industrial software development generally involves documentation, which would be measured in pages. Even for programs, the LOC measure does not cover all cases. Examples of product types where LOC is not generally suitable are menus, files, report pages, or screens. Unless you can devise a suitable size measure, you should use the unit counts and rates as done in Chapter 5.

Also, if you are using a program development aid that generates various kinds of screens, windows, or other standard program elements, counting can be a little more tricky. Here, it is important to count only the LOC you develop and not the LOC generated by the programming aids.

Regardless of the measures used, the principal objective is to estimate development work. For this, you want size measures that relate to the work required to develop the product. That is, product developments that take more time should have proportionately larger size measures.[1]

6.6   Estimating Program Size

While it might seem that you could now estimate the time to write a program, this is not as simple as it seems. For reading textbook chapters, you could count the pages to be read and use the historical average minutes per page to calculate the likely reading times. You might even rank the chapters by reading difficulty and allow a somewhat larger minutes-per-page rate for those chapters that seem more complex or involve less familiar material. By glancing over the new chapter, you assess its relative difficulty and pick a minutes-per-page rate based on past experience.

For writing programs, however, there is no program to count until you have developed it. To estimate the time to write the program, you thus have to first estimate how many LOC the program will likely require and then estimate the number of minutes per LOC the development will likely take. You can then calculate the total estimated time.

While there are various methods for estimating the sizes of programs before developing them, all size-estimating methods involve a lot of judgment. First, examine the requirements for the program to be developed. Then, rank the new pro-

---

[1]For a complete discussion of size measures and size estimating, see Chapters 4 and 5 in my book *A Discipline for Software Engineering* (Reading, MA: Addison-Wesley, 1995).

TABLE 6.3 STUDENT Y PROGRAM-SIZE RANKINGS

Student _Student Y_   Date _9/30/96_

Instructor _Mr. Z_   Class _CS1_

Program	Time	LOC	Minutes/LOC	Functions
4	93	10	9.30	Simple while-loop
2	69	11	6.27	Small case statement
3	114	14	8.14	Larger case statement
5	95	14	6.79	Medium repeat-until
6	151	18	8.39	Small linked list
1	158	20	7.90	Small calculation

gram's relative size among the programs you have already written. Finally, based on your opinion of where the new program will likely fall in this historical size range, estimate its likely LOC.

An example of this procedure is shown in Table 6.3. This is a list of Student Y's previously developed programs, ranked in size order. The list shows the program size in LOC, the development times in minutes, the rates in minutes/LOC, and a brief description of the program's function. By examining such data on your programs, and considering what you know about the program you plan to write, you can judge where the new program would likely fall in the size ranking. This will help you estimate the size range of the new program. Based on the historical minutes per LOC data, you can then estimate the time to develop the new program.

For example, suppose Student Y planned to write a new program containing a moderately complicated while loop. From Table 6.3, she would estimate it as larger than the 14 LOC for program 5 and possibly smaller than the 20 LOC for program 1. She might thus settle on the average of these extremes or (14 + 20)/2 = 17 LOC.

6.7 Making a Larger Size Estimate

While the approach shown in Table 6.3 works reasonably well for small programs of the types you have previously written, it does not work as well for larger programs or new program types. The reason is that even fairly small programs generally contain a mix of functions and procedures. With larger programs, you will thus have progressively more trouble relating a new program to previous developments.

One approach to this problem is to use a form like Table 6.4. Here, various programs or program functions and procedures are listed. With data on a number of programs, you could even break such a list into categories as Student Y did in Table 6.5. Examples of other useful categories are Text, Control, Logic, Display, and Print. The objective is to build a historical record of the previously written elements together with the data on how many lines of code they have each contained. When considering the functions in a new program, you can then estimate the size of each function and add up all these function estimates to get the total program estimate.

With small programs, list each program as shown in Table 6.5. As the programs get larger, they will likely contain multiple functions or procedures. By listing each function and procedure separately, you can quickly build a base of historical estimating data. With more data, it is helpful to keep a separate form like Table 6.4 for each program category. You might have one form for calculations, another for text handling procedures, one for control, and so forth. On each form,

TABLE 6.4 PROGRAM SIZE ESTIMATING FORM

Student _____   Date _____
Instructor_____   Class _____

Program	LOC	Prior Functions	Estimated Functions	Min.	Avg.	Max.
Estimate						

Comments:
_____
_____
_____
_____
_____
_____

TABLE 6.5 STUDENT Y PROGRAM-SIZE ESTIMATE

Student _Student Y_   Date _10/7/96_
Instructor _Mr. Z_   Class _CS1_

Program	LOC	Prior Functions	Estimated Functions	Min.	Avg.	Max.
Loops						
4	10	Simple while-loop				
5	14	Medium repeat-until	Repeat until	7	11	14
Case						
2	11	Small case statement	Case	5	8	11
3	14	Larger case statement				
Data						
6	18	Small linked list				
Calc.						
1	20	Small calculation	Calculation	10	15	20
Estimate				22	34	45

Comments: This program has a simple case statement, a loop, and a calculation. Assume that, at the maximum, it will take the sum of these typical sizes, or 11 + 14 + 20 = 45 LOC.
For the minimum, assume that these functions could be combined more efficiently than when they were separate constructs. Thus pick 22 LOC as the minimum. 34 LOC is about the middle point between these extremes.

list the program functions in order of size and include the name or number of the program that contains it.

An example of how to make a size estimate in this way is shown in Table 6.5. Here, Student Y has grouped data on a number of programs by various categories. Since these programs were all quite small, however, she only listed the complete programs. In estimating the number of LOC a new program will likely contain, she then judged how many LOC of each function type would likely be needed by the new program.

Student Y did this by first examining the requirements for the new program and establishing a general strategy for how to build it. She expected to use a repeat-

until loop and a simple case statement. She also expected to do a fairly simple calculation. In making these estimates, however, she was not entirely sure how big
each of these program parts would be, so she estimated a minimum size, the maximum size, and then the average size for each function. While she would generally
use the average sizes in her estimate, the exercise of thinking about the maximum
and minimum sizes helps to avoid making estimates that are seriously too large or
too small.

While this is not a foolproof size-estimating method, it is much better than
guessing. As you write more programs you can also add to this list of routines.
This growing body of historical data will then help you to make progressively better estimates.

There are no methods that guarantee a good size estimate. Size estimating is
a skill. The key to making good size estimates is to have a substantial amount of
historical data, to make lots of size estimates, and to regularly compare your results with the estimates.

6.8   Using Size Measures in the Job Number Log

When you use size measures instead of unit counts, you should keep the size data
in the Job Number Log, as shown in Tables 6.6 and 6.7. These examples use the
size data in Tables 6.1 and 6.2. Here, instead of just noting that one or two chapters or programs were completed, enter their sizes in the units column. As shown
in Table 6.6, Student Y completed a program of 20 LOC on 9/10, so she entered
20 in the U (units) column. Similarly, on 9/11, she read Chapter 3; since this 12-
page chapter took 28 minutes, she entered 12 in the units column of Table 6.6 and
28 under delta time.

Since you will have the size data in the Job Number Log, it may seem redundant to enter them in the Time Log as well. If your experience is like mine,
however, you will often complete the Job Number Log once or twice a week. You
will then have to search for the size data. At the time you do the work, however, it
generally takes no time to enter the size data in the Time Log.

In Table 6.7, Student Y used these size data to calculate product rates. She did
this using the Job Number Log Instructions given in Table 6.8. For example, for
Job 1 she had no size estimate, so she left the Estimated Units space blank. The
Actual Time remains 158 minutes, but the Actual Units are 20 LOC. This means
that the To Date Units are also 20 LOC and the To Date Rate is 158/20 = 7.90 minutes per LOC. Since this is the first program, the Max and Min values are also
7.90.

For the second program, Job 3, Student Y again made no size estimate, so
the Estimated Units is left blank. The Actual Time for program 2 was 69 minutes

TABLE 6.6 A TIME LOG WITH SIZE DATA

Student ___Student Y_____   Date ___9/9/96_____

Instructor ___Mr. Z_____   Class _____CS1_____

Date	Start	Stop	Interruption Time	Delta Time	Job #	Comments	C	U
9/9	9:00	9:50		50	Class	Lecture		
	12:40	1:18		38	1	Assignment 1		
	2:45	3:53	10	58	1	Assignment 1		
	6:25	7:45		80	2	Read text - Ch 1&2	X	20
9/10	11:06	12:19	6 + 5	62	1	Assignment 1, break, chat	X	20
9/11	9:00	9:50		50	Class	Lecture		
	1:15	2:35	3 + 8	69	3	Assignment 2, break, phone	X	11
	4:18	5:11	25	28	4	Text Ch 3, Chat with Mary	X	12
9/12	6:42	9:04	10 + 6 + 12	114	5	Assignment 3	X	14
9/13	9:00	9:50		50	Class	Lecture		
	12:38	1:16		38	6	Text Ch 4		
0/14	0:15	11:50	5 + 3 + 22	131	Review	Quiz prep, break, phone, chat		
9/16	9:00	9:50		50	Class	Lecture		
	2:10	4:06	4 + 19	93	7	Assignment 4, break, phone	X	10
	7:18	8:49	11	80	6	Read text - Ch 4, chat	X	16
9/17	9:26	11:27	4 + 22	95	8	Assignment 5, break, phone	X	14
9/18	9:00	9:50		50	Class	Lecture		
	4:21	5:43	11	71	9	Text Ch 5, break	X	17
9/19	6:51	9:21	51 + 16 + 6	77	10	Assignment 6		
9/20	9:00	9:50		50	Class	Lecture		
	12:33	1:18	5	40	11	Text Ch 6, break	X	12
	1:24	2:38		74	10	Assignment 6	X	18
9/21	11:18	11:51		33	12	Text Ch 7		

TABLE 6.7 A JOB NUMBER LOG WITH SIZE DATA

Name: _____ Student Y _____   Date: _____ 9/9/96 _____

Job #	Date	Pro-cess	Estimated		Actual			To Date				
			Time	Units	Time	Units	Rate	Time	Units	Rate	Max	Min
1	9/9	Prog	100		158	20	7.90	158	20	7.90	7.90	7.90
Description: Write program 1 (minutes per LOC)												
2	9/9	Text	50	20	80	20	4.00	80	20	4.00	4.00	4.00
Description: Read textbook Chapters 1 and 2 (minutes per page)												
3	9/11	Prog	158		69	11	6.27	227	31	7.32	7.90	6.27
Description: Write program 2												
4	9/11	Text	40	12	28	12	2.33	108	32	3.38	4.00	2.33
Description: Read textbook Chapter 3												
5	9/12	Prog	114		114	14	8.14	341	45	7.58	8.14	6.27
Description: Write program 3												
6	9/13	Text	60	16	118	16	7.38	226	48	4.71	7.38	2.33
Description: Read textbook Chapter 4												
7	9/16	Prog	114		93	10	9.30	434	55	7.89	9.30	6.27
Description: Wrote program 4												
8	9/17	Prog	109		95	14	6.79	529	69	7.67	9.30	6.27
Description: Write program 5												
9	9/18	Text	57	17	71	17	4.18	297	65	4.57	7.38	2.33
Description: Read textbook Chapter 5												
10	9/19	Prog	106		151	18	8.39	680	87	7.82	9.30	6.27
Description: Write program 6												
11	9/20	Text	59	12	40	12	3.33	337	77	4.38	7.38	2.33
Description: Read textbook Chapter 6												
12	9/21	Text	56									
Description: Read textbook Chapter 7												
Description:												
Description:												
Description:												
Description:												
Description:												
Description:												
Description:												

TABLE 6.8 JOB NUMBER LOG INSTRUCTIONS

Purpose	This form is used to track the job numbers for each project. It also records key information on each project. A project is any activity that you wish to track such as developing a program, reading a book, or writing a paper.
General	When starting a project, enter the new job number in this log. Assign sequential numbers starting with 1.
Header	Enter your name. Enter the date this Job Number Log page is started.
Job #	Enter the job number you selected.
Date	Enter the date you start the job.
Process	Enter the type of task. For example, for a technical paper use **Paper,** for a program development use **Prog,** etc.
Estimated Time	Enter the total time in minutes the job was estimated to take. Use the To Date Rate, Max, and Min values as guides. If these rates seem unreasonable, use your judgment.
Estimated Units	Enter the estimated units for the finished job. **For a program development, for example, estimate the number of LOC you expect the finished program to contain.**
Actual Time	Enter the final actual total time the job took.
Actual Units	Enter the final actual number of total units. **For a program, for example, you would count the LOC in the finished program.**
Actual Rates	Enter the Actual Time divided by the Actual Units.
To Date Time	Find the most recent previously completed job of this type. Add the To Date time from that job to the actual time for this most recent job. Enter this total in the To Date Time space for the new job.
To Date Units	Find the most recent previously completed job of this type. Add the To Date units from that job to the actual units for this most recent job. Enter this total in the To Date Units space for the new job.
To Date Rate	Divide the To Date Time by the To Date Units to get the minutes per unit for all the jobs completed to date. Enter this number in the To Date Rate space for this job.
Max	Enter the maximum rate for all jobs completed of each type.
Min	Enter the minimum rate for all jobs completed of each type.
Description	Enter a description of the job to be done. Be sufficiently clear so the job content can be easily identified. The first time data on a task type are recorded, describe the unit of measure.

and the Actual Units for program 2 were 11 LOC. This now gives a To Date Time of 227 minutes as before but the To Date Units is 20 + 11 = 31 LOC. Student Y obtained this number by looking at the To Date Units for the most recent previous task of this type (Job 1) and adding to the 20 LOC shown there the Actual Units of 11 LOC for this job. Now, with 31 To Date LOC and 227 To Date Time, the To Date Rate is 227/31 = 7.32 minutes per LOC. The Max rate for Job 1 was 7.90, which is bigger than 6.27 minutes per LOC for Job 3, so the Max rate remains 7.90. The Min rate for Job 1 was also 7.90, but here the 6.27 minutes per LOC for Job 3 is lower than 7.90, so Min is replaced with the current job's rate of 6.27.

Follow this same procedure for each subsequent program until you have entered all the Job Number data for the programs written to date. In the future, you would estimate and enter the number of LOC for each new program before you wrote it. While this takes a bit of work, the procedure described in Sections 6.6 and 6.7 is relatively easy to follow as long as you have historical data. For reading text, the procedure is identical except that you get the Estimated Units by counting the number of textbook pages to be read.

Using these data, you can see how long it has taken to write programs and to read textbook chapters. You could similarly include other tasks for which you had size and time measures.

6.9   Summary

This chapter introduces product size measures: and shows how size measures fit into the product planning process.

Size measurements are introduced to help estimate product size. The chapter describes how to determine program size in lines of code (LOC). Other size measures, such as menus, files, screens, and report pages, are often needed for industrial software projects.

The first product planning step is to estimate the size of the planned product. To make accurate size estimates, use historical size data. It is helpful to divide the historical size data into functional categories. You can then estimate how many lines of each code category will likely be needed in the new program. As you accumulate more historical data, you will likely make more accurate estimates. The Job Number Log provides a convenient way to record a large volume of historical size and rate data.

6.10   Assignment 6

Review the tasks completed for the assignments so far and count their sizes in LOC and pages. Submit these data in the format of Table 6.1 for the chapter assignments and Table 6.3 for the programs. Also, submit an updated Weekly Activity Summary form and Job Number Log with the rate data in minutes per LOC and minutes per page. If you do not have copies of all your completed programs, include data on at least the last three. Also, submit a copy of any Time Log and Job Number Log pages and Weekly Activity Summaries that you have not previously submitted. From now on, submit all logs and summaries with rates in minutes per LOC and minutes per page, where appropriate.

7

Managing Your Time

This chapter describes time budgets and shows you how to use them. It explains how to make a time budget and suggests some approaches to meeting them. For the chapter assignment, you will make a time budget.

7.1 Elements of Time Management

So far in this course, you have measured the way you spend time over several weeks. You now have a modest amount of data and a pretty good idea how long it takes to do various tasks. This knowledge was not hard to get, and by now you can see how helpful these data can be for making future plans. In this chapter, you will use these data to manage your time as follows:

1. Decide how you want to spend your time.
2. Make a time budget.
3. Track the way you spend time against this budget.
4. Decide what changes to make to bring your actions into agreement with the budget.

These topics are discussed in the following sections.

7.2   Categorizing Your Activities

Review the time categories to see if they cover all of your principal activities. If they do not, add to or revise them. You may find, for example, that you spend significant time analyzing and using the data you have gathered for this course. You might, therefore, want to add a data analysis category to the Weekly Activity Summary.

Although you now have a pretty good idea of the time you spend on weekly tasks, you will not have much data on tasks that only arise occasionally in a month, semester, or school year, such as studying for exams or working on term projects. You cannot gather data on these tasks until you do them, of course, but try to identify these categories now so you can make some provisions for them in your plans.

7.3   Gathering Data on Time Spent by Activity

Your Weekly Activity Summary shows the average, maximum, and minimum times you spend on each activity each week. It's a good idea to examine these categories now to see if some are too broad and others too detailed. An uneven distribution might have one category that takes 50% or more of the time and others that take about 5% or less.

To manage time, you need to focus on those few categories that take the most time. You will need to know in some detail what you do. If you spend 25% of your time on a category labeled Other, you might want to break it into a couple of better defined activities. Without more precise data on these Other activities, you will have trouble controlling how much time you spend on them.

7.4   Evaluating Your Time Distribution

Now that you can see where you spend time, ask yourself whether you are spending time the way you want to. Decide which activities are most important and consider whether you are giving them enough time. Do some tasks take so long that you never get to others that are more important? Are you allowing enough time to read the textbook? Do you have a job? And what are your personal commitments? Do you start work on assignments in time to finish them, or do you often wind up in a last minute crunch? There are no general guidelines on how to spend your time. This very personal decision must balance schoolwork, jobs, recreation, and social life. Some of these components are personal issues that involve complex trade-offs, particularly if you have a job and family responsibilities.

7.5 Making a Time Budget

The time budget is your plan for how to spend time. Starting with the data on how you have previously spent time, you can allocate the amounts of time you would like to spend on each category in the future. Student Y's preliminary time budget is shown in Table 7.1.

Table 7.2 is a copy of Student Y's Weekly Activity Summary from Table 4.4. Looking at line 19, you can compare the time budget in Table 7.1 with the way Student Y has actually spent her time. This leads to several conclusions:

- Student Y's total time on this course has averaged 742 minutes each week so far in the course. That is 12.37 hours. With the new budget, she plans to spend 840 minutes, or 14.0 hours per week—an extra 1.5 hours. This is a reasonably big change and she might have trouble finding this much additional time every week.

- Student Y is budgeting the same amount of time for attending classes as she has been spending, a reasonable plan.

TABLE 7.1 AN EXAMPLE WEEKLY TIME BUDGET

Student __Student Y__ Date __9/23/96__
Instructor __Mr. Z__ Class __CS1__

Activity Category	Budget Minutes	Actual Minutes
Attend Classes	150	
Write Programs	360	
Read Text	180	
Review for Exams	120	
Other	30	
Total	840	

TABLE 7.2 STUDENT Y'S WEEKLY ACTIVITY SUMMARY

	Name Student Y								**Date** 9/23/96	
1	Task	Class	Write	Quiz	Read	Rev.			Other	Total
2	Date		Prog.	Prep.	Text					
3	S 9/15									
4	M	50	93		80					223
5	T		95							95
6	W	50			71					121
7	T		77							77
8	F	50	74		40					164
9	S				33					33
10	Totals	150	339		224					713

11   Period Times and Rates   Number of Weeks (prior number +1): 2

12   Previous Week's Times

13	Total	150	341	134	146				771
14	Avg.	150	341	134	146				771
15	Max.	150	341	134	146				771
16	Min.	150	341	134	146				771

17   Current Week's Times

18	Total	300	680	134	370				1484
19	Avg.	150	340	67	185				742
20	Max.	150	341	134	224				771
21	Min.	150	339	134	146				713

- She plans to spend about 20 minutes more time each week on writing programs. This is also probably reasonable.
- She plans to spend about the same as her prior average time on reading the textbook. This seems reasonable.
- The big additions are in the categories of reviewing for exams and Other. These two add a total of 150 minutes a week, or 2.5 hours. Such a large

change is probably unrealistic. Although it might make sense for Student Y to increase her planned total time to near the 771 maximum minutes she has spent so far on the course, expecting to do much more could be unrealistic.

The key to time management is to gradually rebalance the way you spend time. Even though you may hope to spend a lot more time on some tasks in the future, unless you can identify other areas to cut back, that is often wishful thinking. One important step is to make sure that the time you now spend is used most effectively. People often waste a lot of time deciding what to do next. Establishing personal plans and a time budget will enable you to *know* what to do next. Surprisingly, this will immediately improve your working efficiency.

You may also need more time to do all the things you want to do. Again, however, you need to be realistic. You can usually find some extra time in a crisis, but no one wants to live in perpetual crisis. So allocate reasonable amounts of time for health maintenance, family, friends, hobbies, sleep, and meals. While you will be able to make some adjustments in these areas, you should do so only gradually. I suggest you establish some sustaining level of work that you can continue throughout the school year. You may be able to cut deeply in one or more areas in a crisis, but you cannot do it for very long. If you must spend more time on some activities, you need to take that time from somewhere else. Review your priorities and decide what is most important to you. Then set your time budget accordingly.

7.6 Finding More Time

After you have reviewed the time budget, you may need to increase the total amount of time. How can you do this? You have several options.

First, if your schedule is not very busy, you may easily be able to find a little extra time. Unfortunately, few people are blessed with spare time.

You are more likely to find yourself overcommitted. In this case, take a broad look at all your commitments. You might then wish to track the time you spend on all courses or principal areas of work as well as on leisure activities.

The problem is that there are only 24 hours in a day and there is nothing you can do to increase them. If you need to spend more time on some activities, you must take this time from other activities. Until you know how much time you spend on each category, therefore, it is hard to make realistic adjustments.

7.7   Setting Ground Rules

Now that you have decided how you want to spend time, you need to actually spend it that way. This simple rule takes more effort than you might expect. The reason is that time budgets are only general statements of what you want to do. Actual time management requires making decisions on a minute-by-minute basis. Thus, to actually do what you intend, you need to get very specific.

You have probably noticed that it is easy to manage the amount of time you spend attending classes. The reason is that classes occur at regular, set intervals. When people have specified routines to follow, they generally can do so. Many things we do are in response to rules someone has set. For effective time management, you also need rules. Now, however, you must set them yourself. That, in fact, is what a time-management budget is: rules you have established for managing your own time.

To provide a useful guide to daily behavior, you will thus need a daily time budget. Your budgets for different days and weeks will probably differ. Thus a format like Table 7.3 will be needed.

Now you can see why the budget in Table 7.1 was not very useful. For example, it would make little sense to spend time every week reviewing for exams. You will not want to wait until the day before the exam, nor will you want to do the reviews so far in advance that you forget the material by the time of the exam.

TABLE 7.3 WEEKLY ACTIVITY BUDGET

Name _____   **Date** _____

Budget Week #1

Task									Total
Date									
S									
M									
T									
W									
T									
F									
S									
Totals									

TABLE 7.3 (*Continued*)

Budget Week #2

Task									Total
Date									
S									
M									
T									
W									
T									
F									
S									
Totals									

Budget Week #3

Task									Total
Date									
S									
M									
T									
W									
T									
F									
S									
Totals									

Also, the "Other" category in Table 7.1 was an allowance for unplanned activities. Although it's a good idea to make some allowance for unexpected events, obviously there is no way to make detailed plans for surprises. One way to handle unforeseen contingencies is to allow a little more than the historical average for each activity. The built-in surplus will allow you to handle occasional planning mistakes and unforeseen events.

A more realistic set of time budgets for Student Y might look like Table 7.4.

TABLE 7.4 EXAMPLE WEEKLY ACTIVITY BUDGET

Name Student Y   **Date**   9/23/96

Budget Week #1   Regular weekly budget

Task	Class	Write	Exam	Read	Rev.			Other	Total
Date		Prog.	Prep.	Text					
S									
M	50			40					90
T		120		40					160
W	50			40					90
T		120		40					160
F	50			40					90
S		120							120
Totals	150	360		200					710

Budget Week #2   The week before exams

Task	Class	Write	Exam	Read	Rev.			Other	Total
Date		Prog.	Prep.	Text					
S									
M	50		40						90
T		120	40						160
W	50		40						90
T		120	40						160
F	50		120						170
S			150						150
Totals	150	240	430						820

TABLE 7.4 (*Continued*)

Budget Week #3   Exam Week

Task	Class	Write	Exam	Read	Rev.			Other	Total
Date		Prog.	Prep.	Text					
S									
M			300						300
T			450						450
W	170		150						320
T	50								50
F									
S									
Totals	220		900						1120

7.8   Prioritizing Your Time

One essential step in time management is establishing priorities. Some times are firmly established, like when to attend classes or when to work at your part-time job. You could call these fixed times. Everything else is variable time—activities you do when you can find the time. There are, however, two kinds of variable activities: required and discretionary. Required activities include tasks like doing homework, reading the textbook, or studying for exams. Although they are required, they are variable because you can do them whenever you can find the time and you will spend varying amounts of time on them each week. The discretionary activities are all the other things you do: eating, sleeping, socializing, participating in or watching sports and other entertainment.

As you make an overall time budget, it is helpful to determine just how much time you have spent on each category. Scheduling the fixed items is no trouble; the most common problem is allocating the variable time. If you do not seem to have enough time to get homework done when it is due, for example, the only place to get the additional time is from your discretionary activities. This suggests taking a close look at the fixed, required, and discretionary times to see where you can make adjustments.

A tool for taking a closer look at your personal time distribution is an overall time summary like that shown in Table 7.5. To complete such a summary, you will have to keep track, at least roughly, of how much time you typically spend in each

TABLE 7.5 OVERALL WEEKLY TIME SUMMARY

Name _____Student Y_____   Date _____9/23/96_____

Instructor___Mr. Z_____   Class _____CS1_____

Activity	CS	Physics	Math	English	Eat/Rest	Other	Total
Fixed							
Class	150	150	100	100			500
Required							
Homework	360	240	240	360			1200
Read Text	240	240	180	60			720
Discretionary							
Eating					1260		1260
Sleeping					3150		3150
Sports						600	600
Entertainment						360	360
Relaxation						2290	2290
Total	750	630	520	520	4410	3250	10,080

activity. Although you could use the Time Recording Log, you will not at first need its level of detail. For a start, it is adequate to make a note at the end of each day on where you spent time in each category. If you make sure that the times for each day add up to 24 hours and the total time for the week adds up to 168 hours or 10,080 minutes, your totals will probably be fairly close. If you are unable to make an adequate record this way, you might then want to use the Time Recording Log.

With a total summary like that shown in Table 7.5, you have the basic data to decide where to get the additional time needed. Once again, however, you need to be realistic. Cutting sleeping and eating time, for example, can damage your health and reduce working efficiency. Skipping meals and pulling all-nighters may be a way to meet short-term crises, but it is generally not a good idea to plan on major reductions in these areas.

Being realistic raises another issue: your willingness to actually work to the established plan. A schedule with no time for socializing, relaxation, or physical exercise can get pretty tiresome. While you may need to reduce the time spent on relaxation and entertainment, a certain amount of leisure activity is necessary. It is easy to get tired and depressed when you concentrate exclusively on work. Just as giving up chips, chocolate, and ice cream may cause you to balk at dieting, this could lead you to revolt against the whole idea of managing time. While it is important to budget and track time, ensure that your budget is something you are really willing to live with.

As you continue tracking time, compare the time you actually spend with the time you budgeted. If you can manage time consistently according to your budget, you may not need to make many changes. More likely, however, your initial plan will need adjustment. Don't feel bad about changing budgets and ground rules. Since activities will change from week to week, you will need to make occasional revisions. Remember, however, to write down the new budgets.

7.9 Managing Your Time Budget

To set ground rules for managing time, use the approach illustrated in Table 7.6, listing the times for each category on each day. If you wanted to use two time periods for one category on a single day, either use two columns or make the spaces

TABLE 7.6 EXAMPLE WEEKLY TIME SCHEDULE AND BUDGET

Name Student Y   **Date** 9/23/96

Budget Week #1 Regular weekly budget

Task	Class	Write	Exam	Read	Rev.			Other	Total
Date		Prog.	Prep.	Text					
S									
M	9:00–9:50			10:20–11:00					90
T		8:30–10:30		10:20–11:00					160
W	9:00–9:50			10:20–11:00					90
T		8:30–10:30		10:20–11:00					160
F	9:00–9:50			10:20–11:00					90
S		8:30–10:30		10:20–11:00					160
Totals	150	360		240					750

on this form larger. It's not the format that is important; focus, rather, on establishing a clear and explicit set of ground rules.

Your ability to work according to the time budget will largely depend on personal discipline, but it will also depend on the number and priority of the things you are trying to do. Unexpected events are a natural and normal part of life, especially in software engineering. Crises will periodically disrupt your plans and you will have to make adjustments. For example, to meet an important deadline, you may have to work late into the night or defer planned family, recreational, or social activities.

You may find that the first time you use a time budget, it is not very helpful. This is normal, so don't give up on the time-budgeting process just because it doesn't work the first time. Instead, think about what happened. Was there some unusual event that will not likely recur or was time consumed unexpectedly by some normal occurrence? If there was a true emergency, you may not need to make radical changes in the budget. Just try using it for another week, and then examine the results again. If, however, the budget was disrupted by some regular occurrence, consider adjusting the budget to anticipate such events in the future.

7.10 Suggestions on Managing Variable Time

When establishing ground rules for managing variable time, consider the following questions:

- *What are your highest priority items?* Try to do the most important tasks first. It is natural to put off difficult or unappealing tasks, but they will never get easier. If you find yourself deferring important work, stop and think about what you are doing. You will find that when you defer important tasks, you unconsciously worry about them. Often, in fact, deciding to do them right away will be more efficient and will provide a worthwhile sense of accomplishment. Remember, too, that once you get started on dreaded tasks, they rarely turn out to be as difficult as you had feared.

- *Are there some tasks that should be done at specific times?* Reviewing for an examination, preparing for a laboratory session, or meeting with your faculty advisor are examples. Allocate specific times for these demands in your time budget.

- *Are there activities you want to do as soon as you have the time?* In your engineering notebook, keep a list of things you need to do as soon as possible, like writing assigned programs or reading the next textbook chapter. You can then check them off when you complete them.

To manage your daily time, you need to keep the time management budgets with you all the time. A good way to do this is to carry them in your engineering notebook. Clip them inside the front or back cover or staple them to a notebook page. Whenever you update the budget, date the most recent one, and keep the old copies. Checking previous versions before you make a change will help you guard against overcorrection. To compensate for having overestimated one budgeted task, for example, you are likely to underestimate it the next time. Examining prior budgets will reveal this tendency and help you pick a more informed middle value. A rule to live by in software engineering is this: Do not throw away old plans, data, or programs. Surprisingly often, you will need them later.

7.11   Your Time Management Objective

After you have managed your time in this way for a few weeks, consider simplifying the data-gathering approach by consolidating several time categories into a very few. Your objective at this point is to get an overall picture of your time distribution rather than to know the details. For example, after tracking my own time for several years, I have reduced my work time to only two categories: company projects and personal projects. Since I plan each project separately, detailed period breakdowns don't add much useful information. To me, the most significant question is how much time I can expect to spend on each of my two project categories each week or month.

Remember that the point of gathering time data is to help yourself manage time. If the data you gather prove not to be useful, reconsider the way you gather data. Do this, however, only after you have practiced budgeting your time. Even then, if for some reason your time distribution changes significantly, gather more data until you understand how you currently spend time.

7.12   Summary

To better manage your time: Analyze your own historical time data; establish a budget for spending time; and track your time against the budget. To make a time budget: Decide how you want to spend time and make a schedule that reflects your choices and shows daily times; you may need different budgets for different weeks.

Time budget ground rules can be helpful: Identify your fixed and variable commitments. Break your variable time into tasks that are required and those that are discretionary. Analyze how you currently divide your time in these categories. Remember that your total time is fixed—if you need more time for some activities, you must spend less time on others.

Finally, track performance against the time budget: Continue gathering time data. Review the time budget against your experience. Revise the budget based on your needs and experiences. Make changes only gradually. As you change your time budget, keep the prior versions.

7.13   Assignment 7

Using the data on the way you have spent time, establish a time budget for normal weeks, and also for any special weeks you anticipate during the rest of the semester. For cases where your budget differs substantially from the time averages, briefly explain why you made the various choices. Use budget formats like those in Tables 7.4 and 7.6. Submit copies of these budgets with your homework. Note that the time budget is an optional assignment that you need not complete unless so requested by your instructor.

Submit copies of those Time Recording Log and Weekly Activity Summary pages that you have not already submitted.

8

Managing Commitments

This chapter focuses on commitments, discussing what they are, why they are important, and how to manage them. For the assignment, you will review and list your current commitments.

8.1 Defining Commitment

Being committed is a state of mind. For whatever reason, you have undertaken to do something, and you feel you should do it. A commitment, however, is more than just something you intend to do; there is also someone who expects you to do it. This, in fact, is the key issue with commitments: Who is the person to whom you are committed? In the legal or contractual sense, you are committed to someone else: your professor, your manager, your employer. More important, however, are the deeper commitments you make to yourself.

The principal problem with many software schedules and plans is that management views them as contract-like commitments but the software engineers do not view them as personal commitments. The difference, as we shall see, is largely in how the commitments are made. In this chapter, you will learn how to make contractual commitments so they are also personal commitments.

With a contractual commitment, two or more people must agree on the intended action before it is a commitment. For example, Mr. A and Ms. B agree that Mr. A will provide some product or do some task for Ms. B. An example is your commitment to your teacher to do a homework assignment for this course. Another example would be your agreement to write a program for a customer.

When Mr. A makes a commitment, he agrees with Ms. B to perform a specified task by some defined time and for some reward or compensation. This points out two more elements of commitments. In addition to agreeing on the task, the parties also agreed on the time it is to be done and on the payment or other consideration Mr. A will receive in return. Again, an example would be your agreement to complete and submit homework in one week and the instructor's agreement to give you a grade on the work. Another example could be a customer's obligation to pay you for developing and installing some software.

A key characteristic of personal commitments is that they are voluntary. Suppose, for example, that your customer finds he needs the program sooner and tells you to finish it two weeks earlier than originally agreed. He never asked if you could accomplish this feat, and you did not agree. You were just told the new deadline. Even though you may try to meet the new date, you probably won't feel personally committed to doing so.

To become truly committed, you must have thoughtfully considered the alternatives and decided that this is something you can and will do. Being told by someone that you must do it will not make you personally committed. In fact, when people are ordered to do things, they often feel threatened and angry. They resent the person making the directive and may even want to retaliate. One way to retaliate, of course, would be to not do the demanded action. While such a reaction to a normal business request may seem childish , many people unconsciously respond this way.

True agreement is the most important single characteristic of a personal commitment. The parties must agree on what is to be done, when it will be completed, and what will be given in return.

A true commitment is both personal and contractual and it requires an explicit and voluntary agreement between two or more parties on:

- what will be done,
- the criteria for determining that it is done,
- who will do it,
- when it will be done,
- the compensation or other consideration to be given in return,
- and who will provide this compensation or consideration.

8.2 Responsibly Made Commitments

In addition to the characteristics already described, commitments should be responsibly made and properly managed. You can make sure your commitments are responsible and well managed as follows.

Analyze the job before agreeing to the commitment. Both parties must enter into the commitment in good faith. You are personally committed and really intend to do the job and the other party intends to provide suitable compensation in return. The question, however, is the degree to which you have both made sure you can meet the commitment. For example, have you examined the job in sufficient detail to know you can do it? Similarly, does the other party have the capability to compensate you? Too often, software commitments are based on little more than hope. Even when both parties truly intend to perform, mere good intentions do not provide a reasonable basis for a sound commitment.

Support the commitment with a plan. For a job of any size, the way to responsibly make a commitment is to first make a plan for the work. Planning does involve some effort, but it need not take very long. In fact, if you have had experience in making formal plans, you can usually complete them quite quickly.

Document the agreement. While this may seem obvious, it is not. There is a common misperception that honest people should need only a few words and a handshake. But words are often misunderstood. Even after two people orally agree, they often have trouble agreeing on a written statement of the agreement. This means that their original agreement was superficial and not real. The second problem concerns what the two parties will do in the event of problems. That in fact, is the principal reason for most contracts. You do not need a contract when everything goes according to plan—you need one if there are problems.

If unable to meet the commitment, promptly tell the other party and try to minimize the impact on that person. When you have learned to manage your commitments, you will almost always meet them. Unfortunately, even with the best plans, the job will occasionally be more complex than you expected or something unforeseen may come up.

8.3 Example of a Commitment

Student Y has agreed to do 10 hours of part-time work each week for the University Admissions Office. The steps involved in properly making a commitment are demonstrated by her case.

1. Student Y meets with the office supervisor in the Admissions Office, who explains the job she is expected to do. This is the requirements phase of the commitment process, in which Student Y learns precisely what kind of work is wanted. For an office job, the product of this phase would be a listing of the expected tasks, possibly in a job description.

2. Student Y considers the tasks and concludes that it is a job she is both willing to do and capable of performing.

Having answered the first question—Can you do the job?—The next question is, Can you do it in the time and for the resources required? To answer this question, Student Y does the following:

3. She examines her personal time commitments and concludes that she can find 10 hours (or 600 minutes) during each week to do the job. As you can see by comparing Table 8.1 with Table 7.5 on page 82, she gets this time by reducing her weekly total relaxation time by 600 minutes.

TABLE 8.1 STUDENT Y'S WEEKLY TIME SUMMARY

Name _Student Y_   **Date** _9/30/96_

Instructor _Mr. Z_   **Class** _CS1_

Activity	CS	Physics	Math	English	Eat/Rest	Other	Total
Fixed							
Class	150	150	100	100			500
Job						600	600
Required							
Homework	360	240	240	360			1200
Read Text	240	240	180	60			720
Discretionary							
Eating					1260		1260
Sleeping					3150		3150
Sports						600	600
Entertainment						360	360
Relaxation						1690	1690
Total	750	630	520	520	4410	3250	10,080

4. She reviews her own commitments, shown in Table 8.2, and concludes that the time slot she needs for the job, from 4:00 to 6:00 o'clock Monday through Friday afternoons, is available.

5. Now that she is satisfied that she can do the job, she discusses the pay and the date the Admissions Office supervisor would like her to start work.

6. With all these matters settled, Student Y and the supervisor agree on all the items discussed and the supervisor agrees to provide a letter offer summarizing the key points.

This is a responsible commitment. Student Y took the time to understand the job and her ability to do it. She satisfied herself that she could handle the work and that she could make the time available. She also agreed with the supervisor on the pay rate and other job conditions.

TABLE 8.2 STUDENT Y'S FIXED WEEKLY COMMITMENTS

Name   Student Y   **Date**   9/30/96

Budget Week #1   Fixed time commitments

Task	CS1	Physics	Math	English	Job				Total
Date									
S									
M	9:00–9:50	10:00–10:50			4:00–6:00				220
T			9:00–9:50	10:00–10:50	4:00–6:00				220
W	9:00–9:50	10:00–10:50			4:00–6:00				220
T			9:00–9:50	10:00–10:50	4:00–6:00				220
F	9:00–9:50	10:00–10:50			4:00–6:00				220
S									
Totals	150	150	100	100	600				1100

8.4   An Example in Industry

An engineer for one of the major automobile companies was given a rush software job. Previously, management would simply have given him a date along with the assignment. But since the engineer and his team had just completed PSP training, he asked for time to look over the problem and come back in the morning with a plan.

The engineer then estimated the size of the job and used his PSP data to determine how long the work would likely take. He returned to his manager and explained the plan and why he felt it was realistic. His manager agreed and the engineer finished the work on the schedule he had committed.

Previously, schedules issued by management edict were rarely met. While many of them were unrealistic, the principal problem was the engineers' lack of personal commitment to them. By playing an active role in forming a mutual commitment with management, this engineer was able to establish a reasonable schedule. In the process, he also became personally committed.

8.5   Handling Missed Commitments

After you have become proficient at making plans, you will probably not miss your deadlines very often. You cannot, however, guarantee to never miss a date. Since many of the things software engineers do are original and creative, there is considerable risk. If you were to allow for all possible risks, your estimates would be unreasonably high, hence an occasional schedule or cost miss is unavoidable.

When you must miss a commitment, promptly notify the other party and work together to solve any resulting problems. You could, for example, agree on a longer timeframe or a reduced scope for the work. With software, a common strategy is to deliver a minimum-function version at or near the original schedule and then follow with one or more product enhancements. By properly defining the order and timing of the follow-on functions, you can often minimize the customer's disruption.

The way you handle the occasional missed deadline or unfulfilled commitment is important. Commitment problems are always unpleasant. You will probably feel badly having planned poorly, and the people you committed to could feel misled or cheated. There could be financial consequences and a search for someone to blame. The unpleasantness only worsens with time. Delaying notification in the hope that things will improve usually makes them worse. It is better to face the unpleasantness as soon as you understand the problem.

One caution is important, however: Don't give up without seriously trying to meet the commitment. Have you checked with an independent expert to see if there is a better way? Could added resources accelerate the work? Are there smarter ways to do the design? Thoughtfully examine the alternatives and then, if there is no other way, deal with the problems without delay.

Missed commitments generally lead to inconvenience and unhappiness. This is why people often defer facing up to such problems until the latest possible moment; ostrichlike, they are deferring the unpleasantness in the hope that the problems will somehow go away. Unfortunately, sticking your head in the sand almost always increases the disruption, reduces the customer's options, and maximizes the resulting unhappiness.

8.6   The Importance of Managing Commitments

The principal reason to manage your commitments is so you don't overlook or forget any. Working engineers have many commitments. They participate in reviews, write reports, attend meetings, make program corrections, and submit updates to program modules. They may have to document designs, answer customer calls, meet vendors, or participate on committees. It is not unusual for working engineers to juggle a dozen commitments simultaneously. It is thus important to learn how to manage commitments so you do not drop or forget any of them.

Another reason for managing your commitments is to help you when the work you need to do exceeds the time available. If you plan your work, you shouldn't run out of time too often, but it can be an occasional problem even when you make commitments responsibly. In this situation, quickly identify those commitments that are exposed and promptly notify the other parties.

8.7   The Consequences of Not Managing Commitments

Until you learn to manage your commitments, you will often face some of the following unpleasant consequences:

Work required exceeds time available. You will frequently have more to do than you can accomplish. If you do not keep a list of your commitments, you may take on new commitments when you should not. You might, for example, make a social engagement when you had a homework assignment due the next day. Late in the evening you remember the assignment and then have to stay up all night to get it done. Worse yet, you might not remember it at all.

Failure to meet commitments. Software development jobs are often more complex than expected. When you do not have an orderly way of making commitments, you are likely to assume the job is simpler than it really is. You will then be overcommitted from the moment you start working on the job.

Misplaced priorities. When overcommitted, people often set priorities based on what must be done first rather than what is most important. When there is more to do than you can possibly handle, it is natural to work on the next thing that must be done. Unfortunately, handling the immediate threat is often the wrong strategy. When you are seriously overcommitted, you need to restructure all your commitments to fit what you can do. By deferring or dropping some of the immediate tasks you may be able to meet the more important jobs that come later.

Poor quality work. Under schedule pressure, software engineers often feel pressed to cut corners. This is when careless or silly mistakes are more likely and when attention to quality is most needed. When time is short, engineers should take special care to avoid mistakes. Unfortunately, experience shows that this is the very circumstance when engineers and their managers are least likely to allow the time to do reviews, inspections, or thorough testing.

Loss of trust. If you frequently miss commitments, people will notice. They will learn that when you commit to something, you often don't keep to your word. Such a reputation is hard to repair and will affect your grades, your job ratings, your pay, and even your job security.

Loss of respect for your judgment. When people do not trust what you say, they are unlikely to ask for your opinion and they are more likely to insist that you work to unreasonable schedules.

The most important single asset a software engineer can have is a reputation for meeting commitments. For people to trust your word, you need to say what you plan to do and then do what you say. One important purpose of this book is to provide tools to help you make realistic commitments that you can consistently meet.

8.8   The Way to Manage Commitments

Properly managing commitments starts with making a list of the commitments you already have. Note the date each commitment is due and the amount of time it will likely take. Table 8.3 shows Student Y's commitments list.

In managing commitments in software engineering, it is important to remember several facts of life of the software business:

- If you are falling behind, your schedule will continue to slip unless you do something different.

TABLE 8.3 STUDENT Y'S COMMITMENT LIST

Name   Student Y   **Date**   9/30/96

Instructor   Mr. Z   **Class**   CS1

Date Due	Commitment	To Whom?	Hours	Date Made	Return
Weekly					
MWF	Attend CS1 Class	Instructor	1.5		Grade
MWF	Turn in CS1 homework	Instructor	6.0		Grade
Tu & Th	Read textbook	Instructor	4.0		Grade
M=>F	Part-time job, 4:00–6:00 PM	Admissions	10.0	9/1	Pay
Other					
11/28	Term paper	Instructor	24	9/11	Grade

- Just trying harder will not help. Remember, you were already trying pretty hard.
- If you do not know precisely where you are in a project and how much work remains, you are almost certainly in trouble.
- When you must have good luck in order to meet a commitment, you will not get it.
- When your estimates are wrong, they are almost always too low.
- Almost all changes involve more work.

It is always important to work aggressively to meet commitments, but if you cannot complete the work with a few hours of extra effort, face up to the problem now and deal with it responsibly.

8.9   Summary

This chapter has defined commitment, explained why it is important to meet commitments and how to manage commitments. Two or more parties make a commitment on some task when they agree on what it is, who will do it, when it will be done, and what will be paid in return. In properly made commitments there is reasonable assurance they will be met. They are backed up by a plan, and both the plan and commitment are documented.

You should manage commitments to avoid getting overcommitted. If you become overcommitted, you will fail to meet some commitments and will earn a reputation for being undependable. Consistently missing commitments can damage your career; it will affect your grades and your ability get and keep a job.

The steps to managing commitments are: (1) Make a list of your current commitments, (2) include what is to be done and when, and (3) include an estimate of how much work each commitment will likely take.

Remember the software engineer's facts of life: You will continue to fall behind unless you do something different. Just trying harder will not help. You need to know precisely where you are and how much work remains. You can't count on luck to pull you through. When your estimates are wrong, they are almost always too low. Almost all changes involve more work.

8.10   Assignment 8

Make a list of your commitments. Include a brief summary of what the commitment is, who it is committed to, when it is due, the amount of time you expect to spend to meet the commitment, and what you expect to get in return. Use a format like that shown in Table 8.3. Submit a copy of this list with your homework. Keep a copy of your commitment list in your Engineering Notebook. Note that the commitment list is an optional assignment that you need not complete unless so requested by your instructor.

Submit copies of those Time Log, Job Number Log, and Weekly Activity Summary sheets that you have not previously submitted.

9

Managing Schedules

This chapter shows how to develop and use schedules to track the progress of your work. You will learn how to use checkpoints to track progress against a schedule; and in the chapter assignment, you will identify and describe several checkpoints for tracking progress on a programming project.

9.1 The Need for Schedules

You make schedules in order to meet commitments. A schedule is necessary when you have several commitments to work on at the same time. With small projects or tasks, you can often finish one task before starting the next. Students often can wait to do homework assignments until shortly before they are due, then work on one at a time, finishing each before they start the next. This strategy is feasible for a few tasks, when time is sufficient to complete them all, and when the tasks are all short or simple enough to finish in one sitting. When tasks become larger or more complex, or the workload increases, however, or when there are schedule constraints, more sophisticated time management is needed. You must then alternate between tasks, doing one for a while and then moving to the next.

Suppose, for example, you have a program due in three weeks and a term paper to complete in four weeks. Assume you estimate about five hours to write the program but the work must be done on a particular system that is available only one hour a day. Assume also that the term paper requires some library research and that you must submit an outline in one week. You expect the term paper to take about 10 hours of total work. Since you plan to spend 5 hours a week on these assignments, you expect to finish them both on time in about three weeks.

Following the strategy of completing one task before starting the next, you start the term paper first, since the outline is due in one week. As expected, you do the research, produce the outline, and finish the report in two weeks. Then, you start on the program. After a little work, however, you find that the program will take about 10 hours of work instead of the estimated 5. Unfortunately, even with a crash effort, you cannot get enough computer time to finish the program on schedule.

Suppose, however, that you had done some initial work on *both* assignments during the first week. You would then have seen that the program was larger than expected and would have had three weeks to find the needed extra computer time.

As you work on larger and larger projects, it will be increasingly important to carefully schedule your time. A typical software engineer might have several modules to test for a development project while simultaneously working with a technical writer on product documentation. Questions might arise on a previously developed program, necessitating technical and project review meetings. Engineers somehow must fit many such tasks into their daily schedules without forgetting or slighting any of them. They also must often coordinate their work with many other people. To juggle all this without dropping any balls, they need to keep a personal schedule.

9.2   The Gantt Chart

A schedule is a time-ordered listing of planned events, generally in a format like that shown in Figure 9.1. This is called a **Gantt chart** and it has the following key elements:

- Across the top of the chart are calendar dates. Depending on the desired level of detail, the timeline can be in days, weeks, months, or years. It can even be in hours if you wish.
- The leftmost column contains an identification (ID) number for each task.
- Down the second column from the left are the names of the tasks to be done. These are typically listed in the order in which you expect to do them.

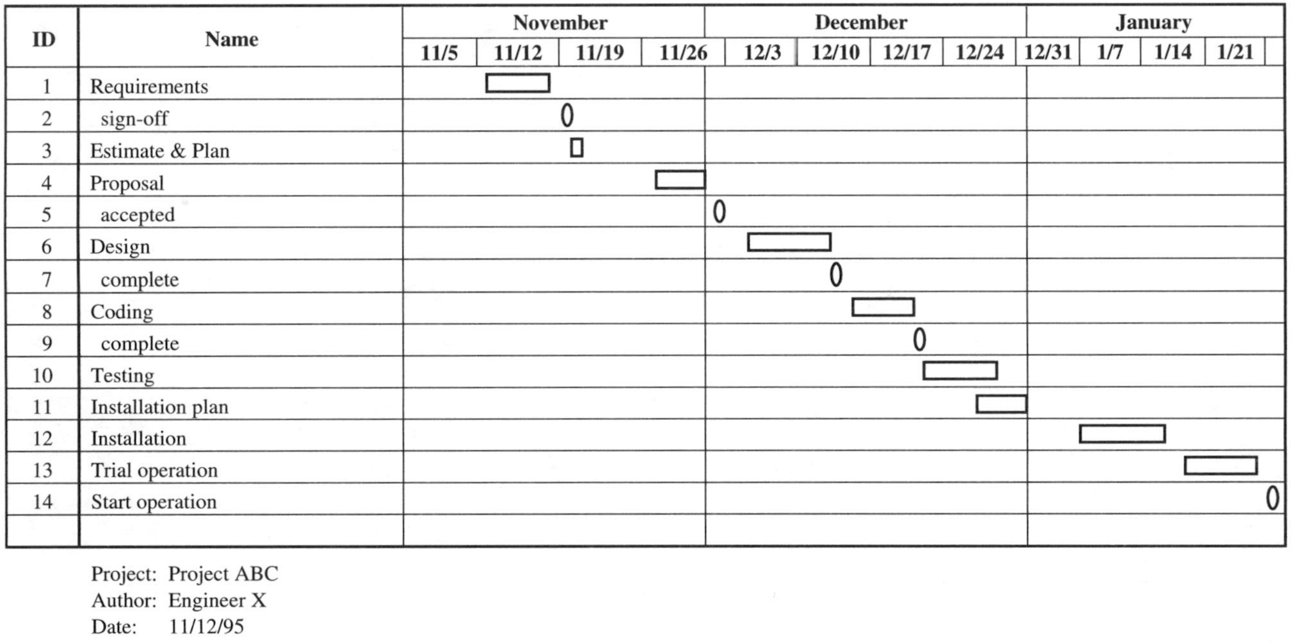

ID	Name	November 11/5	11/12	11/19	11/26	December 12/3	12/10	12/17	12/24	12/31	January 1/7	1/14	1/21
1	Requirements	▭											
2	sign-off		◇										
3	Estimate & Plan		□										
4	Proposal				▭								
5	accepted					◇							
6	Design					▭							
7	complete						◇						
8	Coding						▭						
9	complete							◇					
10	Testing								▭				
11	Installation plan									▭			
12	Installation										▭		
13	Trial operation											▭	
14	Start operation												◇

Project: Project ABC
Author: Engineer X
Date: 11/12/95

FIGURE 9.1 GANTT CHART EXAMPLE

- In the body of the chart, bars show the planned start and end dates for each task.
- At bottom left are the project name, the author of the schedule, and the date the schedule was originally produced.
- Various checkpoints are shown by the small ovals (IDs 2, 5, 7, 9, and 14). Checkpoints are discussed later in this chapter.

As you can see, the Gantt chart is a useful way to present the general flow of a project's tasks. Such charts are particularly useful for coordinating multiple activities. As explained later, the Gantt chart also provides a useful way to track project progress against the plan and schedule.

9.3   Making a Project Schedule

For a project of any size, the first step in making a schedule is to analyze the job in enough detail to identify its several component tasks. Then estimate the size for each of these smaller tasks and determine the amount of work they will likely take. Finally, list each task on a Gantt chart with a schedule bar to show when it will start and end.

When you develop schedules for work that involves several people, you need to take some additional steps:

1. Make sure that each individual knows the tasks he or she is supposed to do.
2. Obtain the committed dates for each of these tasks.
3. Identify the interdependencies among the tasks. What inputs must each person have before being able to proceed with work and from whom do they get these inputs?
4. Document each of these interdependencies.
5. Review the proposed schedule and interdependencies with all the people involved to ensure there are no conflicts, disagreements, or misunderstandings.
6. Also review the schedule to ensure that it covers all the tasks needed to properly complete the overall job.

While you will need more steps to develop schedules for full-scale software projects, these basic principles should help you make plans for your personal work or for any small team projects involving your classmates or colleagues.

9.4 Checkpoints

In planning for any but the smallest projects, it is important to break the work into several parts that can each be estimated and planned. Each of these parts can then be treated as a scheduled item. That is, when each part is completed, you have made a defined level of progress. Measurable schedule points like this are called checkpoints or milestones. Checkpoints are an important part of project planning and project management.

A **checkpoint** is an objectively identifiable point in a project. An example would be completion of some specific project activity or an important action. When a plan includes several checkpoints, each with a planned completion date, you can readily see if you are on schedule or falling behind.

To be useful, checkpoints must be clear and unambiguous. That is, a checkpoint must be a specific action that is either done or not done. Some examples of crisp checkpoints are:

- You have completed and submitted a term paper.
- You have produced and documented the plan to write a program, using a standard planning format.
- You have reviewed the development plan with your instructor and made the suggested modifications.
- You have completed and documented a program's design, using a specified design format.
- You have implemented, compiled, and corrected a program so it compiles without error.

There are many examples of crisp checkpoints that are suitable for planning purposes. The key requirement is that the completion of each checkpoint be objectively verifiable.

General statements that do not meet the criterion of verifiability cannot be used as checkpoints.

Inadequate checkpoints
- You have made a plan to write a program.
- You have designed a program.
- Coding is 90% complete.

While some of these statements could be further refined to meet the criteria of a crisp and unambiguous checkpoint, as written they are too general. For the statement "You have made a plan to write a program," how would you know if the plan contained the needed information? While you could find out by looking at the plan, the checkpoint by itself does not tell you what you want to know. Unless some defined planning framework is used, the plan may or may not be complete. For the second claim, "You have designed a program," do you know what constitutes a complete design? Almost anything from a crude flowchart to a detailed design description could be provided. If, however, the statement added that the design had been documented in a specified format, that could be a suitable checkpoint.

Fred Brooks has described the statement "Coding is 90% complete" as typical of the vague and misleading status reports on many software projects [Brooks]. If anyone tells you that a project is doing fine because coding is nearly done, that is a sure sign of trouble. If, however, the person tells you that he or she has completed, reviewed, compiled, and corrected the code for seven of the nine new modules and started work on the eighth, you can be comfortable that that person knows what he or she is talking about.

Suggestions on Establishing Checkpoints

In making a plan, establish checkpoints for any project involving more than a few hours of work. Try to identify several checkpoints during each week. For example, if a job will take about two weeks, establish at least two checkpoints and preferably four or five. Pick a number of checkpoints consistent with the amount of work involved. More than one checkpoint for a task requiring three to five hours of work would be excessive.

I have found it most helpful to establish a checkpoint for every five hours or so of work. More checkpoints would take up too much time for tracking insignificant activities. For tasks of less than about five hours' duration, manage the task as a complete unit. Under these conditions, project management reduces to time management. As long as you put in the needed hours, you will probably get the work done approximately on schedule. You should, of course, always allow a modest time cushion for each task in case it takes longer than expected.

For tasks of several weeks' duration, set at least one checkpoint each week even if you only expect to spend half an hour or so a week on the task. This checkpoint is needed to remind you to do the work when it is planned. Without such reminders, these small task elements are easy to overlook. If you cannot crisply define a checkpoint for each of these half-hour periods, of course, then the best you can do is manage the amount of time you put in. Until you actually complete a defined checkpoint, you can only generally estimate progress.

Larger projects often take several weeks or months and involve several software engineers. Because the tasks in the project are interdependent, and the project has dependencies on other projects, you may not be able to finish your tasks until other engineers complete theirs. It is thus important for each engineer in a project to have several intermediate checkpoints so that everyone can know the status of all the other work. If some engineers are having trouble, others can then help them or rearrange their work to prevent delaying the overall project.

9.5   Tracking Project Plans

Project tracking is an important part of project management and a key skill for practicing software engineers. While tracking your work can help with small tasks, the principal reason for addressing this topic now is to expose you to the planning and tracking techniques you will later need. The skills you learn with this book will apply directly to the larger jobs you will do as a software engineer.

Tracking a project plan allows you to determine whether the project is on, ahead of, or behind schedule. Crisp checkpoints and a detailed plan can reveal precisely what parts of a project are having trouble and where help is needed to get back on schedule. These concerns become critical as the project size increases. They will also become more significant as the repercussions of missing a commitment become more serious. Crisp status reporting is essential when projects are done for paying customers.

Another reason to track plans is to be able to take timely action in the event of problems. With effective project tracking, you will recognize problems early, see how to fix them, and often be able to recover. In fact, a good tracking system can even help you anticipate problems before they become serious enough to threaten project success.

An Example

A Gantt chart can be used both to portray the project schedule and to post progress against the schedule. In Figure 9.2, for example, Engineer X posts his status on December 13. Notice the following:

- The date of the status update is indicated by the vertical double line through the schedule at 12/13.
- Completed activities are indicated by a horizontal line through the completed task block. For example, the requirements task (ID 1) is shown as complete.
- Partially completed activities are indicated by the portion of the bar covered by a horizontal line. For example, design (ID 6) should have been completed by 12/12 but is shown as only about 80% complete. Until completed, of course, this 80% figure can be only an estimate.

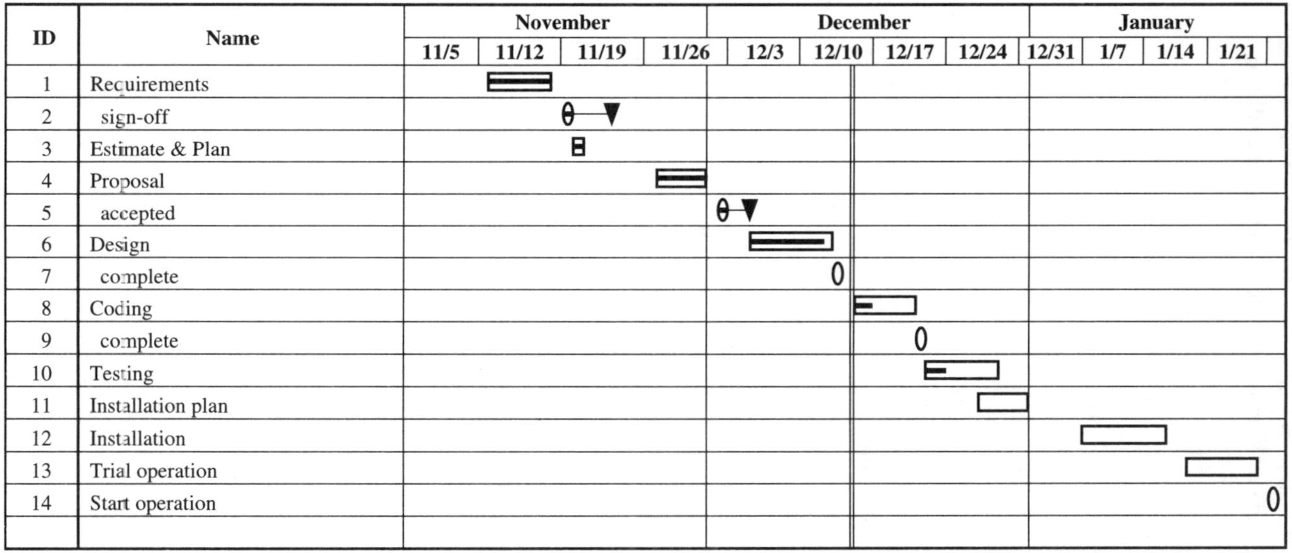

ID	Name	November				December					January		
		11/5	11/12	11/19	11/26	12/3	12/10	12/17	12/24	12/31	1/7	1/14	1/21
1	Requirements												
2	sign-off												
3	Estimate & Plan												
4	Proposal												
5	accepted												
6	Design												
7	complete												
8	Coding												
9	complete												
10	Testing												
11	Installation plan												
12	Installation												
13	Trial operation												
14	Start operation												

Project: Project ABC
Author: Engineer X
Date: 11/12/95
Updated: 12/13/95

FIGURE 9.2 GANTT CHART STATUS

- Project activities that are ahead of schedule are indicated by a progress line that extends beyond the evaluation date. For example, Engineer X started some coding and testing early (IDs 8 and 10).
- Completed checkpoints are shown filled in with an arrow to the actual date they were accomplished (IDs 2 and 5).

With this update, you can see that Engineer X is a little behind schedule with design but a little ahead with coding and testing. The "Design complete" milestone has not yet been met, however, so the project must be considered behind schedule.

Some Suggestions on Schedule Tracking

The major risk with schedule tracking is that people can easily fool themselves. They can get a falsely optimistic view by tracking vague checkpoints or by frequently changing the schedule. Some steps that will help to avoid self-deception are:

- Make sure that the checkpoint definitions are clearly defined and written down.
- Do not change the schedule until you make a complete new plan.
- When posting status against the plan, do not change the plan.
- If you wish to show new estimated completion dates, leave the original schedule in place and note the new dates with dotted lines.
- Keep copies of the original schedule and all updates.

The key is to remember that you are posting status against an original schedule that does not change. That was the plan and you are measuring the work against it. If you alter the original plan, you will have nothing to measure against. That is why, when reviewing status, it is always a good idea to check the date when the schedule was originally produced. If it is too close to the time of the review, then the update does not provide a useful measure of project progress. Ask for the original schedule.

9.6   Tracking Earned Value

One problem with project tracking is that it is often hard to know where you are. Suppose, for example, you were tracking my progress in writing the manuscript for this book. The original plan for the first 10 chapters is shown in Table 9.1. As you can see, the work started with a planning and outline effort, which was expected to

TABLE 9.1 MANUSCRIPT DEVELOPMENT PLAN

Chapter		Plan Minutes	Planned Value		Week		Earned Value
			Unit	Cum.	Plan	Actual	
Plan		681	3.243	3.243	1	1	3.244
Preface	Draft	287	1.367	4.610	2	1	1.367
	Edit	800	3.810	8.420	2	2	3.810
	Rewrite	760	3.619	12.039	3		
Chapter 1	Draft	287	1.367	13.406	3	2	1.367
	Edit	800	3.810	17.216	4	2	3.810
	Rewrite	760	3.619	20.835	4		
Chapter 2	Draft	287	1.367	22.202	4	2	1.367
	Edit	800	3.810	26.012	5	3	3.810
	Rewrite	760	3.619	29.631	6		
Chapter 3	Draft	287	1.367	30.998	7	3	1.367
	Edit	800	3.810	34.808	7	3	3.810
	Rewrite	760	3.619	38.427	8		
Chapter 4	Draft	287	1.367	39.794	10	3	1.367
	Edit	800	3.810	43.604	10	4	3.810
	Rewrite	760	3.619	47.223	10		
Chapter 5	Draft	287	1.367	48.590	11	4	1.367
	Edit	800	3.810	52.400	11	4	3.810
	Rewrite	760	3.619	56.019	12		
Chapter 6	Draft	287	1.367	57.386	12	4	1.367
	Edit	800	3.810	61.196	14		
	Rewrite	760	3.619	64.815	14		
Chapter 7	Draft	287	1.367	66.182	15	4	1.367
	Edit	800	3.810	69.992	16		
	Rewrite	760	3.619	73.611	17		
Chapter 8	Draft	287	1.367	74.978	17		
	Edit	800	3.810	78.788	18		
	Rewrite	760	3.619	82.407	18		
Chapter 9	Draft	287	1.367	83.774	19		
	Edit	800	3.810	87.584	19		
	Rewrite	760	3.619	91.203	20		
Chapter 10	Draft	287	1.367	92.570	20		
	Edit	800	3.810	96.380	20		
	Rewrite	760	3.619	100.0	21		
Total		20,998	100.0				

take 681 minutes. Following the planning, I wrote the preface and each chapter. The task involved writing a chapter draft, editing the draft, and then doing a rewrite. The expected time for each chapter is shown in Table 9.1. Here, the time I expected each task to take is shown under Plan—Minutes and the date I expected to finish is shown under Week—Plan. Week 1 started on Monday, April 17, 1995. This plan was based on data I had gathered while writing two previous books.

After completing this plan, I met with the Computer Science faculty at Embry-Riddle Aeronautical University, who wanted to use the book manuscript to teach courses the following September. That meant that I needed to complete the manuscript for the first 10 chapters by August 10. As is clear from Table 9.1, the plan did not show me completing Chapter 10 until week 21, which started on September 4, or a little over three weeks late.

Rather than redo the plan, I decided to track my work for a few weeks to see if I could make the deadline of the new shortened schedule. I also decided that instead of completing each chapter in turn, I would write and edit the drafts and then get them reviewed by some associates before I did the final rewrite. This approach would have the advantage of getting me informed critiques of the work and would most likely result in a better final product. The drawback was that I could not complete revision of any of the chapters until much later. How then could I tell whether I was proceeding on schedule?

The answer to this problem is something called **earned value.** Basically, I examined the plan and assigned a value to each task based on the amount of time it was planned to take. I did this by calculating each task's percentage of the total 20,998 minutes planned for this part of the project. Thus, the 681-minute planning task would get an earned value of 100*681/20,998 = 3.243%. To meet the accelerated schedule, I had to reach an earned value of 100% by August 10, or week 17, instead of week 21.

After the first four weeks of work, I could see that I would complete the first 10 chapters on time. The way I could tell is shown in Table 9.2 and Figure 9.3. Here, I calculated the projected value by noting that I had earned 37.037 earned value in four weeks, or 9.259 each week. At this rate, I could expect to earn the values in the Projected Values column in Table 9.2. Here, it appears that I would reach the 100% point on week 11, or much ahead of week 17 when it was needed.

The point is, by using earned value, I could do the work in a different order than originally planned and still track progress against the plan. While I could have redone the plan, that would have been a lot of work and would have delayed the project. Since I had added the review task, completion took a little longer than planned and I actually finished the manuscript on week 15 in time for the fall semester.

While you will not be required to use earned value tracking further in this textbook, you will find it a very useful technique for later managing schedules for larger projects. Earned value is discussed more thoroughly in Chapter 6 of the PSP textbook [Humphrey].

TABLE 9.2 BOOK SCHEDULE

Week #	Planned Value	Earned Value	Projected Value
1	3.243	4.610	
2	8.420	14.963	
3	13.406	25.317	
4	22.202	37.037	
5	26.012		46.296
6	29.631		55.556
7	34.808		64.815
8	38.427		74.074
9	38.427		83.333
10	47.223		92.592
11	52.400		101.852
12	57.386		
13	57.386		
14	64.815		
15	66.182		
16	69.992		
17	74.978		
18	82.407		
19	87.585		
20	96.380		
21	100.0		

9.7   Summary

This chapter covers schedules and checkpoints, explaining why schedules are needed and how Gantt charts are produced and used for scheduling. Checkpoints are an important part of project planning and management: A checkpoint identifies the completion of a specific project event; it must be specific and have established completion criteria. You should have a checkpoint for at least every 5 to 10 hours of work, and at least one or two checkpoints for every project week. Check-

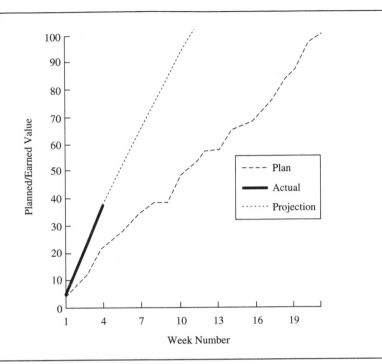

FIGURE 9.3 BOOK MANUSCRIPT—ACTUAL AND PROJECTION

points help you to see where a project stands and take corrective action when a project is falling behind. Earned value helps you to precisely track project status and accurately estimate when you will finish.

9.8   Assignment 9

Define three or more checkpoints for the work to write a modest-sized program. Submit a brief report describing each checkpoint and how someone else could tell that it has been met. Note that the checkpoint assignment is optional and that you need not complete it unless so requested by the instructor.

Submit copies of those Time Log, Job Number Log, and Weekly Activity Summary sheets that you have not previously submitted.

References

[Brooks] Brooks, Frederick P. *The Mythical Man-Month, Essays on Software Engineering, Anniversary Edition.* Reading, MA: Addison-Wesley Publishing Company, 1995.

[Humphrey] Humphrey, W. S. *A Discipline for Software Engineering.* Reading, MA: Addison-Wesley, 1995.

10

The Project Plan

This chapter extends the discussion of product planning to include time estimating. The Project Plan Summary form is introduced for recording both estimated and actual program size and development time. For the assignment, you will produce a project plan for the next program you write.

10.1 The Need for Project Plans

The project plan defines the work and how it will be done. It provides a definition of each major task, an estimate of the time and resources required, and a framework for management review and control. The project plan is also a powerful learning vehicle. When properly documented, it is a benchmark to compare with actual performance. This comparison permits the planners to see their estimating errors and to improve their planning accuracy [Humphrey 89].

The project plan is thus an essential part of a project. The larger the project, the more important it is to have a plan. The reason you make project plans in this course is to learn how. As you get more experience, your ability to produce accurate plans will improve and you will be able to produce one quickly when needed. For now, the project plans you make will only include a product size estimate and the time you estimate to do the work. After you finish the job, you will also enter the actual size and time data.

Once you have made a time estimate, write it down so that when you finish the job, you can compare the estimate with the time it actually took to do the work. Analyzing such comparisons will help you make better estimates for future tasks. If, for example, your estimates are generally too low, you can adjust them upward, or conversely, if the estimates are consistently too high, you can adjust them downward. Be careful making these adjustments, however, as it is easy to overcorrect.

10.2   The Project Plan Summary

The form you use to record planned and actual project data is shown in Table 10.1. In later chapters items will be added to this relatively simple form. To keep from introducing new forms with each chapter, we will actually use the Project Plan Summary form shown in Table 10.2, in which the entries that will later be introduced are shaded. Ignore the shading for now.

TABLE 10.1 PROJECT PLAN SUMMARY

Student	_____	Date	_____
Program	_____	Program #	_____
Instructor	_____	Language	_____

Summary	Plan	Actual
Minutes/LOC	_____	_____
LOC/Hour	_____	_____

Program Size (LOC):	Plan	Actual
Total New & Changed	_____	_____
Maximum Size	_____	
Minimum Size	_____	

Time in Phase (min.)	Plan	Actual
Total	_____	_____
Maximum Time	_____	
Minimum Time	_____	

TABLE 10.2 PSP PROJECT PLAN SUMMARY

Student _____   Date _____

Program _____   Program # _____

Instructor _____   Language _____

Summary	Plan	Actual	To Date
Minutes/LOC			
LOC/Hour			
Defects/KLOC			
Yield			
A/FR			

Program Size (LOC):

	Plan		To Date
Total New & Changed			
Maximum Size			
Minimum Size			

Time in Phase (min.)	Plan	Actual	To Date	To Date %
Planning				
Design				
Code				
Code Review				
Compile				
Test				
Postmortem				
Total				
Maximum Time				
Minimum Time				

Defects Injected	Plan	Actual	To Date	To Date %	Def./Hour
Planning					
Design					
Code					
Code Review					
Compile					
Test					
Total					

Defects Removed	Plan	Actual	To Date	To Date %	Def./Hour
Planning					
Design					
Code					
Code Review					
Compile					
Test					
Total					

To complete the form, fill in the **Plan** parts before starting a programming project. When finished, complete the **Actual** entries. The chapter assignments will ask you to turn in a filled-out Project Plan Summary form with each completed program from now on. Save copies of these forms so you have data on your work for use in future assignments. The following paragraphs explain how to complete the Project Plan Summary form in Table 10.2.

10.3   The Summary

The Summary section holds the rate data used to make the plan. It also provides a place to record the actual rate data after job completion. The top entry in the Summary section is Minutes/LOC (minutes per line of code). Under the Plan column, enter the Minutes/LOC rate used in making the plan. As shown in the example in Table 10.3, Student X used his historical data from the prior program or the Job Number Log to get the rate of 7.82 Minutes/LOC for this program. Of course, if he had no historical data, he would have had to guess.

Unless you have a good reason to do otherwise, use your historical average rate for the latest program in the Job Number Log. You might need to use a different value if a new program seems particularly difficult and likely to take longer than average. Or you might need to use a different value in the converse case, if a new program is so similar to one you have recently written that it will probably take much less effort. By checking the average, maximum, and minimum time values for the most recent programming job, you can select an appropriate value for the new program.

The next entry in the Summary section is LOC/Hour (lines of code per hour). Again, enter the planned value before starting the work and the actual value after job completion. The LOC/Hour are calculated from Minutes/LOC by dividing 60 by Minutes/LOC. In the example in Table 10.3, Student X's planned Minutes/LOC rate is 7.82, and so the planned LOC/Hour number is $60/7.82 = 7.67$. The LOC/Hour rate is commonly used by engineers to analyze development productivity.

10.4   Program Size

The Program Size (LOC) section of the Project Plan Summary form contains the estimated and actual data on the program's size and the likely size ranges. Using the methods described in Chapter 6, estimate the finished size of the program you plan to develop and enter it under Plan in the Total New & Changed row. In completing the Project Plan Summary for program 8, Student X made a size estimate, as shown in Table 10.4.

The reason the size entry is labeled Total New & Changed is that you should only record the numbers of LOC that you will actually write. At first, each pro-

TABLE 10.3 PROJECT PLAN SUMMARY EXAMPLE

Student	Student X	Date	10/7/96
Program		Program #	8
Instructor	Mr. Z	Language	Ada

Summary	Plan	Actual	To Date
Minutes/LOC	7.82	7.21	
LOC/Hour	7.67	8.32	
Defects/KLOC			
Yield			
A/FR			

Program Size (LOC):			
Total New & Changed	26	19	
Maximum Size	36		
Minimum Size	18		

Time in Phase (min.)	Plan	Actual	To Date	To Date %
Planning				
Design				
Code				
Code Review				
Compile				
Test				
Postmortem				
Total	203	137		
Maximum Time	282			
Minimum Time	141			

Defects Injected	Plan	Actual	To Date	To Date %	Def./Hour
Planning					
Design					
Code					
Code Review					
Compile					
Test					
Total					

Defects Removed	Plan	Actual	To Date	To Date %	Def./Hour
Planning					
Design					
Code					
Code Review					
Compile					
Test					
Total					

gram you write will generally be entirely new. After a few programs, however, you will begin to use library routines to perform standard functions or you may develop a new program by adding to or modifying a previous program. To save development time, you may also copy parts of previously developed programs. You might, for example, decide to reuse a function in a program that you had already

TABLE 10.4 STUDENT X PROGRAM SIZE ESTIMATE

Student _Student X_ Date _10/7/96_
Instructor _Mr. Z_ Class _CS1_

Program	LOC	Prior Functions	Estimated Functions	Min.	Avg.	Max.
Case						
2	11	Simple case statement				
4	18	Medium case statement	Large case statement	12	17	24
Loops						
1	5	Simple do while	Small loop	3	4	5
6	11	Medium repeat until				
Calc.						
3	23	Large calculation				
Text						
5	7	Small text string	Simple text string	3	5	7
7	24	Medium text string				
Estimate				18	26	36

Comments: This program has a fairly large case statement for selecting among a number of text conditions. The case statement is thus about the size of the one in program 4 but could be larger. A simple loop is needed to cycle through the case conditions for each text input, and a simple text string analyzer is needed to format the text for the final result. Assume that the maximum sizes for the loop and text functions are about the sizes of the prior programs and that the case statement is somewhat larger. Also assume that the minimum size is about half the maximum size.

written. Rather than write it all over again, you merely copy that code and reuse it in the new program.

None of these previously developed lines of code are counted when you estimate the size of the new program. The reason is that you want to track the program LOC you actually write. This is what takes the most time and this is how the productivity rate in Minutes/LOC is calculated. This row in the Project Plan Summary is thus called Total New & Changed because that is the only type of code to count—both the new LOC written and any LOC in previously written code that are changed. Then, to estimate how long it will take to develop a new program, multiply the planned Minutes/LOC times the planned New & Changed LOC.

For example, if you copied 25 LOC from a previous program while developing 30 LOC of new code, this would only be 30 LOC of new and changed code. On the other hand, if you copied 25 LOC from a previous program and modified 7 of these LOC, that would be 37 New and Changed LOC: 7 LOC of changed code plus 30 LOC of new code.

The reason to count only New & Changed LOC this way is that the amount of code you use from libraries or from your previously developed programs will vary widely. Also, the time in minutes/LOC for including this code is generally much less than normally required to develop new code or modify existing code. Thus, if you ignore these reused and copied LOC, you will generally ignore a relatively small part of the total job and your estimates will probably be more accurate. While the subject of how to count modified and reused code can get complex, for now you will include all the new and changed LOC in the size estimates but none of the reused code. Ignore any LOC taken from various system libraries or from previously developed programs. If, however, the time spent on reusing previously developed programs seems too large to ignore, consult the fuller discussion of this subject in Chapters 4 and 5 of the PSP text [Humphrey 95].

Maximum and Minimum Size

The maximum and minimum size numbers in the Program Size (LOC) section are obtained from a size estimate that is made in the way that was described in Chapter 6. In the example in Table 10.4, Student X used the sum of the sizes of programs 1 and 5 as the maximum sizes for two of the functions and selected a somewhat larger number than program 4 for the other function. To compute the minimum, he assumed that the combined new functions would be about half the total size of the maximum. He then selected a most likely size as about at the midpoint between these numbers. He thus picked the maximum size as 36 and the minimum size as 18 LOC and the most likely size as 26 LOC.

These maximum and minimum size numbers are useful for judging the likely time range for a development estimate. For example, if you were particularly anxious to complete a new program on the committed date, consider the maximum size as an indication of how big the program could become. If you had estimated the likely size for a new program was 26 LOC and the maximum size was 36 LOC, you might want to allow some leeway in the schedule in case the program turned out close to the maximum value.

The minimum size value is also obtained as described in Chapter 6. The main reason for calculating this number is to encourage you to think about the likely size range of the planned program. Generally, however, base plans and commitments on the average and maximum size numbers.

Note also that the maximum and minimum values are based purely on the ranges of the size estimate. They were thus not statistically derived and cannot be relied on to provide statistical limits. Until you have a substantial amount of data, only use the maximum and minimum size estimates for general planning guidance. When you have more data, consider using the prediction interval calculations given in Chapter 5 and Appendix A of the PSP text [Humphrey 95].

10.5   Time in Phase

The next section of the Project Plan Summary form in Table 10.3 is called Time in Phase because it is later used for data on the phases of the software development process. Until the next chapter, however, use only total program development time.

To calculate the total planned development time for a new program, estimate the program size in LOC and then multiply it by the planned Minutes/LOC from the top of the form. This gives an estimate of the total minutes to develop the program. These numbers are also shown in the example in Table 10.3. Total planned time is obtained by multiplying the planned Minutes/LOC by the planned New & Changed LOC: 7.82*26 = 203.32, or 203 minutes.

Also calculate minimum and maximum times and enter them in the Plan column. Get these values by multiplying the minimum and maximum sizes by the Minutes/LOC to give the minimum and maximum times respectively. For the minimum, 7.82*18 = 140.76, and for the maximum, 7.82*36 = 281.52.

Note that you could also obtain maximum-maximum and minimum-minimum values by multiplying the maximum and minimum LOC by the maximum and minimum Minutes/LOC rates from the Job Number Log. Since these values generally provide too wide limits for useful guidance we will not use them in the Project Plan Summary. They may, however, give you some idea of the worst case and best case development times you can expect.

Complete and enter these Plan data on the Project Plan Summary before you actually develop the program and then complete the Actual data when you are done. As you do the work, track the time and, when finished, enter the total on the Total row under the Actual column. Also, count the New & Changed LOC in the finished program and calculate the actual Minutes/LOC and LOC/Hour. To review the way the Project Plan Summary is completed, consult the instructions in Table 10.5.

10.6   Estimating Accuracy

Your initial size and time estimates will probably not be very accurate. This is normal. The first objective is to learn to make unbiased estimates. That is, for every 10 estimates, you want about 5 to be overestimates and 5 to be underestimates.

TABLE 10.5 PROJECT PLAN SUMMARY INSTRUCTIONS

Purpose	This form holds the estimated and actual project data in a convenient and readily retrievable form.
Header	Enter the following: • Your name and today's date • The program name and number • The instructor's name • The language you will use to write the program
Summary Minutes/LOC	Prior to development • Enter the Minutes/LOC planned for this project. After development • Divide the total development time by the actual program size to get the actual Minutes/LOC. • For example, if the project took 266 minutes and you produced 34 LOC, the Minutes/LOC would be 266/34 = 7.82.
LOC/Hour	Prior to development • Calculate the LOC per hour planned for this program by dividing 60 by the Plan Minutes/LOC. After development • For Actual LOC/Hour, divide 60 by the Actual Minutes/LOC. • For Actual Minutes/LOC of 7.82, Actual LOC/Hour are 60/7.82 = 6.76.
Program Size (LOC)	Prior to development • Enter under plan the estimated Total, Maximum, and Minimum New & Changed LOC. After development • Count and enter the Actual New & Changed LOC.
Time in Phase Plan	For Total development time, multiply Total New & Changed LOC by Minutes/LOC. For example, with 7.82 Minutes/LOC and Total New & Changed LOC of 26 LOC, Total = 26*7.82 = 203 minutes. For Maximum time, multiply the Maximum size by Minutes/LOC. For example, with 7.82 Minutes/LOC and Maximum Size of 36 LOC, Maximum Time = 36*7.82 = 282 minutes. For Minimum time, multiply the Minimum size by Minutes/LOC. For example, with 7.82 Minutes/LOC and Minimum Size of 18 LOC, Minimum Time = 18*7.82 = 141 minutes.
Actual	At job completion, enter the actual development time in minutes. Get these data from the time log.

Although you would prefer that they all be exactly correct, such accuracy is not likely. Estimate fluctuations will reduce only gradually, but you should soon be able to make unbiased estimates—that is, to make about as many overestimates as underestimates. With experience, you can then gradually reduce the average size of the estimating error.

Document your estimates, study them, and learn from them. This will help you to make better estimates. Some engineers are better estimators than others. As you measure estimating accuracy, you will know how big an allowance to make for under- and overestimates. This will help you judge the risk of making commitments you cannot meet.

10.7   Summary

This chapter shows how to make project plans. It describes the product planning process, defines the needed data and forms, and gives an example of a completed project plan. Documenting project plans enables you to compare the estimated and actual development time and size of a program and learn to make better plans.

To make good plans, you need an estimate of how the job at hand compares with previous jobs, historical data on how long similar tasks have taken, and a form on which to record the plan. To obtain the data to make plans, measure the sizes of the completed products, estimate the size of the next job, estimate the likely development rate for this job, calculate the time the new job will likely take, and determine the likely size and development time ranges for the new job.

10.8   Assignment 10

Make a plan for writing the next program. Base this plan on your historical data, and use the planning form in Table 10.2. In the future, make and submit a plan for every programming assignment. In that plan, record the original estimate before you start development and then enter the actual sizes and times when you have finished the work. Also, submit a copy of the program size estimate using the form shown in Table 10.4.

Submit a copy of any Time Recording Log, Job Number Log, and Weekly Activity Summary sheets that you have not previously submitted. From now until the end of the semester, submit these completed forms for every program you develop for this course.

References

[Humphrey 89] Humphrey, W. S. *Managing the Software Process.* Reading, MA: Addison-Wesley, 1989.

[Humphrey 95] Humphrey, W. S. *A Discipline for Software Engineering.* Reading, MA: Addison-Wesley, 1995.

11

The Software Development Process

Following a systematic process will help you to plan and manage your work more effectively. This chapter explains how to use a process to develop software. For the assignment, you will produce a plan and write a program, using the process described in this chapter.

11.1 Why We Use Processes

In helping a number of software organizations improve their performance, one of the principal problems I have found is determining the organization's current performance. One group, for example, could not even tell how many projects had been late or over budget. Without such data, there was no way they could tell if they were getting better or getting worse. To address this problem, they started gathering data using the methods you will learn in this chapter.

A process is a defined set of steps for doing a job. Each step or phase of a job has specified entry criteria that must be satisfied before starting the phase. Similarly, each phase has exit criteria to be satisfied before completing the phase. The process steps then define the tasks and how they are done. The design and management of processes is important in software engineering because the quality of an engineer's process largely determines the quality and productivity of the engineer's work. The objective of the personal process defined in this book is to help you be a more effective software engineer.

The process used in this course is called the Personal Software Process (PSP). The PSP is a framework that helps software engineers measure and improve the way they work. Its two objectives are to help you develop programs and to show you how using processes can improve the way you work. Later, when you develop larger and more complex programs, you can extend the PSP to help you with that work. While this book does not describe how to define and extend processes, the methods are well known and are covered in the larger PSP textbook [Humphrey 95].

11.2   Some Definitions

In discussing processes, we use the terms defined in Chapter 5 and a few more:

- □ A **product** is something you produce for a co-worker, an employer, or a customer.
- □ A **project** typically produces a product.
- □ A **task** is a defined element of work.
- □ A **process** defines the way to do projects.
- □ Processes have various **phases** or steps, like planning, developing, and testing.
- □ A process phase could be composed of multiple tasks or activities, like integration test, product test, and system test.
- □ Note that a process may have only one phase or many and a phase may have only one task or activity or many.
- □ Plans describe the way a specific project is to be done: how, when, and at what cost. You can also plan individual tasks.
- □ A **job** is something you do, either a project or a task.

When a process is fully described, it is called a *defined process*. Defined processes are typically composed of scripts, forms, templates, and standards. A process script is a written set of steps the process users or agents follow when using the process. Various forms, such as logs and summaries, are used to record and store project data. In the remaining chapters of this book, you will use the PSP. The elements of the PSP are shown in Figure 11.1. Note that, although this figure shows both time and defect logs, you will not start gathering defect data until Chapter 12.

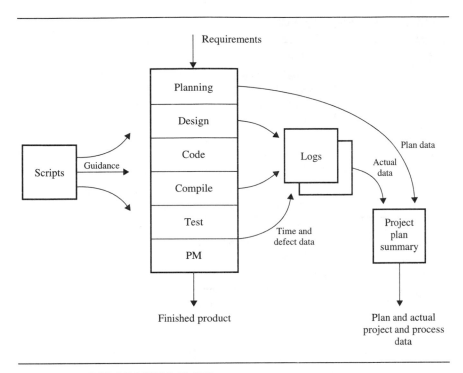

FIGURE 11.1 PSP PROCESS FLOW

11.3   The Process Script

The initial PSP script is presented in Table 11.1. This is the first of several PSP script versions. In subsequent chapters, this script is enhanced to include additional steps. The phases of the PSP process are described below and summarized in Table 11.1.

Planning.   First obtain the requirements for the project and then complete the unshaded Plan portions of the Project Plan Summary form. Finally, enter the time you took to do this planning in the Time Recording Log.

Design.   Design the program. While a design need not be elaborate, think through the program logic before starting to write the code. Record the design in

TABLE 11.1 PSP PROCESS SCRIPT

	Purpose	To guide you in developing small programs
	Entry criteria	The problem description PSP Project Plan Summary form Actual size and time data for previous programs Time Recording Log
1	Planning	Obtain a description of the program functions. Estimate the Max., Min., and total LOC required. Determine the Minutes/LOC. Calculate the Max., Min., and total development times. Enter the plan data in the Project Plan Summary form. Record the planning time in the Time Recording Log.
2	Design	Design the program. Record the design in the specified format. Record design time in the Time Recording Log.
3	Code	Implement the design. Use a standard format for entering the code. Record coding time in the Time Recording Log.
4	Compile	Compile the program. Fix all defects found. Record compile time in the Time Recording Log.
5	Test	Test the program. Fix all defects found. Record testing time in the Time Recording Log.
6	Postmortem	Complete the Project Plan Summary form with actual time and size data. Record postmortem time in the Time Recording Log.
	Exit criteria	A thoroughly tested program A properly documented design A complete program listing A completed Project Plan Summary Completed time logs

a flowchart, in pseudocode, or in any other format your instructor specifies. At the end of the design phase, record the design time in the Time Recording Log. The design process and various kinds of design representations are discussed further in Chapter 17.

Code.   Implement the design by coding in the selected programming language. Use a consistent coding format and follow the coding standards your instructor specifies. At the end of the coding phase, record the coding time in the Time Recording Log.

Compile.   Compile the program and correct all the defects found. Continue compiling and fixing defects until the program compiles properly without any error messages. All the time spent in this phase is counted as compile time, even when correcting the code or changing the design. At the end of the compile phase, record the compile time in the Time Recording Log.

Test.   Run enough tests to ensure that the program meets all its requirements and runs a comprehensive set of tests without error. All the time spent in this phase is counted as test time, including correcting the code, changing the design, and re-compiling. At the end of the test phase, record the test time in the Time Recording Log.

Postmortem.   Complete the actual entries in the Project Plan Summary form as described in the remainder of this chapter. Since you have to record the post-mortem time before you have actually finished the postmortem phase, complete as much of the work as you can and then allow a few minutes to make the final cal-culations and enter an estimated postmortem time. Use this estimated postmortem time to compute the total development time and all the other calculations.

11.4   Checkpoints and Phases

Checkpoints were introduced in Chapter 9 to help in making and tracking project schedules. By defining explicit and clearly recognizable project checkpoints, you can make better plans. The reason these plans are better is that the checkpoints provide precise reference points for measuring project status while you are doing the work.

The software development process further extends the checkpoint idea from a few points to all the process phases. With a defined process, each phase produces a specified result and hence the completion of a phase is a measurable checkpoint. By using a defined process, you will have many checkpoints to help in planning and tracking your work.

11.5.   The Updated Project Plan Summary Form

The Project Plan Summary in Table 11.2 is one of the forms for the PSP process. Its instructions are given in Table 11.3. As before, parts of the Project Plan Sum-mary are shaded. These parts can be ignored now because they will not be used

TABLE 11.2 PSP PROJECT PLAN SUMMARY

Student _____   Date _____

Program _____   Program # _____

Instructor _____   Language _____

Summary	Plan	Actual	To Date
Minutes/LOC	_____	_____	_____
LOC/Hour	_____	_____	_____
Defects/KLOC	_____	_____	_____
Yield	_____	_____	_____
A/FR	_____	_____	_____

Program Size (LOC):

Total New & Changed	_____	_____	_____
Maximum Size	_____		
Minimum Size	_____		

Time in Phase (min.)	Plan	Actual	To Date	To Date %
Planning	_____	_____	_____	_____
Design	_____	_____	_____	_____
Code	_____	_____	_____	_____
Code Review	_____	_____	_____	_____
Compile	_____	_____	_____	_____
Test	_____	_____	_____	_____
Postmortem	_____	_____	_____	_____
Total	_____	_____	_____	_____
Maximum Time	_____			
Minimum Time	_____			

Defects Injected	Plan	Actual	To Date	To Date %	Def./Hour
Planning	_____	_____	_____	_____	
Design	_____	_____	_____	_____	
Code	_____	_____	_____	_____	
Code Review	_____	_____	_____	_____	
Compile	_____	_____	_____	_____	
Test	_____	_____	_____	_____	
Total	_____	_____	_____	_____	_____

Defects Removed	Plan	Actual	To Date	To Date %	Def./Hour
Planning	_____	_____	_____	_____	
Design	_____	_____	_____	_____	
Code	_____	_____	_____	_____	
Code Review	_____	_____	_____	_____	_____
Compile	_____	_____	_____	_____	_____
Test	_____	_____	_____	_____	_____
Total	_____	_____	_____	_____	

TABLE 11.3 PSP PROJECT PLAN SUMMARY INSTRUCTIONS

Purpose	This form holds the estimated and actual project data in a convenient and readily retrievable form.
Header	Enter the following: • Your name and today's date • The program name and number • The instructor's name • The language you will use to write the program
Minutes/LOC	Prior to development • Enter the Minutes/LOC planned for this project.*Use the To Date rate from the most recent program in the Job Number Log or the most recent Project Plan Summary* After development • Divide the total development time by the actual program size to get the actual Minutes/LOC. • For example, if the project took 196 minutes and you produced 29 LOC, the Minutes/LOC would be 196/29 = 6.76.
LOC/Hour	Prior to development • Calculate the LOC per hour planned for this program by dividing 60 by the Plan Minutes/LOC. After development • For Actual LOC/Hour, divide 60 by the Actual Minutes/LOC. • For Actual Minutes/LOC of 6.76, Actual LOC/Hour are 60/6.76 = 8.88.
Program size (LOC)	Prior to development • Enter under plan the estimated Total, Maximum, and Minimum New & Changed LOC. After development • Count and enter the Actual New & Changed LOC. • *For To Date, add Actual New & Changed LOC to the To Date New & Changed LOC for the previous program.*
Time in Phase Plan	For Total development time, multiply Total New & Changed LOC by Minutes/LOC. For Maximum time, multiply the Maximum size by Minutes/LOC. For Minimum time, multiply the Minimum size by Minutes/LOC. *From the Project Plan Summary for the most recent program, find the To Date % values for each phase.* *Using the To Date % from the previous program, calculate the plan time for each phase.*
Actual	At job completion, enter the actual time in minutes spent *in each development phase.* Get these data from the time log.
To Date	*For each phase, enter the sum of actual time and To Date time from the most recent previous program.*
To Date %	*For each phase, enter 100 times the To Date time for that phase divided by the Total To Date time.*

until later chapters. To identify the changes from one process version to the next, the additions are shown in ***Bold Italics.*** By comparing Tables 10.2 and 11.2, you can see that several sections that were previously shaded are now used. For example, under Time in Phase, the Planning, Design, Code, Compile, Test, and Postmortem rows are now included in the form. Also, the To Date and To Date % columns are used. To indicate that these are new additions to the form, the new column and row headings are given in ***Bold Italics.***

The Time in Phase section of the new Project Plan Summary form has a row for each phase of the process. This row holds the planned and actual times for each process phase. During the planning phase, enter all the Plan data on this form. During the postmortem phase, enter the Actual data. When recording time in the Time Recording Log, note in the comments section the process phase you are in. Then, during the postmortem, enter these times in the Actual Time in Phase column for each phase.

Before starting a project, complete the Plan portion of the Project Plan Summary form just as in Chapter 10. The only difference now is that you need to estimate the time to be spent in each phase. The way to do this is to allocate the total development time to the phases in proportion to the way you have spent time on previous projects. The first time you use this PSP version, you won't have actual data to do this, so you will have to guess. For subsequent projects, however, you can use the data from previous projects to estimate the time for each phase of the new project. This is the reason for the To Date % values in the Project Plan Summary form.

The To Date and To Date % columns in the Project Plan Summary form provide a simple way to calculate the percent distribution of development time by process phase. The To Date column contains the total of all the time spent in each phase for all the completed programs. The To Date % column holds the percentage distribution of the times in the To Date column. The example in Section 11.7 shows how to calculate the To Date and To Date % entries.

11.6   A Planning Example

Table 11.4 shows how Student X completed the plan part of the Project Plan Summary form for program 9. He used the data from the Project Plan Summary for program 8 in Table 11.5. The plan entries in Table 11.4 are obtained as follows:

- □ *Minutes/LOC.* In planning program 9, look at the Actual Minutes/LOC for the previous program, which is program 8 in Table 11.5, and find the rate of 7.21 Minutes/LOC.

TABLE 11.4 PSP PROJECT PLAN SUMMARY

Student	Student X		Date	10/21/96
Program			Program #	9
Instructor	Mr. Z		Language	Ada

Summary	Plan	Actual	To Date
Minutes/LOC	7.21		
LOC/Hour	8.32		
Defects/KLOC			
Yield			
A/FR			

Program Size (LOC):

	Plan	Actual	To Date
Total New & Changed	23		
Maximum Size	31		
Minimum Size	15		

Time in Phase (min.)	Plan	Actual	To Date	To Date %
Planning	5			
Design	0			
Code	74			
Code Review				
Compile	25			
Test	52			
Postmortem	10			
Total	166			
Maximum Time	224			
Minimum Time	108			

Defects Injected	Plan	Actual	To Date	To Date %	Def./Hour
Planning					
Design					
Code					
Code Review					
Compile					
Test					
Total					

Defects Removed	Plan	Actual	To Date	To Date %	Def./Hour
Planning					
Design					
Code					
Code Review					
Compile					
Test					
Total					

Unless you have a good reason to do otherwise, use these prior actual rates in planning new projects. In the future, rather than using the actual rate for the previous program, you will use the average rates for all the programs developed to date. When the To Date rates are included in the PSP in Chapter 12, they provide these data.

- □ *LOC/Hour.* Student X calculated the LOC/Hour as $60/7.21 = 8.32$.
- □ *Program Size.* In the same way as in Chapter 6, Student X estimated the program's Total New & Changed (N) LOC and the Max. and Min. LOC. In the example in Table 11.4, these sizes are 23, 31, and 15 LOC respectively.
- □ *Time in Phase—Total.* Using the estimated size of 23 LOC and the rate of 7.21 minutes/LOC, the likely development time is $7.21*23 = 166$ minutes.
- □ *Maximum Time.* The maximum time is Minutes/LOC times Maximum Size or: $7.21*31 = 224$ minutes.
- □ *Minimum Time.* The minimum time is Minutes/LOC times Minimum Size, or $7.21*15 = 108$ minutes.

With a total estimated development time of 166 minutes, use the To Date % data from Table 11.5 to estimate the likely times by phase in developing program 9. Student X made these calculations as follows:

- □ *Planning.* Estimated planning time is $2.9*166/100 = 4.81$, or about 5 minutes.
- □ *Design.* Planned design time is $0*166/100 = 0$.
- □ *Code.* Planned coding time is $44.6*166/100 = 74.04$, or 74 minutes.
- □ *Compile.* Planned compile time is $15.3*166/100 = 25.40$, or 25 minutes.
- □ *Test.* Planned test time is $31.4*166/100 = 52.12$, or 52 minutes.
- □ *Postmortem.* Planned postmortem time is $5.8*166/100 = 9.63$, or 10 minutes.

Remember that on the first program developed with the PSP, you will not have prior data to use as a guide. Since Student X had no previous history when planning program 8, he had to guess. As you can see by comparing the plan and actual times in Table 11.5, his actual time distribution was quite different from his guess. A little data can make a big difference in planning. For program 9, Student X's plan was much closer to his actual times.

11.7 An Example of To Date Calculations

In the postmortem phase for program 9, Student X counted 29 new and changed LOC and recorded this number in the Actual space in the Project Plan Summary form in Table 11.6. Next, he found the actual times for each phase in the Time

TABLE 11.5 PSP PROJECT PLAN SUMMARY

Student   Student X   Date   10/7/96

Program   Program #   8

Instructor   Mr. Z   Language   Ada

Summary	Plan	Actual	To Date
Minutes/LOC	7.82	7.21	7.21
LOC/Hour	7.67	8.32	8.32
Defects/KLOC			
Yield			
A/FR			

Program Size (LOC):			
Total New & Changed	26	19	19
Maximum Size	36		
Minimum Size	18		

Time in Phase (min.)	Plan	Actual	To Date	To Date %
Planning	10	4	4	2.9
Design	19	0	0	0
Code	118	61	61	44.6
Code Review				
Compile	12	21	21	15.3
Test	29	43	43	31.4
Postmortem	15	8	8	5.8
Total	203	137	137	100.0
Maximum Time	282			
Minimum Time	141			

Defects Injected	Plan	Actual	To Date	To Date %	Def./Hour
Planning					
Design					
Code					
Code Review					
Compile					
Test					
Total					

Defects Removed	Plan	Actual	To Date	To Date %	Def./Hour
Planning					
Design					
Code					
Code Review					
Compile					
Test					
Total					

TABLE 11.6 PSP PROJECT PLAN SUMMARY

Student _____Student X_____   Date _____10/21/96__

Program _____   Program # _9_____

Instructor __Mr. Z_____   Language _Ada___

Summary	Plan	Actual	To Date
Minutes/LOC	7.21	6.76	
LOC/Hour	8.32	8.88	
Defects/KLOC			
Yield			
A/FR			

Program Size (LOC):

Total New & Changed	23	29	29
Maximum Size	31		
Minimum Size	15		

Time in Phase (min.)	Plan	Actual	To Date	To Date %
Planning	5	11	15	4.5
Design	0	12	12	3.6
Code	74	85	146	43.9
Code Review				
Compile	25	28	49	14.7
Test	52	49	92	27.6
Postmortem	10	11	19	5.7
Total	166	196	333	100.0
Maximum Time	224			
Minimum Time	108			

Defects Injected	Plan	Actual	To Date	To Date %	Def./Hour
Planning					
Design					
Code					
Code Review					
Compile					
Test					
Total					

Defects Removed	Plan	Actual	To Date	To Date %	Def./Hour
Planning					
Design					
Code					
Code Review					
Compile					
Test					
Total					

Recording Log and recorded them in the Project Plan Summary form. This time, both the size and time estimates were reasonably close to the actual result. Student X took somewhat longer than expected to develop the program, but his Actual LOC per hour rates were very close to his historical rates. Also, the time distribution was not too far from the plan.

To complete the To Date column in Table 11.6, Student X added the actual times on this form to the To Date times for program 8 in Table 11.5. He also calculated the To Date % numbers in Table 11.6 by dividing the To Date number in each phase by the Total To Date time of 333 minutes and multiplying by 100. His calculations for these numbers were as follows:

- □ Total New & Changed LOC To Date New and Changed LOC = 19 + 29 = 48.
- □ Planning To Date planning time = 4 + 11 = 15.
  To Date %, planning = 100*15/333 = 4.5.
- □ Design To Date design time = 0 + 12 = 12.
  To Date %, design = 100*12/333 = 3.6.
- □ Code To Date coding time = 61 + 85 = 146.
  To Date %, coding = 100*146/333 = 43.9.
- □ Compile To Date compile time = 21 + 28 = 49.
  To Date %, compile = 100*49/333 = 14.7.
- □ Test To Date test time = 43 + 49 = 92.
  To Date %, test = 100*92/333 = 27.6.
- □ Postmortem: To Date postmortem time = 8 + 11 = 19.
  To Date %, postmortem = 100*19/333 = 5.7.
- □ Total To Date total development time = 137 + 196 = 333.

With data from program 9, Student X can now estimate the times to be spent in each phase of the next project. To be most useful, however, he should average these times over several projects. The To Date and To Date % columns do just that. For program 8 in Table 11.5, the To Date column held the actual times Student X spent on that project. When he developed program 9, however, he added the actual times for programs 8 and 9 to get new To Date values. The new To Date % distribution thus gives the average time distribution for programs 8 and 9. Similarly, when the Project Plan Summary for program 10 is completed, it will have the average time distribution for programs 8, 9, and 10, and so on.

From project to project, total development times will vary. The time distribution among the phases will likely be more stable, however. This, of course, depends on the quality of your process. When you spend a lot of time compiling and testing, for example, the planned phase times will be less accurate because of the large and unpredictable amount of time spent fixing defects. When averaging these times over several programs, however, the average amount of time spent in compile and test will not change as much. That is, it won't change until you change the process. When initially using the PSP, you will likely spend from one-third to one-half your time finding and fixing defects during compile and test. As you use the PSP methods in later chapters, you will reduce the number of defects found in compile and test and thus reduce compile and test times. This will save development time, improve process predictability, permit more accurate plans, and produce better programs.

11.8   Summary

This chapter defines a process, describes the basic PSP process, and shows how a defined process can help you make better plans. The Project Plan Summary form is expanded to include times for the project phases, and to calculate the To Date time and the percentage of development time spent in each phase. In making project plans, you will want to estimate the time to be spent in each phase based on past experience, using the To Date % values from the previous program. In using the PSP, you will produce a Project Plan Summary for each project, complete the Plan portions before starting the work, enter the Actual data when finished, and complete the To Date and To Date % entries.

11.9   Assignment 11

Using the Project Plan Summary form shown in Table 11.2, make a plan for writing the next program. First, estimate the program's size as described in Chapter 6. For this first PSP program, guess the time distribution by phase. In the future, use the To Date % figures in the Project Plan Summary form for the most recently developed program to make this estimate. Record the estimate before doing the work and record the actual sizes and phase times when finished.

Also, submit a copy of any Time Recording Log, Job Number Log, and Weekly Activity Summary sheets that you have not previously submitted.

Reference

[Humphrey 95] Humphrey, W. S. *A Discipline for Software Engineering.* Reading, MA: Addison-Wesley, 1995.

12

Defects

This chapter introduces the subject of software defects (see Section 12.4 to learn why not to call them bugs). Defects can cause serious problems for users of software products and they can be expensive to find and fix. Because defects are caused by developers' mistakes, engineers need to understand the defects they inject and learn how to manage them. The first step in managing defects is to gather data on the defects you are injecting in your programs. With these data, you can better devise ways to find and fix them. For the chapter assignment, you will gather and report data on the defects in your programs.

So far in this book, we have only talked about methods for managing cost and schedule. This, however, is only half the story. Starting with this chapter, we address the need to deliver quality software products. First, we will need a definition of quality.

12.1 What Is Software Quality?

Software quality affects development costs, delivery schedules, and user satisfaction. Because software quality is so important, we need to first discuss what we mean by the word *quality*. The quality of a software product must be defined in terms that are meaningful to the product's users. Thus a product that provides the capabilities that are most important to its users is a quality product. Users' needs are often stated in requirements documents. Because they are so important, the development, clarification, and refinement of requirements is a major subject in itself. We do not, therefore, address requirements further in this book. It is essential to remember, however, that until you have clear requirements, you cannot develop a quality program. While you may not start with clear requirements, you must understand the requirements before you can finish.

Software quality is an enormous subject that this book only partially addresses. The book does, however, provide the skills and practices you will need to understand the defects you inject. This will equip you to efficiently find and fix most of your defects and it will also provide the data to help prevent these defects in the future. Finally, once you can efficiently manage defects, you can devote more attention to those quality concerns that affect the usefulness and value of the programs you develop.

12.2   Defects and Quality

Recall, from Chapter 1, that a software engineer's job is to deliver quality products for their planned costs and on schedule. Recall too that software products must both meet the user's functional needs and reliably and consistently do the user's job. Doing the job is a key point. While the software functions are most important to the program's users, these functions are not usable unless the software runs. To get the software to run, you must remove its defects. Thus, while there are many aspects to software quality, your first quality concern must necessarily be with its defects. This does not mean that defects are your only concern or even that they are most important, but just that you must deal with most of the defects before you can satisfy any of the program's other objectives. Even after you get the programs to work, if they have more than a very few defects, they will not work in large systems and no one will use them, regardless of their other qualities.

The reason defects are so important is that people make a lot of mistakes. In fact, even experienced programmers typically make a mistake for every seven to ten lines of code they develop. While they generally find and correct most of these defects when they compile and test their programs, often a lot of defects still remain in the finished product. Clearly, then, your first priority is to understand the defects you inject and to prevent as many of them as you can. To do this, you need to be fluent with the programming languages you use, to thoroughly understand your development support systems, and to have mastered the kinds of applications you will develop. These steps and more are required to reduce the number of defects you inject.

12.3   What Are Defects?

The term *defect* refers to something that is wrong with a program, such as a syntax error, a misspelling, a punctuation mistake, or an incorrect program statement. Defects can occur in programs, in designs, or even in the requirements, specifications, or other documentation. Defects can be redundant or extra statements, incorrect statements, or omitted program sections. A defect, in fact, is anything that detracts from the program's ability to completely and effectively meet the user's needs. A defect is thus an objective thing. It is something you can identify, describe, and count.

Simple coding mistakes can produce very destructive or hard-to-find defects. Conversely, many sophisticated design defects are often easy to find. The sophistication of the design mistake and the impact of the resulting defect are thus largely independent. Even trivial implementation errors can cause serious system problems. In fact, the source of most software defects is simple programmer oversights and mistakes. While design issues are always important, when first written, programs typically have few design defects compared to the number of simple oversights, typos, and goofs. To improve program quality, it is thus essential that engineers learn to manage all the defects they inject in their programs.

It is important to separate the question of finding or identifying defects from determining their causes. Simply counting and recording defects in software products is not specifying causes or placing blame. Defects do, however, have causes. You may have misspelled a parameter name, omitted a punctuation mark, or incorrectly called a procedure. These mistakes all cause defects. All defects, in fact, result from human errors and many of the errors that software engineers make cause program defects.

Errors are incorrect things that people do and, regardless of when or who produced them, defects are defective elements of programs. Thus, people *make* errors or mistakes while programs *have* defects. When engineers make errors that result in defects, we refer to this as injecting defects. This means that to reduce the number of defects you inject in your products, you must change what you do. To remove the defects in your products, however, often you merely have to find them. Defect removal is, therefore, a more straightforward process than defect prevention. Defect prevention is an important and a major topic that requires a comprehensive study of the entire software development process [Humphrey 89]. The remainder of this book concentrates on defect removal.

Unless engineers find and correct the defects they inject, these defects will end up in their finished products. The problem is that it takes a lot of time and money to find and fix software defects. To produce fewer defects, you must learn from the defects you have injected, identify the mistakes that caused them, and learn how to avoid repeating the same mistakes in the future. Since defective products can be expensive to test, difficult to fix, and possibly even dangerous to use, it is important that you learn to minimize the number of defects you leave in your products. This book shows you how to do this.

Defects should be important to every software engineer not only because they affect the users but also because more than half a typical software organization's effort is devoted to finding and fixing defects. Because testing time is hard to predict, defects are often a major cause of cost and schedule problems.

12.4   Defects Versus Bugs

Some people mistakenly refer to software defects as bugs. When called bugs, they seem like pesky things that should be swatted or even ignored. This trivializes a critical problem and fosters the wrong attitude. Thus, when an engineer says there are only a few bugs left in a program, the reaction is one of relief. Suppose, however, that we called them time bombs instead of bugs. Would you feel the same sense of relief if a programmer told you that he had thoroughly tested a program and there were only a few time bombs left in it? Just using a different term changes your attitude entirely.

Defects are more like time bombs than bugs. And though not all of them will have explosive impact, some of them could. When programs are widely used and are applied in ways that their designers did not anticipate, seemingly trivial mistakes can have unforeseeable consequences. As widely used software systems are enhanced to meet new needs, latent problems can be exposed and a trivial-seeming defect can truly be destructive.

At this point, those readers who have written several programs will likely shake their heads and feel I am overstating the case. In one sense, I am. The vast majority of trivial defects have trivial consequences. Unfortunately, however, some small percentage of seemingly silly mistakes can cause serious problems. In one example, a simple initialization mistake caused a buffer to overflow. This caused a railroad control system to lose data. Then, when there was an outage, the system could not be quickly restarted and all the trains on several thousand miles of track had to stop for several hours while the needed data were reentered.

Some percentage of the defects in a program will likely have unpredictable consequences. If we knew in advance which ones these were, then we could just fix them and not worry about the rest. Unfortunately, there is no way to do this and any overlooked defect may potentially have serious consequences. Although it is true that many programs are not used in applications where failure is more than an annoyance, an increasing number are. Thus, while defects may not be an important issue for you now, they soon could be. It is important that you learn to manage defects now so you will be ready when you truly need to produce high-quality programs.

The software engineer who writes a program is best able to find and fix its defects. It is thus important that software engineers take personal responsibility for the quality of the programs they produce. Learning to write defect-free programs is, however, an enormous challenge. It is not something that anyone can do quickly or easily. It takes data, effective technique, and skill. By using the methods described in this book you can develop and hone your ability to produce high-quality programs. After all, if you don't strive to produce defect-free work, you probably never will.

12.5 Defect Types

In analyzing defects, it is helpful to divide them into categories. This book classifies defects into 10 general types. By categorizing defects into a few types, you can quickly see which categories cause the most trouble and better focus on their prevention and removal. That, of course, is the key to defect management. Focus on the few defect types that are most troublesome. Once these types are under control, identify the next set and work on them, and so on indefinitely.

The defect types used in this book are shown in Table 12.1. This list is derived from the work of Chillarege and his colleagues at IBM Research [Chillarege]. He has studied the defects in a wide variety of IBM products and identified their prin-

TABLE 12.1 DEFECT TYPE STANDARD

Defect Types		
Type Number	Type Name	Description
10	Documentation	comments, messages
20	Syntax	spelling, punctuation, typos, instruction formats
30	Build, package	change management, library, version control
40	Assignment	declaration, duplicate names, scope, limits
50	Interface	procedure calls and references, I/O, user formats
60	Checking	error messages, inadequate checks
70	Data	structure, content
80	Function	logic, pointers, loops, recursion, computation, function defects
90	System	configuration, timing, memory
100	Environment	design, compile, test, other support system problems

cipal categories. These same types have also been found helpful for the PSP [Humphrey 95].

In Table 12.1, the defect categories refer to generic kinds of problems. For example, type 20 syntax defects refers to all those constructs that do not meet the programming language specifications. Examples would be missing semicolons, incorrectly structured `if` statements, spelling errors, or improper declarations. A type 20 syntax defect is any defect that results in incorrect program syntax, regardless of how that defect was caused or found. Another defect category would be type 80, function. An example here would be a `do-while` loop with incorrect logic in the while condition.

The type hierarchy in Table 12.1 is ordered by the general sophistication of the probable defect causes. For example, the type 10, 20, and 30 defects typically result from simple oversights and mistakes. Type 80, 90, and 100 defects, however, typically involve more sophisticated design or system issues.

Rather than refining each of these 10 PSP defect type categories into subcategories, wait until you have gathered defect data for a number of programs. Then you can see where more detail would help and what specific additional information are needed. For example, you could divide the type 20 syntax defects into subtypes 21 for semicolon mistakes, 22 for other punctuation errors, 23 for Boolean expression problems, 24 for incorrect instruction formats, and so forth. Before defining finer levels of detail for each defect type, wait until you have gathered data on at least 100 or more defects. Even then, you will likely find that these initial defect data types are adequate.

12.6 Understanding Defects

The first step in managing defects is to understand them. To do that, you must gather defect data. Then you can understand these mistakes and figure out how to avoid them. You can also figure out how to best find, fix, or even prevent the defects you still inject.

To gather data on defects in your program, do the following:

- Keep a record of every defect you find in a program.
- Record enough information on each defect so you can later understand it.
- Analyze these data to see what defect types caused the most problems.
- Devise ways to find and correct these defects.

The defects you inject and find in your own programs are only part of the story. You will someday need to learn about the defects that other people find in your programs. Since these defects will have escaped all your defect prevention and detection efforts, they will be most important in understanding and addressing the weaknesses in your personal process. These defects are called escapes because they have escaped all your defect-removal efforts. As your personal process improves, escapes will ultimately be the principal source of data for your personal improvement.

12.7 The Defect Recording Log

The Defect Recording Log is designed to help gather defect data. The log is shown in Table 12.2, and its instructions are shown in Table 12.3. Use this log to gather defect data for every program you write. Describe each defect in enough detail so you can later understand it. After you have completed each program, analyze the data to see where you injected and removed defects and which defect types caused the most trouble. Before using this log, read the rest of this chapter and the instructions in Table 12.3. The following paragraphs use the Defect Recording Log example in Table 12.4 to show how to complete the log:

1. *When starting to develop a program,* get several Defect Recording Log pages and fill in the header data on the first page. After you use all the spaces on the first page, complete the header before starting on the second page.

2. *When you first encounter a defect,* enter its number in the log, but do not enter the rest of the data until you have fixed the defect. When Student X first tried to compile program 10, the compiler displayed more than a dozen error messages. Although he did not at first know what the problem was, he knew that there was at least one mistake. He thus noted the time and entered a 1 under Number in the first line of the defect log. This was for the first defect of program 10. These numbers will later help you analyze the defect data. In larger programs, defect numbers are used to track problems with incorrect fixes and to aid in defect prevention.

3. *Use a separate line for each defect.* Do not group multiple identical defects on the same line.

4. *Enter the date the defect was found.* If you find several defects on the same day, it is acceptable to leave the subsequent date entries blank until the first entry of the next day. In Table 12.4, Student X found all the defects on 10/28. He thus did not need to keep reentering the date since it is assumed to repeat until changed.

5. *After fixing the defect, enter the defect type.* While you may be confused about which type is appropriate, use your best judgment. Don't waste time worrying about the precise defect type. Do, however, try to be reasonably consistent. On defect 1 in Table 12.4, for example, Student X found that the

```
Defect Types
10  Documentation   60  Checking
20  Syntax          70  Data
30  Build, Package  80  Function
40  Assignment      90  System
50  Interface      100  Environment
```

TABLE 12.2 DEFECT RECORDING LOG

Student _____   Date _____
Instructor_____   Program # _____

Date	Number	Type	Inject	Remove	Fix Time	Fix Defect
[ ]	[ ]	[ ]	[ ]	[ ]	[ ]	[ ]

Description: _____

Date	Number	Type	Inject	Remove	Fix Time	Fix Defect
[ ]	[ ]	[ ]	[ ]	[ ]	[ ]	[ ]

Description: _____

Date	Number	Type	Inject	Remove	Fix Time	Fix Defect
[ ]	[ ]	[ ]	[ ]	[ ]	[ ]	[ ]

Description: _____

Date	Number	Type	Inject	Remove	Fix Time	Fix Defect
[ ]	[ ]	[ ]	[ ]	[ ]	[ ]	[ ]

Description: _____

Date	Number	Type	Inject	Remove	Fix Time	Fix Defect
[ ]	[ ]	[ ]	[ ]	[ ]	[ ]	[ ]

Description: _____

Date	Number	Type	Inject	Remove	Fix Time	Fix Defect
[ ]	[ ]	[ ]	[ ]	[ ]	[ ]	[ ]

Description: _____

Date	Number	Type	Inject	Remove	Fix Time	Fix Defect
[ ]	[ ]	[ ]	[ ]	[ ]	[ ]	[ ]

Description: _____

Date	Number	Type	Inject	Remove	Fix Time	Fix Defect
[ ]	[ ]	[ ]	[ ]	[ ]	[ ]	[ ]

Description: _____

TABLE 12.3 DEFECT RECORDING LOG INSTRUCTIONS

Purpose	This form holds data on each defect as you find and correct it. Use these data to complete the Project Plan Summary.
General	Record all review, compile, and test defects in this log. Record each defect separately and completely. If you need additional space, use another copy of the form.
Header	Enter the following: • Your name • Today's date • The instructor's name • The number of the program
Date	Enter the date when the defect was found.
Number	Number each defect. For each program, use a sequential number starting with 1 (or 001, etc.).
Type	Enter the defect type from the defect type list in Table 12.1 (also summarized in the top left corner of the Defect Recording Log). Use your judgment in selecting which type applies.
Inject	Enter the phase during which the defect was injected. Use your judgment.
Remove	Enter the phase during which the defect was removed. This would generally be the phase during which you found and fixed the defect.
Fix time	Estimate or measure the time required to find and fix the defect. You can use a stopwatch if you wish.
Fix defect	You may ignore this entry at this time. If you injected this defect while fixing another defect, record the number of the improperly fixed defect. If you cannot identify the defect number, enter an X in the Fix Defect box.
Description	Write a succinct description of the defect. Make the description clear enough to later remind you about the error that caused the defect and why you made it.

problem was a missing semicolon. Once he had resolved the problem, he entered the number 20 under Type for defect 1.

6. *Enter the phase of the process when you injected the defect.* While this may not always be clear, it should not be a problem for small programs. Use your best judgment and don't waste time worrying about it. In the example, Student X was confident that he had made the semicolon mistake when he was coding the program, so he entered the word *code* in the Inject space.

Defect Types	
10 Documentation	60 Checking
20 Syntax	70 Data
30 Build, Package	80 Function
40 Assignment	90 System
50 Interface	100 Environment

TABLE 12.4 DEFECT RECORDING LOG EXAMPLE

Student ___Student X_____ Date ___10/28/96__
Instructor__Mr. Z_____ Program # ____10__

Date	Number	Type	Inject	Remove	Fix Time	Fix Defect
10/28	1	20	code	compile	1 min	
Description:	missing;					

Date	Number	Type	Inject	Remove	Fix Time	Fix Defect
	2	20	code	compile	1 min	
Description:	missing;					

Date	Number	Type	Inject	Remove	Fix Time	Fix Defect
	3	40	design	compile	1 min	
Description:	wrong type on RHS of binary operator, must cast integers as float					

Date	Number	Type	Inject	Remove	Fix Time	Fix Defect
	4	40	code	compile	1	
Description:	wrong type on RHS, constant literal should be 0.0 not 0					

Date	Number	Type	Inject	Remove	Fix Time	Fix Defect
	5	40	code	compile	1	
Description:	wrong type on RHS, had to cast an integer as a float					

Date	Number	Type	Inject	Remove	Fix Time	Fix Defect
	6	40	design	compile	7	
Description:	exponent must be an integer, researched and used math lib for sqrt. integral is not calculated correctly.					

Date	Number	Type	Inject	Remove	Fix Time	Fix Defect
	7	80	code	test	14	
Description:	answer (std. dev.) incorrect - eqn not coded properly, subtracted when I should have divided.					

Date	Number	Type	Inject	Remove	Fix Time	Fix Defect
	8	80	code	test	28	
Description:	loop did not terminate on negative exponent, forgot to change sign on subtracting					

7. *Enter the process phase when you removed the defect.* This is typically the phase when you found the defect. After starting the *compile* phase, for example, enter the word *compile* for the phase removed. Here, for defect 1, Student X was in the compile phase when he found and fixed the defect, so he entered the word *compile* in the Remove space.

8. *For the defect fix time, estimate the time from when you first were aware* of and started working on the defect until you had finished fixing and checking it. When he started to fix defect 1, Student X noted the time on his watch. Once he had fixed the problem and checked to make sure it was a proper fix, he again checked his watch and saw that he had only spent about a minute. Generally, for compile defects, fix time will be only a minute or so. For defects found in test, however, the correcting can take much longer. You could use a clock or a stopwatch to measure the fix time, but for short fixes your judgment will generally be adequate.

9. *The Fix Defect entry* is for defects injected while fixing other defects. While this will be important later, ignore it for now.

10. *Write a brief description of the defect in the description section.* Make this as brief and simple as possible but describe the defect clearly. For example, merely enter a ";" to designate a missing semicolon. For a more sophisticated logic defect, however, write several lines, overflowing onto subsequent lines of the defect log if needed. For defect 1, Student X simply noted "missing ;." For most of the defects in Table 12.4, he had to provide a more substantial description. Since this description is only for your use, however, it is not necessary to write any more than is needed to remind you of the problem.

People are often confused about defect types and think there should be a special type for misunderstandings and confusion. For example, if you didn't understand the requirements or were not familiar with the development environment, you would likely make many mistakes. This issue is important, but it relates to defect *causes*. As far as the *type* of the defect is concerned, there are only two questions: Was something wrong in the product and if so, what type of product defect was it? So, while understanding the cause is necessary for preventing defects, the defect type only describes what was wrong in the product.

12.8 Counting Defects

While the definition of a defect may seem obvious, it is not. During compiling, for example, count only the changes you make. That is, if the compiler provides 10 error messages for a missing semicolon, the missing semicolon is the only defect. Thus, enter one defect in the Defect Recording Log for every program correction, regardless of the nature of the correction and regardless of the number of compiler error messages.

Similarly, when you find a design defect while writing code, that is a design defect. While designing, however, you may often change your mind on how to do something. If you are correcting a mistake in the requirements or specifications, that would be a requirements or specification defect. If, however, you have thought of a better way to do the design, that would not be a defect. You will also often catch and correct mistakes as you make them. Such adjustments are natural parts of creative thinking and are not defects. The key is to record those defects you leave in the product when you have finished the initial design or completed coding.

For example, if you enter a line of code and immediately see and correct a misspelled parameter name, that misspelling is not a defect. If, however, you finished coding the program and later noticed the mistake, the same misspelling *would* be a defect and you would count it. Thus, if your normal practice is to check every line right after you enter it, then the defects you find this way need not be counted.

Start counting defects whenever you complete a phase for a product or part of a product. After the design phase, for example, you would count all design defects. Suppose, however, that you are coding two program procedures. After coding the first, you decide to code the second before starting compiling. Part way through coding the second procedure, you realize that you have misnamed a parameter in the first procedure. This is a defect because even though you are still in the coding phase, you had actually completed coding the first procedure.

Note that in this book you are not required to count the defects found during the design or coding phases. Initially, it is important to concentrate on those defects found during compiling or testing. Once you are accustomed to gathering defect data, you will better know why these defect data are needed. Then you may want to learn more about the mistakes you make and correct during the design and coding phases. Since you will likely make the most mistakes while designing and coding, these are the phases where you must look to understand the defect causes and see how to prevent them. For the moment, however, start with only those defects you find in compile and test.

12.9   Using the Defect Recording Log

Why should you count defects? As you gather defect data, remember why you are doing so:

- *To improve your programming.* These defect data are to help improve the way you write programs. While it is easy to get defensive about defects, you cannot manage defects if you don't understand them. This means you must gather accurate data about them. If you make excuses or pretend, for example, that syntax errors don't count if they are caught by a syntax checker instead of a compiler, you will only fool yourself. If you are willing to fool yourself, don't expect to improve.

- *To reduce the number of defects in your programs.* Everyone injects defects but, by using care and proper methods, you can reduce the number of defects you inject.

- *To save time.* Mistakes cause more mistakes. The longer defects stay in a program, the more time they take to find and the harder they are to fix. Requirements problems lead to improper designs. Design errors cause implementation mistakes. Implementation mistakes inject program defects. This is why it is important to remove defects as soon as possible after you inject them.

- *To save money.* Defects are expensive. After unit test, the costs of finding and fixing defects increase by about 10 times with every subsequent testing or maintenance phase.

- *To do your job responsibly.* Defects are injected by engineers and it is their responsibility to find and fix them.

12.10 The Updated PSP Process

The updated PSP process script is shown in Table 12.5. The principal addition is the gathering and recording of defect data. The updated Project Plan Summary form is shown in Table 12.6 and its instructions are in Table 12.7. Note that there is no space for recording defects injected or removed during the postmortem phase. Although you are not likely to find or inject defects during the postmortem, it is possible. One example could be that you noticed a defect while counting the New and Changed LOC. You might even inject a defect during the postmortem if you made a mistake while fixing the first defect. The following paragraphs explain how the new parts of the Project Plan Summary in Table 12.8 are completed.

During the postmortem phase, review the defect log and count the number of defects injected in each phase. From the Defect Recording Log in Table 12.4, Student X first counted defects 3 and 6 as injected in design so he entered a 2 under Actual in the design row of Table 12.8. The other six defects were all injected in coding, so he entered a 6 in the code row. The total is then eight injected defects. While you will initially inject almost all the defects in coding, you may inject a few in design, compile, or test. Occasionally, with more complex programs, you may even inject some defects during planning.

Next, count the number of defects removed in each phase. Student X counted six defects removed in compile and two in test so he entered a 6 and a 2 in these

TABLE 12.5 PSP PROCESS SCRIPT

	Purpose	To guide you in developing small programs
	Entry criteria	The problem description PSP Project Plan Summary form Actual size and time data for previous programs Time Recording Log ***Defect Recording Log***
1	Planning	Obtain a description of the program functions. Estimate the Max., Min., and total LOC required. Determine the Minutes/LOC. Calculate the Max., Min., and total development times. Enter the plan data in the Project Plan Summary form. Record the planning time in the Time Recording Log.
2	Design	Design the program. Record the design in the specified format. Record design time in the Time Recording Log.
3	Code	Implement the design. Use a standard format for entering the code. Record coding time in the Time Recording Log.
4	Compile	Compile the program. Fix ***and record*** all defects found. Record compile time in the Time Recording Log.
5	Test	Test the program. Fix ***and record*** all defects found. Record testing time in the Time Recording Log.
6	Postmortem	Complete the Project Plan Summary form with actual time, size, ***and defect*** data. Record postmortem time in the Time Recording Log.
	Exit criteria	A thoroughly tested program A properly documented design A complete program listing A completed Project Plan Summary Completed time ***and defect*** logs

rows of the defects removed section. Again, the total is 8. With the PSP, you will probably start out finding most defects during compile. Test, however, will generally take more time because it is harder to find and to fix defects in test.

After recording the number of defects injected and removed, complete the To Date and To Date % columns in the same way you fill the same columns with time data. (See Section 11.7 of Chapter 11.) You will not need the To Date and To Date % defect data until Chapter 15, when you will start to estimate the number of injected and removed defects.

TABLE 12.6 PSP PROJECT PLAN SUMMARY

Student _____   Date _____

Program _____   Program # _____

Instructor _____   Language _____

Summary	Plan	Actual	To Date
Minutes/LOC	_____	_____	_____
LOC/Hour	_____	_____	_____
Defects/KLOC	_____	_____	_____
Yield	_____	_____	_____
A/FR	_____	_____	_____

Program Size (LOC):

Total New & Changed	_____	_____	_____
Maximum Size	_____		
Minimum Size	_____		

Time in Phase (min.)	Plan	Actual	To Date	To Date %
Planning	_____	_____	_____	_____
Design	_____	_____	_____	_____
Code	_____	_____	_____	_____
Code Review	_____	_____	_____	_____
Compile	_____	_____	_____	_____
Test	_____	_____	_____	_____
Postmortem	_____	_____	_____	_____
Total	_____	_____	_____	_____
Maximum Time	_____			
Minimum Time	_____			

Defects Injected	Plan	Actual	To Date	To Date %	Def./Hour
Planning	_____	_____	_____	_____	
Design	_____	_____	_____	_____	
Code	_____	_____	_____	_____	
Code Review	_____	_____	_____	_____	
Compile	_____	_____	_____	_____	
Test	_____	_____	_____	_____	
Total	_____	_____	_____	_____	

Defects Removed	Plan	Actual	To Date	To Date %	Def./Hour
Planning	_____	_____	_____	_____	
Design	_____	_____	_____	_____	
Code	_____	_____	_____	_____	
Code Review	_____	_____	_____	_____	
Compile	_____	_____	_____	_____	
Test	_____	_____	_____	_____	
Total	_____	_____	_____	_____	

With the To Date % data, it is surprising how accurately engineers can estimate the numbers of defects they inject and remove. People are creatures of habit and our habits govern our mistakes. As long as we do not change these habits, we will continue to make similar mistakes. Thus, unless you make some major change like using a different process, working on more complex applications, or modify-

TABLE 12.7 PSP PROJECT PLAN SUMMARY INSTRUCTIONS

Purpose	This form holds the estimated and actual project data in a convenient and readily retrievable form.
Header	Enter the following: • Your name and today's date • The program name and number • The instructor's name • The language you will use to write the program
Minutes/LOC	Prior to development • Enter the Minutes/LOC planned for this project. Use the To Date rate from the most recent program in the Job Number Log or the most recent Project Plan Summary. After development • Divide the total development time by the actual program size to get the actual **and To Date** Minutes/LOC. • For example, if the project took 196 minutes and you produced 29 LOC, the Minutes/LOC would be 196/29 = 6.76.
LOC/Hour	Prior to development • Calculate the LOC per hour planned for this program by dividing 60 by the Plan Minutes/LOC. After development • For Actual **and To Date** LOC/Hour, divide 60 by the Actual **To Date** Minutes/LOC. • For Actual Minutes/LOC of 6.76, Actual LOC/Hour are 60/6.76 = 8.88.
Program size (LOC)	Prior to development • Enter under plan the estimated Total, Maximum, and Minimum New & Changed LOC. After development • Count and enter the Actual New & Changed LOC. • For To Date, add Actual New & Changed LOC to the To Date New & Changed LOC for the previous program.

(Continued)

ing the development environment, you will probably inject about the same numbers of defects in the next program as you did in the last.

The remainder of the Project Plan Summary is completed in much the same way as before. There are, however, a few considerations to keep in mind: First, the To Date entry for Minutes/LOC is calculated by taking the ratio of the To Date total development time and the To Date New & Changed LOC; thus, 682/105 = 6.50 Minutes/LOC. Second, the To Date LOC/Hour is calculated by dividing 60

TABLE 12.7 *(Continued)*

Time in Phase Plan	For total development time, multiply Total New & Changed LOC by Minutes/LOC. For Maximum time, multiply the Maximum size by Minutes/LOC. For Minimum time, multiply the Minimum size by Minutes/LOC. From the Project Plan Summary for the most recent program, find the To Date % values for each phase. Using the To Date % from the previous program, calculate the plan time for each phase.
Actual	At job completion, enter the actual time in minutes spent in each development phase. Get these data from the time log.
To Date	For each phase, enter the sum of actual time and To Date time from the most recent previous program.
To Date %	For each phase, enter 100 times the To Date time for that phase divided by the Total To Date time.
Defects Injected *Actual*	*After development, find and enter the actual number of defects injected in each phase.*
To Date	*For each phase, enter the sum of the actual defects and the To Date defects from the most recent program.*
To Date %	*For each phase, enter 100 times the To Date defects for that phase divided by the total To Date defects.*
Defects Removed *Actual*	*After development, find and enter the actual number of defects removed in each phase.*
To Date	*For each phase, enter the sum of the actual defects and the To Date defects from the most recent programs.*
To Date %	*For each phase, enter 100 times the To Date defects for that phase divided by the total To Date defects.*

by the To Date Minutes/LOC, thus, 60/6.50 = 9.23 LOC/Hour. Note that with these To Date rates, you no longer need to track the program development Units and Rates on the Job Number Log. Since this log is a very convenient reference for project information, however, I suggest you continue tracking program job numbers. If your experiences are like mine, you will quickly accumulate a large amount of data. I have now tracked over 200 jobs, and I store my project data by job number. I thus find that the Job Number Log is the most convenient way to identify historical data or to find data on a particular project.

TABLE 12.8   PSP PROJECT PLAN SUMMARY EXAMPLE

Student	Student X		Date	10/28/96
Program			Program #	10
Instructor	Mr. Z		Language	Ada

Summary	Plan	Actual	To Date
Minutes/LOC	6.76	6.12	6.50
LOC/Hour	8.88	9.80	9.23
Defects/KLOC			
Yield			
A/FR			

Program Size (LOC):

	Plan	Actual	To Date
Total New & Changed	44	57	105
Maximum Size	58		
Minimum Size	30		

Time in Phase (min.)	Plan	Actual	To Date	To Date %
Planning	13	18	33	4.8
Design	11	43	55	8.1
Code	130	162	308	45.2
Code Review				
Compile	44	21	70	10.2
Test	82	73	165	24.2
Postmortem	17	32	51	7.5
Total	297	349	682	100.0
Maximum Time	392			
Minimum Time	203			

Defects Injected	Plan	Actual	To Date	To Date %	Def./Hour
Planning					
Design		2	2	25.0	
Code		6	6	75.0	
Code Review					
Compile					
Test					
Total		8	8	100.0	

Defects Removed	Plan	Actual	To Date	To Date %	Def./Hour
Planning					
Design					
Code					
Code Review					
Compile		6	6	75.0	
Test		2	2	25.0	
Total		8	8	100.0	

12.11   Summary

Software quality is meeting the user's needs and reliably and consistently doing the user's job. This requires that the software you produce have few if any defects.

A software defect is something in the product that is incorrect. Defects are caused by human errors. Because defects are expensive to find and fix, it is most efficient when engineers promptly find and fix the defects they inject.

The first step in managing defects is to understand them. For this, the programmer needs to gather defect data, analyze these data, and determine how to better prevent, find, and fix these defects.

The Defect Type Standard is a simplified standard used in this book to help you identify your most important defect categories. After you have some defect data, you may wish to augment these categories. Use the Defect Recording Log to gather defect data. Record every defect using one entry in the log for each defect. For each program, summarize these data in the Project Plan Summary form.

12.12   Assignment 12

Use the Defect Recording Log to record every defect you find in the programs you write. Identify the program where you found the defect, list each defect as a separate entry, and completely describe each defect. Summarize the defect data in the Project Plan Summary for each program.

Also, submit a copy of any Time Recording Log, Job Number Log, and Weekly Activity Summary sheets that you have not previously submitted and turn in a completed planning form and Defect Recording Log for each newly developed program.

References

[Chillarege] Chillarege, Ram, Inderpal S. Bhandari, Jarir K. Chaar, Michael J. Halliday, Diane S. Moebus, Bonnie K. Ray, and Man-Yuen Wong. "Orthogonal Defect Classification—A Concept for In-Process Measurements." *IEEE Transactions on Software Engineering,* vol,. 18, no. 11, Nov. 1992, pp. 943–956.

[Humphrey 89] Humphrey, W. S. *Managing the Software Process.* Reading, MA: Addison-Wesley, 1989.

[Humphrey 95] Humphrey, W. S. *A Discipline for Software Engineering.* Reading, MA: Addison-Wesley, 1995.

13

Finding Defects

There are various ways to find defects. This chapter briefly summarizes the principal alternatives and shows how one particular method, code reviews, can help improve the productivity and quality of your work. For the assignment, you will do code reviews for the next programs you write.

13.1 A Personal Commitment to Quality

In spite of all the available tools and methods, the most important single factor in program quality is the personal commitment of the software engineer to developing a quality product. When engineers are committed to quality, they take more care with their work and they take pride in the quality of the products they produce. The PSP can help you produce quality products by showing you how to use effective quality methods. Your first step is to understand the defects you have injected in prior programs. Then, using the PSP methods, you learn to quickly find and fix these defects. This and subsequent chapters describe how to do this.

13.2   The Steps in Finding Defects

Although there is no way to stop injecting defects, it is possible to find and remove almost all defects early in development. After you have learned the PSP, you
will find that removing defects early will both save time and produce better products. For example, if you could find and correct a design defect before producing
the code, you would not waste time implementing an incorrect design. Similarly,
when you fix coding defects before compile and test, you save the time you would
have spent finding and fixing these defects during compile and test. This chapter
shows you how to find defects early in the development process and it provides
data you can use to evaluate the effectiveness of these defect-removal methods.

There are various ways to find the defects in a program. In essence, these
methods all involve the following steps:

1. Identify the defect symptoms.
2. Deduce from these symptoms the location of the defect.
3. Figure out what is wrong with the program.
4. Decide how to fix the defect.
5. Make the fix.
6. Verify that the fix has resolved the problem.

13.3   Ways to Find and Fix Defects

Various tools and aids have been devised to help engineers with these steps. The first
tool that engineers generally use is a compiler. To understand how and why a compiler helps to find defects, it is important to discuss its purpose. Fundamentally, the
compiler's job is to generate code. Thus, a compiler will scan through the source
code to see if it can generate code. If it can, it will, whether the code is correct or not.

Thus, the compiler will generate code until it hits some characters it cannot interpret. For example, if you put the character string ABC in a source program and
had not declared it, the compiler will flag this string as an error. Compilers can identify most syntax defects, but they cannot tell what you intend. Thus compilers often
provide many error messages for seemingly simple defects. Compilers, however,
only provide defect symptoms and you must figure out where and what the problem
is. While you will often do this quickly, occasionally it can take much longer.

Compilers will not detect every spelling, punctuation, or other syntax defect.
The reason is that compilers can often generate code from defective source programs. While most of these missed defects are improper design, some could be

simple syntax mistakes. It may seem unlikely that a compiler would miss syntax errors, but my data from several thousand C++ defects show that this happened for about 9.4% of the syntax errors I made. Just as a spell-checking program does not catch all spelling mistakes, the compiler will not catch all syntax defects.

A second way to find defects is through testing. While there are many kinds of tests, they all require that testers provide test data and test conditions (sometimes called test cases or test scenarios). The quality of the test is thus governed by the degree to which these scenarios cover all important program functions. The testers then run these test cases to see if the program produces the proper results. This implies another tester responsibility: to figure out what the results of the test would look like if the program worked correctly.

While tests can be used to verify almost any program function, they have several disadvantages. First, as with compilers, testing only addresses the first step of the defect fixing process. That is, you still have to get from symptoms to problems before you can start to work on the fix. Another problem is that each test verifies only one set of program conditions. That is, if the program multiplies two numbers, x and y, and you tested it with $x - 11$ and $y = 18$, you would only know that it works for these values. You would not know, for example, how the program works with negative numbers, or zero, or the largest positive or negative numbers in the number system, or in fact with any other pair of numbers. Testing all these possibilities would take a lot of tests. Since even simple programs involve many possible combinations of data and operational conditions, comprehensive testing is time consuming. In fact, for any but the simplest programs, comprehensive testing is practically impossible.

The third way to find defects is all too common. That is to ship defective programs and wait for the users to identify and report the defects. This, it turns out, is the most expensive strategy. For example, in one year, IBM spent about $250 million repairing and reinstalling fixes to 13,000 customer-reported defects. That is about $20,000 for each defect.

Finally, the most effective way to find and fix defects is by personally reviewing the source program listing. While this may seem like a difficult way to clean up a defective program, it turns out to be fastest and most efficient. This chapter explains why.

13.4 Code Reviews

A code review is a way to find defects quickly. To do a code review, you study the source code to find mistakes. It is best to do this after producing the source code and before starting to compile or test it. Since most software defects result from simple oversights and goofs, they are easiest to find right after you produce the design or the code. This is when you will most likely remember what was intended and when you will most probably know how to fix any problems.

While there are many ways to do a code review, the most common approach is to print a source code listing and review every line. You could review the code on the computer screen, but engineers generally find it more convenient to review even small programs when they are printed on a listing. Listings also allow you to quickly move between code segments, make notes, or check off completed sections.

Even though code reviews are time consuming, they are much more efficient than testing. Data from both students and engineers show that code reviews are between three and five times as efficient as running the initial or unit tests. A typical engineer, for example, will find only about 2 to 4 defects in an hour of unit testing but will find 6 to 10 defects in each hour of reviewing code.

The reason code reviews are efficient is that, when doing reviews, you see problems not symptoms. That is, while going through the code, you think about what the program is supposed to do. Thus when something doesn't look right, you see the likely problem and can quickly verify the code. Since the time required to get from symptom to problem is the bulk of the cost of finding and fixing defects during compiling and testing, reviews can save a lot of time.

Reviews also have disadvantages. The two principal disadvantages are that code reviews are time consuming and they are hard to do properly. Reviewing, however, is a skill that can be taught and improved with practice. Even with experience, however, you will probably only find an average of 75% to 80% of the defects in a program. It will also take at least 30 minutes to thoroughly review each 100 LOC of source code. When doing reviews much more quickly, you will usually miss a lot of defects. The rest of this chapter describes the code review process. The next several chapters discuss measurements and techniques that will help improve the way you do code reviews and provide data to demonstrate their effectiveness.

13.5   Why Find Defects Early?

There are many reasons to review programs before compiling and testing them. The most important is that you simply cannot hack out a defective program and later turn it into a quality product. Once you have produced a defective program, it will always be defective. You may fix all the known problems and you may make it work according to the specifications you have tested, but it will then be a defective program with a lot of patches.

As an example, suppose you were buying a new car. Before closing the deal, you visited two manufacturers' assembly plants. At one plant, you saw lots of beautiful cars coming off the line and going into test. While the cars looked great coming out of production, testing found an average of 10 defects per car. These defects were all fixed and the cars were sent to the dealers.

At the second plant, the cars rolling off the line looked much the same as those at the first plant. Here, however, testing only found one defect for every 10 cars. Even if the cars from the second plant cost a bit more, you would probably prefer them, almost regardless of any other differences. You know that testing will not find all the problems and that if the production process produced a lemon, that car will probably always be a lemon, regardless of the amount of final test and inspection.

Programs are no different. When engineers tolerate defective work, they will produce poor-quality products. An attitude of "I'm too busy, we can fix it later," is unlikely to produce a superior product. To produce quality software, every software development step must be of high quality. While such rigorous quality practices may seem expensive, they will actually save time.

13.6   The Costs of Finding and Fixing Defects

In typical software projects, the product is divided into many small program elements or modules. Each engineer then develops one or more of these modules. After module design, implementation, and compiling, the engineers do an initial or unit test. After these private unit tests, the modules are combined into larger components and integration tested. Various levels of component testing follow before the components are combined into products for product testing. Finally, the products are assembled into systems for system testing. While the type, duration, and complexity of the integration, component, product, and system testing will vary with the size and complexity of the system, the same general process is used for almost all large-scale software products.

The average cost of finding and fixing a defect increases about 10 times with every step of the development process. While defect fix times vary enormously, these averages hold true regardless of defect types. Some trivial syntax defects like misplaced semicolons or misspelled names can get past the compiler and be extraordinarily hard to find in test. In code reviews, you will find and fix defects in an average of 1 to 2 minutes. In initial testing, defect fix times will average between 10 to 20 or more minutes. These are, however, an average of a lot of 1- and 2-minute fixes and a few that take many minutes or even several hours.

The time to find defects in integration, component, or system test will also vary with the size and complexity of the system. More time is typically required to find and fix defects in larger and more complex systems. In integration test, for example, each defect can cost an hour or more, and in system test each defect can cost as much as 10 to 40 or more engineer hours. Once products are shipped to customers, the costs of finding and fixing defects can be much more, depending on the kinds of products and the types and numbers of customers. My personal data on the times to find and fix C++ defects are shown in Figure 13.1. The following examples show the enormous cost of waiting until test to clean up defective programs.

- A small commercial software house developed a program with several components. Those developed by PSP-trained engineers completed integration testing in a couple of weeks. One component, however, was developed by a group that had not yet been PSP trained and its integration testing took several months. The testing time to find and fix 36 defects was 300 hours. Since testing took much longer than planned, customer delivery was two months late.

- One aerospace systems development group spent an average of 40 engineer hours to find and fix each defect in the system test of a navy avionics system.

- At Digital Equipment Corporation, for one system, the minimum time to find and fix each customer-reported defect was 88 engineering hours.

In addition to cost, an equally important reason to find defects early is that compiling, debugging, and testing are only marginally effective. Compilers are the fastest defect detection tools we have, yet they only find about 90% of the syntax defects and very few of the logic defects. Unit testing is typically the most effec-

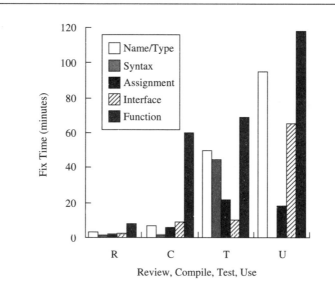

FIGURE 13.1 DEFECT FIX TIMES

tive testing stage, but it typically finds only about half the defects in the program at test entry. After unit test, testing effectiveness declines, with system test typically finding only about 30% to 40% of the defects that were in the product at system test entry.

Thus, if you want to produce a high-quality product, you will either have to produce a clean program at the outset or expect to spend a lot of time in test.

13.7   Using Reviews to Find Defects

You may find it hard to believe that tracking and checking your defects will improve your work, but other students have reduced the numbers of defects they find in compile and test by 5 to 10 times. They do this by following the steps outlined in this and the following chapters. Code reviews work so well that after you have used them in this course and seen the data on how well they work, you will likely make reviews a normal part of your personal process.

The first step in doing reviews is to understand the kinds of defects you inject. This is the principal reason for gathering defect data. The kinds of defects in the next program will be much like the defects you injected in previous programs. This will be true as long as you continue developing software in the same way. On the other hand, as you gain skill and experience, or if you change the process, the numbers and types of defects will likely change.

Because the kinds of defects you inject could differ from those injected by other people, your review strategy should be based on your personal defect profile. Just as skilled typists make fewer typing mistakes, experienced software engineers make fewer programming mistakes. You will naturally improve just by getting more practice, but there is some point beyond which improvement becomes more difficult. Then, you must study the defects. That will help you see how to better find and fix them.

The objectives of code reviews are to find as many defects as early as possible in the software process. You also want to find each defect in as little time as possible. A script for doing code reviews is shown in Table 13.1. While this script is self-explanatory, it is important that you use the following practices when you review code:

- ☐ Do the review before the first compile.
- ☐ Do the review on a printed source code listing.
- ☐ Record every defect found in the Defect Recording Log.
- ☐ During the review, check for the types of defects you have previously found in compile and test. An orderly method for doing this is described in Chapter 14.

TABLE 13.1 CODE REVIEW SCRIPT

	Entry criteria	Check that the following are on hand: • The requirements statement • The program design • The program source code • The coding standards
1	Review procedure	First produce the finished program source code. Before compiling or testing the program, print out a source code listing. Next, do the code review. During the code review, carefully check every line of source code to find and fix as many of the defects as you can.
2	Fix the defects	Fix all defects found. Check the fixes to ensure they are correct. Record the defects in the Defect Recording Log.
3	Review for coverage	Verify that the program design fulfills all the functions described in the requirements. Verify that the source code implements all the design.
4	Review the program logic	Verify that the design logic is correct. Verify that the program correctly implements the design logic.
5	Check names and types	Verify that all names and types are correctly declared and used. Check for proper declaration of integer, long integer, and floating point data types.
6	Check all variables	Ensure that every variable is initialized. Check for overflow, underflow, or out-of-range problems.
7	Check program syntax	Verify that the source code properly follows the language specifications.
	Exit criteria	At completion you must have: • The completed and corrected source code • Completed Time Recording Log • Completed Defect Recording Log

13.8   Reviewing Before Compiling

There are several reasons to review programs before compiling them. In essence, they are:

1. It will take about as long to do a thorough code review whether you do it before or after compiling.

2. Reviewing first will save a lot of compile time. Before they do code reviews, engineers typically spend from 12% to 15% of their development time com-

piling. Once they learn to do code reviews, their compile time drops to 3% or less.

3. Once engineers have compiled their programs, their reviews are generally not as thorough.

4. Compiling is equally effective before or after the code review.

5. Experience shows that when programs have a lot of defects in compiling, they generally have a lot of defects in test.

The argument for reviewing before you compile is essentially: "Do it this way and you will see." If, after this course, you would like to try compiling before reviewing, then write a few programs each way and compare your performance. Then, using the methods described in Chapters 18 and 19, evaluate the product and process data to see which approach is more effective. The important point is not to just follow your intuition or do what everyone else does. Gather data on your own work and make a logical decision based on these facts.

13.9   Data on Compile and Test Defects

The engineers on one project had all been PSP trained. They were developing six components of a new product and each component had 600 to 2500 LOC. In their process they did a unit test after coding and compiling and then a development test. The product was then delivered to the customer and any customer-reported defects were recorded as postdevelopment defects.

The data on the compile and test defects for these components are shown in Figures 13.2. 13.3, and 13.4. An engineer who had been adamantly opposed to doing code reviews found nearly 200 defects during compile. As Figure 13.2 shows, his unit test had many more defects than the other components. What is interesting is that this same component also had the most defects in integration and system test. Even though the customer had only run a brief acceptance test on these components, the same component again had the most defects. Finally, this one defective component took twice as long to develop as planned. All the other components were delivered on or ahead of schedule, while this one was five weeks late.

Careful work pays off. When engineers feel personally responsible for the quality of their programs, they will not depend on compilers or other tools to find their defects. When you are committed to producing a quality product, your commitment will show in the number of defects you find in compile, the number you find in test, and in the quality of your finished programs.

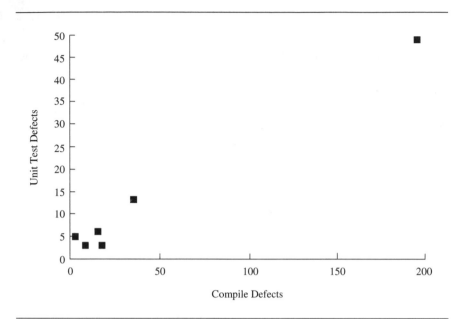

FIGURE 13.2 COMPILE VS. UNIT TEST DEFECTS

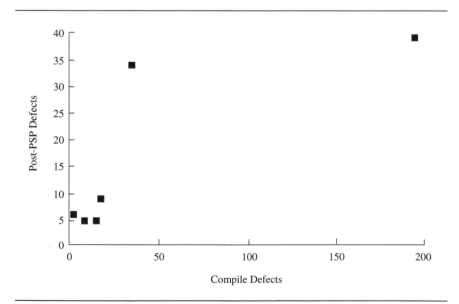

FIGURE 13.3 COMPILE VS. POST-PSP DEFECTS

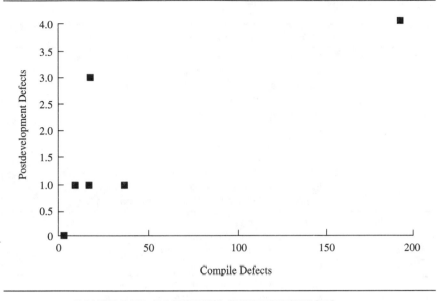

FIGURE 13.4 COMPILE VS. POSTDEVELOPMENT DEFECTS

13.10   The Updated PSP Project Plan Summary Form

The PSP process is now enhanced to include code reviews. This is done in the modified process script shown in Table 13.2. The Project Plan Summary form is also updated as shown in Tables 13.3, 13.4, and the example summary in Table 13.5.

These tables are self-explanatory, but one point deserves mention. In completing the To Date and To Date % columns for this process, remember that the introduction of code reviews will change your time and defect distributions. When planning a new program, you may thus want to adjust the calculated time estimates to account for these changes.

13.11   Other Kinds of Reviews

In software organizations, a common practice is to have several engineers review one another's programs. These are called peer reviews or inspections. Well-run inspections typically find from 50% to 70% of the defects in a program. While

TABLE 13.2 PSP PROCESS SCRIPT

	Purpose	To guide you in developing small programs
	Inputs required	The problem description PSP Project Plan Summary form Actual size and time data for previous programs Time Recording Log Defect Recording Log
1	Planning	Obtain a description of the program functions. Estimate the Max., Min., and total LOC required. Determine the Minutes/LOC. Calculate the Max., Min., and total development times. Enter the plan data in the Project Plan Summary form. Record the planning time in the Time Recording Log.
2	Design	Design the program. Record the design in the specified format. Record design time in the Time Recording Log.
3	Code	Implement the design. Use a standard format for entering the code. Record coding time in the Time Recording Log.
4	Code review	***Completely review the source code.*** ***Follow the code review script.*** ***Fix and record every defect found.*** ***Record review time in the Time Recording Log.***
5	Compile	Compile the program. Fix and record all defects found. Record compile time in the Time Recording Log.
6	Test	Test the program. Fix and record all defects found. Record testing time in the Time Recording Log.
7	Postmortem	Complete the Project Plan Summary form with actual time, size, and defect data. Record postmortem time in the Time Recording Log.
	Exit criteria	A thoroughly tested program A properly documented design A complete program listing A completed Project Plan Summary Completed time and defect logs

TABLE 13.3 PSP PROJECT PLAN SUMMARY

Student	_____	Date	_____
Program	_____	Program #	_____
Instructor	_____	Language	_____

Summary	Plan	Actual	To Date
Minutes/LOC	_____	_____	_____
LOC/Hour	_____	_____	_____
Defects/KLOC	_____	_____	_____
Yield	_____	_____	_____
A/FR	_____	_____	_____

Program Size (LOC):

	Plan	Actual	To Date
Total New & Changed	_____	_____	_____
Maximum Size	_____		
Minimum Size	_____		

Time in Phase (min.)	Plan	Actual	To Date	To Date %
Planning	_____	_____	_____	_____
Design	_____	_____	_____	_____
Code	_____	_____	_____	_____
Code Review	_____	_____	_____	_____
Compile	_____	_____	_____	_____
Test	_____	_____	_____	_____
Postmortem	_____	_____	_____	_____
Total	_____	_____	_____	_____
Maximum Time	_____			
Minimum Time	_____			

Defects Injected	*Plan*	Actual	To Date	To Date %	*Def./Hour*
Planning		_____	_____	_____	
Design		_____	_____	_____	
Code		_____	_____	_____	
Code Review		_____	_____	_____	
Compile		_____	_____	_____	
Test		_____	_____	_____	
Total		_____	_____	_____	

Defects Removed	*Plan*	Actual	To Date	To Date %	*Def./Hour*
Planning		_____	_____	_____	
Design		_____	_____	_____	
Code		_____	_____	_____	
Code Review		_____	_____	_____	
Compile		_____	_____	_____	
Test		_____	_____	_____	
Total		_____	_____	_____	

TABLE 13.4 PSP PROJECT PLAN SUMMARY INSTRUCTIONS

Purpose	This form holds the estimated and actual project data in a convenient and readily retrievable form.
Header	Enter the following: • Your name and today's date • The program name and number • The instructor's name • The language you will use to write the program
Minutes/LOC	Prior to development • Enter the Minutes/LOC planned for this project. Use the To Date rate from the most recent previous program. After development • Divide the total development time by the actual program size to get the actual and To Date Minutes/LOC. • For example, if the project took 196 minutes and you produced 29 LOC, the Minutes/LOC would be 196/29 = 6.76.
LOC/Hour	Prior to development • Calculate the LOC per hour planned for this program by dividing 60 by the Plan Minutes/LOC. After development • For Actual and To Date LOC/Hour, divide 60 by the Actual To Date Minutes/LOC. • For Actual Minutes/LOC of 6.76, Actual LOC/Hour are 60/6.76 = 8.88.
Program size **(LOC)**	Prior to development • Enter under plan the estimated Total, Maximum, and Minimum New & Changed LOC. After development • Count and enter the Actual New & Changed LOC. • For To Date, add Actual New & Changed LOC to the To Date New & Changed LOC for the previous program.

(Continued)

inspections can take a lot of time, they can be extraordinarily effective at finding defects. The reason is that engineers often have trouble seeing their own design mistakes. They created the design and they know what it is supposed to do. If their concept was flawed or they made an erroneous design or implementation assumption, they often have trouble detecting it. Inspections can help to overcome this problem. Data on times to find defects in inspections are shown in Table 13.6.

TABLE 13.4 *(Continued)*

Time in Phase Plan	For total development time, multiply Total New & Changed LOC by Minutes/LOC. For Maximum time, multiply the Maximum size by Minutes/LOC. For Minimum time, multiply the Minimum size by Minutes/LOC. From the Project Plan Summary for the most recent program, find the To Date % values for each phase. Using the To Date % from the previous program, calculate the plan time for each phase.
Actual	At job completion, enter the actual time in minutes spent in each development phase. Get these data from the time log.
To Date	For each phase, enter the sum of actual time and To Date time from the most recent previous program.
To Date %	For each phase, enter 100 times the To Date time for that phase divided by the Total To Date time.
Defects Injected Actual	After development, find and enter the actual number of defects injected in each phase.
To Date	For each phase, enter the sum of the actual defects and the To Date defects from the most recent program.
To Date %	For each phase, enter 100 times the To Date defects for that phase divided by the total To Date defects.
Defects Removed Actual	After development, find and enter the actual number of defects removed in each phase.
To Date	For each phase, enter the sum of the actual defects and the To Date defects from the most recent program.
To Date %	For each phase, enter 100 times the To Date defects for that phase divided by the total To Date defects.

For very small classroom exercises, inspections are generally not warranted, but for larger projects or any industrial program, inspections should always be done. The optimum strategy is to do a personal code review before compiling, and then to compile the program. Next, before any testing, conduct an inspection. While this book does not further discuss inspections, there are several useful references on the subject [Fagan, Gilb, Humphrey 89].

TABLE 13.5 PSP PROJECT PLAN SUMMARY EXAMPLE

Student _Student X_   Date _11/4/96_

Program   Program # _11_

Instructor _Mr. Z_   Language _Ada_

Summary	Plan	Actual	To Date
Minutes/LOC	6.50	5.88	6.30
LOC/Hour	9.23	10.20	9.52
Defects/KLOC			
Yield			
A/FR			

Program Size (LOC):

	Plan	Actual	To Date
Total New & Changed	53	48	153
Maximum Size	72		
Minimum Size	35		

Time in Phase (min.)	Plan	Actual	To Date	To Date %
Planning	17	15	48	5.0
Design	28	28	83	8.6
Code	156	132	440	45.6
Code Review	0	36	36	3.7
Compile	35	7	77	8.0
Test	83	38	203	21.1
Postmortem	26	26	77	8.0
Total	345	282	964	100.0
Maximum Time	468			
Minimum Time	228			

Defects Injected	*Plan*	Actual	To Date	To Date %	*Def./Hour*
Planning					
Design		1	3	21.4	
Code		5	11	78.6	
Code Review					
Compile					
Test					
Total		6	14	100	

Defects Removed	*Plan*	Actual	To Date	To Date %	*Def./Hour*
Planning					
Design					
Code					
Code Review		3	3	21.4	
Compile		2	8	57.2	
Test		1	3	21.4	
Total		6	14	100.0	

TABLE 13.6   HOURS TO FIND A DEFECT

Reference	Inspection	Test	Use
Ackerman	1	2–10	
O'Neill	.26		
Ragland		20	
Russell	1	2–4	33
Shooman	.6	3.05	
vanGenuchten	.25	8	
Weller	.7	6	

13.12   Summary

This chapter describes how and why to find defects early in development. The most important single factor in program quality is the engineer's personal commitment to quality. With this commitment, engineers remove defects early, even before they compile or test their programs.

   The principal defect-removal method introduced with the PSP is the personal code review. Here, you first print a program listing and then review it line by line to fix as many of the defects as you can find. To be most efficient, look for those defect types that have caused you the most problems in compiling and testing prior programs. Since people tend to repeat the same mistakes, your defect data will help you find all or most of a program's defects before you first compile and test it.

   Experience has shown that when engineers thoroughly review their code before the first compile, they reduce compile times by about 10% of development time and they cut testing time even more. While thorough code reviews take time, they will save at least as much time as they cost and they will produce much better products.

13.13   Assignment 13

For the next program, review the source code before compiling and testing it. Follow the code review script shown in Table 13.1. Record all the defects found in the Defect Recording Log and record the project data in the updated Project Plan Summary form.

Submit copies of those Time Recording Log and Weekly Activity Summary sheets you have not previously submitted. Also, turn in completed copies of the Project Plan Summary form and Defect Recording Logs for every program you develop. Include both planned and actual development times and actual defects injected and removed.

References

[Ackerman] Ackerman, Frank A., Lynne S. Buchwald, and Frank H. Lewski. "Software Inspections: An Effective Verification Process." *IEEE Software,* May 1989, pp. 31–36.

[Fagan] Fagan, Michael. "Design and Code Inspections to Reduce Errors in Program Development." *IBM Systems Journal,* vol. 15, no. 3, 1976.

[Gilb 93] Gilb, Tom, and Dorothy Graham. *Software Inspection.* Edited by Susannah Finzi, Reading, MA: Addison-Wesley, 1993.

[Humphrey 89] Humphrey, W. S. *Managing the Software Process.* Reading, MA: Addison-Wesley, 1989.

[O'Neill] O'Neill, Don. Personal communication.

[Ragland] Ragland, Bryce. "Inspections Are Needed Now More Than Ever." *Journal of Defense Software Engineering,* 38. Software Technology Support Center, U.S. Department of Defense, Nov. 1992.

[Russell] Russell, Glen W. "Experience with Inspections in Ultralarge-Scale Developments." *IEEE Software,* Jan. 1991, pp. 25–31.

[Shooman] Shooman, M. L., and M. I. Bolsky. "Types, Distribution, and Test and Correction Times for Programming Errors." *Proceedings of the 1975 Conference on Reliable Software.* Catalog no. 75 CHO 940-7CSR, IEEE, New York: p. 347.

[vanGenuchten] vanGenuchten, Michael. Personal communication.

[Weller] Weller, E. F., "Lessons Learned from Two Years of Inspection Data." *IEEE Software,* Sept. 1993, pp. 38–45.

14

The Code Review Checklist

The key to conducting effective code reviews is having an efficient review procedure. This chapter describes code review checklists, and explains how they can help you to quickly and efficiently find the defects in your programs and how to develop a checklist for your personal use. For the assignment, you will design a checklist for the defects you typically inject and then use this checklist when you review your programs.

14.1 Why Do Checklists Help?

A checklist contains a series of procedural steps that you want to follow precisely. When people have important things that they want to do exactly as specified, they often use checklists. Airline pilots, for example, use them for the preflight check before taking off. Even if they had just checked the same aircraft an hour before, they do it again. A study of accidents at one U.S. Air Force base found that in every case, the preflight checklist had not been rigorously followed. Another example of a complete and complex checklist is the countdown used by NASA before every shuttle flight. This procedure takes several days and follows hundreds of steps. It is so complex that computers are used to monitor countdown progress.

When it is essential to find and correct every defect in a program, you must follow a precise procedure. A checklist can help ensure that procedure is followed. In this chapter, we deal with a very special kind of checklist: one designed to help you find defects when doing a code review of a program you have written. You will see how to make a code review checklist that is tailored to find the precise defects that have previously caused you the most problems.

Checklists can also be a source of ideas. When you follow a personal checklist, you know how you review code. If you use the list properly, you also know how many defects you found with each checklist step. You will be able to measure the efficiency of the review procedure and improve the checklist. Comparing your own checklist with those of other engineers may also suggest helpful review approaches.

The checklist encapsulates personal experience. By regularly using and improving a personal checklist, you will get better at finding the defects in your programs. The checklist will also help you find these defects in less time.

14.2   An Example Code Review Checklist

The code review checklist that I designed for reviewing my C++ programs is shown in Table 14.1. A similar checklist for the Ada language is shown in Table 14.2. These checklists suggest a number of points to consider as you develop and use your own personal checklist:

A useful first step is to ensure that the code implements all the functions included in the design. In larger programs, it is easy to neglect to code some procedure or operation. Such oversights are common errors and can occasionally get past all subsequent reviews, compilations, and tests. They are generally easy to find with a checklist.

Overall checks for `includes` (or `withs`), initialization, procedure calls, and names are also effective. These are common problem areas that you should check unless historical data indicate that you NEVER make such mistakes.

Also consider checking the code against coding standards to ensure that you have not left out key comments, used an improper format, or omitted important process or product information. While coding standards may seem unimportant, they can be a great help for later work, such as program repair, enhancement, or reuse. Since these are major activities for most software organizations, you should get in the habit of following coding standards. (See in Section 14.7).

The principal danger with checklists is that you generally find what you look for. While this is useful, the problem is that, if you only do the checks on the checklist, you will only find what is on the checklist. Often, however, serious problems are unexpected, such as global interactions among programs, unanticipated

TABLE 14.1 C++ CODE REVIEW GUIDELINE AND CHECKLIST

Program Name and #:

Purpose	To guide you in conducting an effective code review.	#	#	#	#	To Date	To Date %
General	As you complete each review step, note the number of defects of that type found in the box to the right. If none, put a check in the box at the right. Complete the checklist for one program, class, object, or method before you start to review the next.						
Complete	Verify that all the functions in the design are coded.						
Includes	Verify that `includes` are complete.						
Initialization	Check variable and parameter initialization: • at program initiation • at start of every loop • at function/procedure entry						
Calls	Check function call formats: • Pointers • Parameters • Use of '&'						
Names	Check name spelling and use: • Is it consistent? • Is it within declared scope? • Do all structures/classes use '.' reference?						
Strings	Check that all strings are: • identified by pointers • terminated in NULL						
Pointers	Check that pointers are: • initialized NULL • only deleted after new • always deleted after use if new						
Output format	Check the output format: • Is line stepping proper? • Is spacing proper?						
{} Pairs	Ensure that the {} are proper and matched.						
Logic operators	Verify the proper use of ==, =, ||, etc. Check every logic function for proper ()						
Line-by-line check	Check every line of code: • Instruction syntax • Proper punctuation						
Standards	Ensure that the code conforms to the coding standards.						
File open and close	Verify that all files are: • properly declared • opened • closed						
Overall	Do an overall scan of the program to check system issues and unexpected problems.						
Totals							

TABLE 14.2 ADA CODE REVIEW GUIDELINE AND CHECKLIST

Program Name and #:

Purpose	To guide you in conducting an effective code review.	#	#	#	#	To Date	To Date %
General	As you complete each review step, note the number of defects of that type found in the box to the right. If none, put a check in the box at the right. Complete the checklist for one program, class, object, or method before you start to review the next.						
Complete	Verify that all the functions in the design are coded.						
Includes	Verify that the `with` statements are complete.						
Initialization	Check variable and parameter initialization: • at program initiation • at start of every loop • at procedure entry						
Calls	Check procedure call formats: • Punctuation • Parameters						
Names	Check name spelling and use: • Is it consistent? • Is it within declared scope? • Do all structures/packages use '.' reference?						
Strings	Check that all strings make proper use of slices.						
Pointers	Check that pointers are: • only deleted after new • always deleted after use if new						
Output format	Check the output format: • Is line stepping proper? • Is spacing proper?						
() Pairs	Ensure that the () are proper and matched.						
Logic operators	Verify the proper use of all logic operators. Check every logic function for proper ()						
Line-by-line check	Check every line of code: • Instruction syntax • Proper punctuation						
Standards	Ensure that the code conforms to the coding standards.						
File open and close	Verify that all files are: • properly declared • opened • closed						
Overall	Do an overall scan of the program to check for system issues and unexpected problems.						
Totals							

timing issues, complex memory utilization problems, or unusual operating conditions. It is thus a good idea to do at least one overall scan of the program to look for the unexpected. When you do, try to look from a systems or user perspective.

14.3   Using a Code Review Checklist

To use a code review checklist, read each item in turn and do the prescribed actions precisely as stated. When you complete each action, check it off on the checklist. At the end, review the entire checklist to ensure that you have checked every item. If you have not, go back and perform the missing actions, check them off, and again scan the list to make sure you did not miss anything else. In using a checklist, the following practices should be helpful:

1. Go through the program completely for each item on the checklist. For the checklist in Table 14.1, for example, first review the entire program to ensure that it completely implements the design. During this review, if you see other defects, fix them. Your intention, however, is to check the program completely against the design. Next, review for the next item on the checklist, and so forth.

2. When you find defects during any check, note that fact with a vertical mark in the first unused # box at the right. For a second defect, enter a second mark in the same box. Thus, after the complete review, you can look back to see how many defects you found with each review step.

3. After completing each check, if you have found no defects, put an x in the first unused # box at the right.

4. When reviewing a program with several functions, objects, or procedures, it is often a good idea to review each one separately. That is, review the first procedure completely and fill in the boxes in the first # column on the right with an x mark or the numbers of defects for that procedure. For the second procedure, again do it completely as a unit and fill in the boxes in the second # column. Continue in this way until you have reviewed all the functions, objects, or procedures.

5. As noted before, it is always a good idea to do a final overall scan of the entire program to look for the unexpected, new kinds of problems, or system or user issues.

The general process to follow with a code review checklists is shown in the updated Code Review Script in Table 14.3. The updated PSP Process Script is shown in Table 14.4. These scripts have only a couple of changes from the last chapter to include the checklist and require that it be completed when doing the re-

TABLE 14.3 CODE REVIEW SCRIPT

	Entry criteria	Check that the following are on hand: • The requirements statement • The program design • The program source code • The coding standards • *A copy of the Code Review Checklist*
	General	*Use the Code Review Checklist.* *Follow the checklist instructions during the review* *At review completion, fill in the To Date and To Date %* *columns and the Totals row.*
1	Review procedure	First produce the finished program source code. Before compiling or testing the program, print out a source code listing. Next, do the code review. During the code review, carefully check every line of source code to find and fix as many of the defects as you can.
2	Fix the defects	Fix all defects found. Check the fixes to ensure they are correct. Record the defects in the Defect Recording Log.
3	Review for coverage	Verify that the program design fulfills all the functions described in the requirements. Verify that the source code implements all the design.
4	Review the program logic	Verify that the design logic is correct. Verify that the program correctly implements the design logic.
5	Check names and types	Verify that all names and types are correctly declared and used. Check for proper declaration of integer, long integer, and floating point data types.
6	Check all variables	Ensure that every variable is initialized. Check for overflow, underflow, or out-of-range problems.
7	Check program syntax	Verify that the source code properly follows the language specifications.
8	Scan program	Do an overall scan of the program to check for system issues and unexpected problems.
	Exit criteria	At completion you must have: • the completed and corrected source code • completed Time Recording Log • completed Defect Recording Log

TABLE 14.4 PSP PROCESS SCRIPT

	Purpose	To guide you in developing small programs
	Inputs required	The problem description PSP Project Plan Summary form ***A copy of the Code Review Checklist*** Actual size and time data for previous programs Time Recording Log Defect Recording Log
1	Planning	Obtain a description of the program functions. Estimate the Max., Min., and total LOC required. Determine the Minutes/LOC. Calculate the Max., Min., and total development times. Enter the plan data in the Project Plan Summary form. Record the planning time in the Time Recording Log.
2	Design	Design the program. Record the design in the specified format. Record design time in the Time Recording Log.
3	Code	Implement the design. Use a standard format for entering the code. Record coding time in the Time Recording Log.
4	Code review	Completely review the source code. Follow the code review script ***and checklist***. Fix and record every defect found. Record review time in the Time Recording Log.
5	Compile	Compile the program. Fix and record all defects found. Record compile time in the Time Recording Log.
6	Test	Test the program. Fix and record all defects found. Record testing time in the Time Recording Log.
7	Postmortem	Complete the Project Plan Summary form with actual time, size, and defect data. ***Review the defect data and update the code review checklist.*** Record postmortem time in the Time Recording Log.
	Exit criteria	A thoroughly tested program A properly documented design ***A completed Code Review Checklist*** A complete program listing A completed Project Plan Summary Completed time and defect log

view. The PSP Project Plan Summary form and instructions are unchanged from the previous chapter.

14.4 Building a Personal Checklist

To build a personal code review checklist, first review the defect data and see which defect types have caused the most problems. While you will initially have a limited amount of defect data, you will get more with each new program. To be most effective, remember that the checklist must be designed for you, for the language you use, and for the types of defects you typically find and miss. While someone else's checklist may help to get started, it will not likely be as efficient as one tailored to your specific needs.

Here are some hints that may help you to produce a useful personal checklist.

1. Make a list by type of the numbers of defects found in each phase of the software process. See, for example, the Student X data in Table 14.5. Here, in the lower part of the table, he listed the defects found by phase for each program. This made it easy to check that all the defects were counted.

TABLE 14.5 STUDENT X'S DEFECT DATA ANALYSIS

Type	Injected			Removed			Missed
	Design	Code	Other	Review	Compile	Test	in Review
10							
20		8		4	4		4
30							
40	2	3		1	4		4
50		2			1	1	2
60							
70							
80	2	3			1	4	5
90							
100							
Total	4	16		5	10	5	15
Program							
10	2	6			6	2	8
11	1	5		3	2	1	3
12	1	5		2	2	2	4

2. Rank the defect types in descending order of the number of defects found in compile and test. An example of this listing is shown in Table 14.6.

3. For those few defect types with the most defects, examine the Defect Recording Logs to see what specific problems caused the most trouble. From Table 14.6, these would be type 80 function defects, type 20 syntax defects, and type 40 assignment defects.

4. For defects resulting from these most important problems, determine the steps to take in the code review to find them. Suppose that for the type 20 syntax defects, Student X found that his most common problem was missing or misplaced semicolons. He might then decide to add a check as a reminder to look at every source program line to check specifically for semicolons.

5. Make entries in the Code Review Checklist to ensure that you take these steps. Here, for example, Student X could add a semicolon item to the checklist that said: Review each source program line to verify that semicolons are properly used.

6. After using the new checklist, examine the defect data again in the same way.

7. If the checklist was effective at finding these most important defects, add another type and use it again.

8. If the checklist was not effective at finding some defect types, try to change it to better address these defects and try it again. In this case, if Student X found he had frequently typed a colon instead of a semicolon, he could add a reminder to check each semicolon to ensure that it was not mistakenly typed as a colon. His updated checklist is shown in Table 14.7.

(List continues on page 185.)

TABLE 14.6 STUDENT X'S RANKED DEFECT DATA

Type	Injected			Removed			Missed
	Design	Code	Other	Review	Compile	Test	in Review
80	2	3			1	4	5
20		8		4	4		4
40	2	3		1	4		4
50		2			1	1	2
60							
100							
30							
10							
70							
90							
Total	4	16		5	10	5	15

TABLE 14.7 STUDENT X's UPDATED ADA CHECKLIST

Program Name and #:

Purpose	To guide you in conducting an effective code review.	#	#	#	#	To Date #	To Date %
General	As you complete each review step, note the number of defects of that type found in the box to the right. If none, put a check in the box at the right. Complete the checklist for one program, class, object, or method before you start to review the next.						
Complete	Verify that all the functions in the design are coded.	X					
Includes	Verify that the `with` statements are complete.	X					
Initialization	Check variable and parameter initialization: • at program initiation • at start of every loop • at procedure entry	X					
Calls	Check procedure call formats: • Pointers • Parameters	X					
Names	Check name spelling and use: • Is it consistent? • Is it within declared scope? • Do all structures/packages use '.' reference?	1				2	40
Strings	Check that all strings are: • identified by pointers • terminated in NULL	X					
Pointers	Check that pointers are: • initialized NULL • only deleted after new • always deleted after use if new	X					
Output format	Check the output format: • Is line stepping proper? • Is spacing proper?	X					
() Pairs	Ensure that the () are proper and matched.	X					
Logic operators	Verify the proper use of all logic operators. Check every logic function for proper ()	X					
Line-by-line check	Check every line of code: • Instruction syntax • Semicolons are properly used • Check that semicolons are not typed as colons • Other punctuation	1				3	60
Standards	Ensure that the code conforms to the coding standards.	X					
File open and close	Verify that all files are: • properly declared • opened • closed	X					
Overall	Do an overall scan of the program to check system issues and unexpected problems.	X					
Total		2				5	100

9. In developing or updating the checklist, group similar checks together and do not duplicate them. If a particular check is not working well, replace it instead of adding an additional check for the same thing. In the example in Table 14.7, Student X included the semicolon checks with the other punctuation checks.

10. After developing each new program, briefly examine your defect data and the checklist in this same way to identify useful changes or additions.

11. It is also a good idea to consider what steps might prevent these defects in the future. Examples would be updating the coding standard or adding a step to the design process.

In Tables 14.5 and 14.6, Student X listed all the defects he had injected and removed since he started gathering defect data. While this included only 20 defects, it was all the data he had. In Table 14.5, he first listed the program totals from the Project Plan Summaries and then went through the defect logs to get the type information. In Table 14.6, he sorted Table 14.5 in the order of the number of defects listed in the right-hand column. The top item thus lists the type that had the most defects missed in code review and the next item has the type with the second largest number, and so forth. This type of listing is called a Pareto distribution. These distributions list the items in a priority order determined by the data. Note also that since Student X did not do a code review for program 10, he counted all the defects found in compile and test as defects missed in code review.

14.5 Improving the Checklist

Make a habit of regularly reviewing your defect data and reexamining the checklist. When steps are effective, retain them. When some step does not work well, figure out how to make that step more effective and update the checklist. The checklist thus becomes an encapsulation of personal experience. It also helps you to consistently follow the steps you have personally devised to find and fix defects.

The following paragraphs suggest ways to improve your personal checklist.

After completing a program, fill in the To Date column at the right of the checklist. Add the To Date value from the most recent previously completed checklist to the number of defects found in each step of this review. Enter this number in the To Date column for each row. Student X's updated checklist in Table 14.7 shows how this is done.

Complete the To Date % column by first totaling the To Date column and entering the total in the total row at the bottom of the checklist under To Date. Next, calculate the percentage each To Date row entry is of the To Date total and enter it in that row of the To Date % column. Again, Table 14.7 shows an example.

During the postmortem phase for each program, compare the checklist with the defect log to see where and how the checklist should be enhanced to better find defects. Also consider dropping review steps that have not found or missed any defects for the most recent five to ten programs. Here, for example, Student X would review the defect log from program 12 in Table 14.8 to see if he should change the checklist to better find the defects he missed. It is this check that convinced him to add the semicolon entry to the checklist in Table 14.7.

I suggest you gather data on more than 20 defects before updating the checklist; nonetheless, review the defect data during every program postmortem. When you have seen the same defect several times in compile or test, consider updating the checklist to address that specific problem.

Periodically prune the checklist. Checklists, by their nature, grow over time. The power of a checklist, however, is that it focuses attention. When it grows too large, you will lose focus. It is thus important to review the defect data periodically and eliminate checklist items that are not finding problems. You may want to group these removed items in a miscellaneous category to consider as you review the other items.

The personal checklist method recognizes that every engineer is different and that the practices one engineer uses may not necessarily be effective for others. Design your own checklist and periodically examine it to make it more effective. As long as you continue to miss defects in code reviews, continue to look for ways to improve the checklist. Remember, however, that improvements will come slowly. Initially, your ability to find defects will improve with each review. Thereafter, improvement will become more difficult. Keep gathering and analyzing defect data and thinking about what you could do to prevent or better find the defects missed. As long as you continue to do this, you will continue to get better at doing reviews. You will also continue to improve the quality of the programs you produce.

14.6   Coding Standards

One reason checklists are effective is that they provide a standard against which to review programs. While the principal code review standard is the programming language syntax specification, this does not specify coding styles or formats. For these, you need a coding standard.

Defect Types	
10 Documentation	60 Checking
20 Syntax	70 Data
30 Build, Package	80 Function
40 Assignment	90 System
50 Interface	100 Environment

TABLE 14.8 STUDENT X DEFECT RECORDING LOG EXAMPLE

Student ___Student X_____   Date ____11/11/96___
Instructor__Mr. Z_____   Program # ____12___

Date	Number	Type	Inject	Remove	Fix Time	Fix Defect
11/11	1	20	code	compile	1 min	
Description:	missing;					

Date	Number	Type	Inject	Remove	Fix Time	Fix Defect
	2	20	code	review	1 min	
Description:	misspelled variable X_ axis as X_ axes					

Date	Number	Type	Inject	Remove	Fix Time	Fix Defect
	3	20	code	compile	1 min	
Description:	; entered as :					

Date	Number	Type	Inject	Remove	Fix Time	Fix Defect
	4	50	code	compile	1	
Description:	incorrectly formatted call for procedure Normalize					

Date	Number	Type	Inject	Remove	Fix Time	Fix Defect
	5	80	code	text	11	
Description:	forgot to initialize variables X_ axis and Y_ axis					

Date	Number	Type	Inject	Remove	Fix Time	Fix Defect
	6	80	design	test	7	
Description:	while loop did not step on negative value X_ axis					

Date	Number	Type	Inject	Remove	Fix Time	Fix Defect
Description:						

Date	Number	Type	Inject	Remove	Fix Time	Fix Defect
Description:						

A **standard** is an officially accepted basis for comparison. A **coding standard** thus defines an accepted set of coding practices which can serve as a model for your work. This standard should be used as a guide when you write the source code. Such standards will typically specify the way the source code is formatted, what statements go on separate text lines, and how statements are indented. Practices for writing comments are commonly defined, including when explanatory comments are needed. Typically, the engineer's name, the date of the work, the program name, and the project name and version are also entered in a header comment at the top of the program listing. An example C++ coding standard is shown in Table 14.9.

Coding standards can also be helpful in preventing defects. Here, for example, you might list certain practices to avoid, like using `go-to` statements, having multiple exits from procedures, or using recursive routines. Some practices are also generally helpful like always initializing variables at loop entry or when declaring them. Poor naming practices can be a major source of error. Only use names that clearly relate to the variable's functions, and names should be different enough so they cannot easily be confused. Two confusing and error-prone names would be XY34B and XY35C. Better choices would be AZIM34 and UPDATE_AZIM.

If your professor has established a coding standard, get a copy and use it. It will help you produce more readable and easily understood programs. Readable code also helps in testing and debugging programs and it will help anyone who wants to use or modify your programs.

14.7   Summary

This chapter introduces code review checklists and describes how you can develop and use one of your own. A checklist contains a series of steps you want to follow precisely. When you use a checklist developed from your own defect data, you will do more efficient reviews. The checklist not only helps you to find more defects, it also helps you to find them faster.

In constructing a Code Review Checklist, tailor it to the language you use, design it from your defect data, and adjust it as your skills and experience change.

Some guides on using checklist are: Do the reviews in steps. Complete each program or procedure before starting the next. Check off each checklist step when you complete it. When you find defects, note the number found with each checklist step. When done, complete the To Date and To Date % entries. After finishing each program, review the data and checklist to see how to improve it.

TABLE 14.9 C++ CODING STANDARD

Purpose	To guide the development of C++ programs
Program headers	All programs begin with a descriptive header.
| Header format | ```
/**********************************************/
/* Program Assignment: the program number    */
/* Name:               your name             */
/* Date:               the date program      */
/*                     development started   */
/* Description:        a short description of */
/*                     the program           */
/*                     function              */
/**********************************************/
``` |
| Listing contents | Provide a summary of the listing contents. |
| Contents example | ```
/**********************************************/
/* Listing Contents:                         */
/*    Reuse instructions                     */
/*    Includes                               */
/*    Class declarations:                    */
/*       CData                               */
/*       ASet                                */
/*    Source code in c:\classes\CData.cpp:   */
/*       CData                               */
/*       CData()                             */
/*       Empty()                             */
/**********************************************/
``` |
| Reuse instructions | Describe how the program is used. Provide the declaration format, parameter values and types, and parameter limits.
Provide warnings of illegal values, overflow conditions, or other conditions that could potentially result in improper operation. |
| Example | ```
/**********************************************/
/* Reuse Instructions                        */
/*    int PrintLine(char *line_of_character) */
/*    Purpose: to print string,              */
/*     'line_of_character', on one print line */
/*    Limitations: the maximum line length is */
/*       LINE_LENGTH                          */
/*    Return: 0 if printer not ready to print, */
/*       else 1                              */
/**********************************************/
``` |
| Identifiers | Use descriptive names for all variables, function names, constants, and other identifiers. Avoid abbreviations or single letter variables. |
| Identifier example | ```
int number_of_students;   /* This is GOOD */
float x4, j, ftave;       /* These are BAD */
``` |

(Continued)

TABLE 14.9 (*Continued*)

Comments	Sufficiently document the code so the reader can understand its operation. Comments should explain both the purpose and behavior of the code. Comment variable declarations to indicate their purpose.

Good comment	<pre>if(record_count > limit) /* have all the */
	/* records been processed? */</pre>

Bad comment	<pre>if(record_count > limit) /* check if record_ */
	/* count is greater than limit */</pre>

Major sections	Major program sections should be preceded by a block comment that describes the processing that is done in the next section.

Example	<pre>/***/
	/* This program section will examine the */
	/* contents of the array "grades" */
	/* and will calculate the average grade */
	/* for the class */
	/***/</pre>

Blank space	Write programs with sufficient spacing so they are easy to read. Separate every program construct with at least one space.
Indenting	Indent every level of bracket from the previous one. Open and closing brackets should be on lines by themselves and aligned with each other.

Indenting example	<pre>while (miss_distance > threshold)
	{
	  success_code=move_robot (target_location);
	  if (success_code==MOVE_FAILED)
	  {
	      printf("The robot move has failed.\n");
	  }
	}</pre>

Capitalization	All defines are capitalized. All other identifiers and reserved words are lowercase. Messages being output to the user can be mixed-case so as to make a clean user presentation.

Capitalization example	<pre>#define DEFAULT_NUMBER_OF_STUDENTS 15
	
	int class_size=DEFAULT_NUMBER_OF_STUDENTS;</pre>

14.8   Assignment 14

Construct a checklist to find the defect types that caused the most trouble during compile and test. Restrict this initial checklist to a few defect types and use it on the next program. Submit the completed checklist, along with the program and its completed Project Plan Summary form. Also submit a copy of the defect data used to construct the checklist. Use a format similar to that shown in Table 14.6 for analyzing the defect data.

Submit copies of those Time Recording Log and Weekly Activity Summary sheets not previously submitted. Also, turn in completed copies of the Project Plan Summary form, the Defect Recording Logs, and the Code Review Checklist for every program you develop. Include both planned and actual development times and actual defects injected and removed.

15

Projecting Defects

This chapter discusses ways to analyze and use your defect data to help improve both planning accuracy and product quality. It also gives examples of useful ways to analyze these defect data. For the exercise, you will prepare a brief report on the defect data for the programs you have developed so far in this course.

The principal reason for using defect data is to determine how best to prevent or find the defects you inject. In later chapters, we introduce measures to help control the quality of your work. This will help you to more consistently produce high-quality programs.

15.1 Defect Rates

Defect injection rates for experienced software engineers typically range from about 50 up to around 250 defects/KLOC. Figure 15.1 shows the defects/KLOC that a group of 38 engineers injected in one small programming exercise. This was before they had started to measure, track, and control the numbers of defects they injected. This figure thus reflects the rate at which these engineers injected defects before they were trained in the PSP.

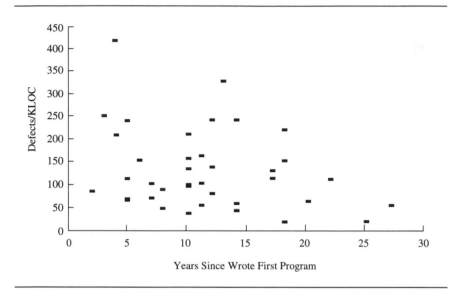

FIGURE 15.1 DEFECTS/KLOC VS. YEARS—BEFORE PSP TRAINING

Note also that Figure 15.1 shows defect density as a function of the years since each engineer wrote his or her first program. While some of the least experienced engineers had higher defect levels than the others, except for these few engineers, years of experience had little relationship to defect levels. This implies that there are some quality practices that most engineers learn with experience. Some pick them up very quickly and others take a little longer. Then, after some base level of experience, defect levels are largely a matter of personal discipline.

Figure 15.2 shows data for the same 38 engineers after they had completed a course on the PSP [Humphrey 95]. At this point, they had all tracked their defects for a total of 10 small programs, and had made two studies of the types, distributions, and fix times of their defects. As a result, they understood the numbers and types of defects they typically injected and how much time they took to fix. This helped them to appreciate the importance of disciplined personal practices, and it motivated them to be more careful in designing and coding their programs. As a result, they reduced their total defect injection rates. The data in Figures 15.1 and 15.2 suggest that personal discipline, coupled with defect tracking and analysis, are much more effective than years of experience in reducing the number of injected defects.

Another message from Figures 15.1 and 15.2 is that software engineers inject a lot of defects. With few exceptions, average defect injection rates for software groups are around 100 defects/KLOC or more. Even engineers who have learned defect management inject an average of about 50 defects/KLOC. That is 1 defect

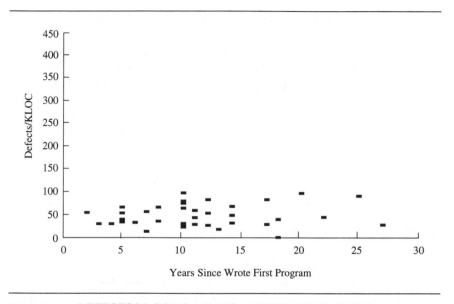

FIGURE 15.2 DEFECTS/KLOC VS. YEARS—AFTER PSP TRAINING

for every 20 LOC. While this may not seem like a lot, it would be 50 defects in a 1000 LOC program, 500 in a 10,000 LOC program, and 50,000 in a 1,000,000 LOC program. All these defects must be found and fixed before you can be sure the program will operate properly. To repeat a key point, since defect injection is a natural consequence of being human, all software engineers inject defects. All engineers should therefore understand the number and types of defects they inject.

15.2   Using Defect Data

To date, you have gathered defect data to help understand the defects you have injected. You then used these data to design a personal checklist for doing code reviews. In this chapter, you will use these defect data to estimate the number of defects you will inject in a new program. By using historical data, you will also see how to make reasonably good projections of the number of defects you will inject and remove in each phase of a programming project.

Accurate estimates of defect levels are important. You can always run another test or do another code review. The only way to decide to do such tests and reviews is to analyze defect data. By comparing the data on the current project with your historical experience, you can determine the likely quality of the program being developed. You can then decide whether additional defect-removal steps are needed.

All these measurements and plans will not help very much, however, unless you are personally committed to producing defect-free programs. While it is hard to produce such high-quality programs, and you will rarely be able to do so at first, with enough practice, you will produce defect-free programs most of the time. This is important because someday you will likely work on a project where defect-free work is essential. I suggest you consider every program you develop as practice for that day.

15.3   Defect Density

The basic defect measure used in the PSP is the defects per thousand lines of code (KLOC). This is called defect density (Dd) and it is measured in units of defects/KLOC. Here, the K stands for 1000. To calculate the total defects/KLOC found in a program, do the following:

1. Add up the total numbers of defects (D) found in all phases of the process.
2. Count the number (N) of new and changed LOC in the program.
3. Calculate the defects per KLOC as Dd = 1000*D/N.

For example, if a 96 LOC program had a total of 14 defects, then the defect density would be 1000*14/96 = 145.83 defects/KLOC.

In calculating defect densities, it is important to use the right size measures. As described in Chapter 6, this book counts program size in numbers of new and changed LOC. That is, if you use a library routine or copy part of a program, do not count these LOC. Do, however, count all the new LOC as well as any modified LOC in these copied programs.

15.4   Projecting Defect Rates

When developing a new program, you will likely have trouble estimating how many defects you will inject. The reason is that this number will vary from one program to the next. There are several causes for this. First, with experience, your skills will improve. When starting to program, you faced many problems you had not previously encountered. You may not be sure how some function or procedure works, you may be confused by a language construct, or you may encounter new compiler or environment issues. These problems will cause your development times and defect injection rates to fluctuate. With experience, you will gradually overcome these early problems and make fewer mistakes. This will both reduce the total numbers of defects and reduce the variation in these numbers. Some initial reduction in defect levels will thus result from more experience and improved language fluency. Beyond this initial improvement, however, you will need to gather and analyze defect data to continue improving.

The second reason for fluctuating defect rates is that your process is not stable. That is, as you learn to write programs, you are also learning new methods and procedures. Your working practices are thus evolving. This will cause fluctuations in the time to do various programming tasks and in the numbers of defects you inject. Finally, the defects themselves are a source of variation. The more defects you inject, the more time you spend repairing them. Since engineers typically inject six to eight defects per hour while writing code, every hour spent fixing defects increases the chances of injecting more defects. Since defect repair time is widely variable, a process that injects many defects is inherently unpredictable.

As your process improves, however, it will stabilize, and this stability will improve the accuracy of your defect projections. If you spend a sufficient amount of time in code reviews, your process will quickly settle down to a more stable pattern. Once your process is reasonably stable, it will also be more predictable. Then, by tracking the number of defects/KLOC you injected and removed in the most recent programs, you can fairly accurately estimate the number of defects you will likely inject and remove in the future.

15.5 Defect Estimation

When planning a new program, first estimate the number of new and changed LOC the program will likely have. Next, calculate the average defects/KLOC for previously developed programs. With these numbers, you can now calculate the expected number of defects/KLOC in the new program as

$$Dd_{\text{plan}} = 1000(D_1 + \ldots + D_i)(N_1 + \ldots + N_i).$$

Suppose, for example, you had the data for five programs shown in Table 15.1. Now, the value of Dd_{plan} is calculated as follows:

$$Dd_{\text{plan}} = 1000*(6 + 11 + 7 + 9 + 5)/(37 + 62 + 49 + 53 + 28)$$
$$= 1000*38/229 = 165.94 \text{ defects/KLOC}$$

Assuming the new program will have this same defect density, calculate its expected number of defects as

$$D_{plan} = N_{plan}*Dd_{plan}/1000.$$

Now, using this same example, and assuming the LOC estimated for the new program was 56, calculate the expected number of defects as

$$D_{plan} = 56*165.94/1000$$
$$= 9.29 \text{ defects.}$$

Using these data, you would thus anticipate nine defects for a programming project with a planned 56 LOC.

The To Date size and defect data in the Project Plan Summary form were designed to help make these calculations.

$$D_{plan} = N_{plan}*D_{ToDate}/N_{ToDate}.$$

Or, using the data from Table 15.1, this equation gives

$$D_{plan} = 56*38/229 = 9.29,$$

which is the same answer as before.

With the expected number of total defects for the new program, you can calculate the expected number of defects to be injected and removed in each phase. To get these numbers, multiply the total expected number of defects by the To Date % value for each phase and divide by 100. This gives the expected number of defects for that phase of the new project. This was the reason for calculating the defect To Date and To Date % values. They provide the historical data needed for defect estimating. Section 15.7 gives an example of these calculations with the updated Project Plan Summary form.

TABLE 15.1 EXAMPLE DEFECT DATA

Program Number	Defects (D)	LOC (N)
1	6	37
2	11	62
3	7	49
4	9	53
5	5	28
Total To Date	38	229

15.6   The Updated Project Plan Summary Form and Example

The new PSP Process Script and a Project Plan Summary form now includes defect planning. These are shown in Tables 15.2 and 15.3. The Project Plan Summary Instructions are shown in Table 15.4. The new items in these tables are shown in **_Bold Italics_**. The additions are the Plan column for defects injected and defects removed and the defects/KLOC row in the summary.

Table 15.5 shows an example of Student X's Project Plan Summary Form for program 13. The following paragraphs describe how he used data from the previously completed program 12 summary in Table 15.6 to complete this form. Various of the values in these tables are labeled with letters of the alphabet to help identify the source of the data. First, during planning:

1. Student X first estimated the size of the new program as 58 LOC (a) and the maximum and minimum LOC as 72 (a) and 41 (a) LOC.

2. He next looked on the Project Plan Summary form for program 12 to find the To Date minutes/LOC. As shown, this was 5.92 (b) minutes/LOC. He used this as the planning rate for program 13.

3. With a total estimated LOC of 58 (a), the estimated total project time is then 58*5.92 = 343.36 or 343 minutes (c).

4. Student X then calculated the maximum and minimum development times by multiplying the maximum and minimum sizes (a) by 5.92 (b) to get 426 and 243 (d) minutes, respectively.

5. For the time in phase, he took the To Date % times from the program 12 summary (e) and multiplied them by the total estimated time of 343 minutes (c), then divided the result by 100. This gave the times for each phase as shown at (f). For convenience, he rounded off to the nearest minute.

6. For total defects injected and removed, Student X found the To Date Defects/KLOC on the program 12 Project Plan Summary in Table 15.6 as 94.79 (g). As shown below, this is calculated from the To Date LOC (h) and To Date Defects (i).

7. With 94.79 defects/KLOC (i) and 58 planned LOC (a), he calculated the total expected number of defects as 94.79*58/1000 = 5.50, or about 6 defects (j).

8. Based on the To Date % values for defects injected and defects removed from program 12 (k), he calculated the expected number of defects to be injected and removed by phase (l).

This now completes the defect projections for program 13.

TABLE 15.2 PSP PROCESS SCRIPT

	Purpose	To guide you in developing small programs
	Inputs required	The problem description PSP Project Plan Summary form A copy of the Code Review Checklist Actual size and time data for previous programs Time Recording Log Defect Recording Log
1	Planning	Obtain a description of the program functions. Estimate the Max., Min., and total LOC required. Determine the Minutes/LOC. Calculate the Max., Min., and total development times. ***Estimate the defects to be injected and removed by phase.*** Enter the plan data in the Project Plan Summary form. Record the planning time in the Time Recording Log.
2	Design	Design the program. Record the design in the specified format. Record design time in the Time Recording Log.
3	Code	Implement the design. Use a standard format for entering the code. Record coding time in the Time Recording Log.
4	Code review	Completely review the source code. Follow the code review script. Fix and record every defect found. Record review time in the Time Recording Log.
5	Compile	Compile the program. Fix and record all defects found. Record compile time in the Time Recording Log.
6	Test	Test the program. Fix and record all defects found. Record testing time in the Time Recording Log.
7	Postmortem	Complete the Project Plan Summary form with actual time, size, and defect data. Review the defect data and update the code review checklist. Record postmortem time in the Time Recording Log.
	Exit criteria	A thoroughly tested program A properly documented design A completed Code Review Checklist A complete program listing A completed Project Plan Summary Completed time and defect log

TABLE 15.3 PSP PROJECT PLAN SUMMARY

Student _____   Date _____

Program _____   Program # _____

Instructor _____   Language _____

Summary	Plan	Actual	To Date
Minutes/LOC	_____	_____	_____
LOC/Hour	_____	_____	_____
Defects/KLOC	_____	_____	_____
Yield	_____	_____	_____
A/FR	_____	_____	_____

Program Size (LOC):			
Total New & Changed	_____	_____	_____
Maximum Size	_____		
Minimum Size	_____		

Time in Phase (min.)	Plan	Actual	To Date	To Date %
Planning	_____	_____	_____	_____
Design	_____	_____	_____	_____
Code	_____	_____	_____	_____
Code Review	_____	_____	_____	_____
Compile	_____	_____	_____	_____
Test	_____	_____	_____	_____
Postmortem	_____	_____	_____	_____
Total	_____	_____	_____	_____
Maximum Time	_____			
Minimum Time	_____			

Defects Injected	*Plan*	Actual	To Date	To Date %	*Def./Hour*
Planning	_____	_____	_____	_____	
Design	_____	_____	_____	_____	
Code	_____	_____	_____	_____	
Code Review	_____	_____	_____	_____	
Compile	_____	_____	_____	_____	
Test	_____	_____	_____	_____	
Total	_____	_____	_____	_____	

Defects Removed	*Plan*	Actual	To Date	To Date %	*Def./Hour*
Planning	_____	_____	_____	_____	
Design	_____	_____	_____	_____	
Code	_____	_____	_____	_____	
Code Review	_____	_____	_____	_____	
Compile	_____	_____	_____	_____	
Test	_____	_____	_____	_____	
Total	_____	_____	_____	_____	

TABLE 15.4 PSP PROJECT PLAN SUMMARY INSTRUCTIONS

Purpose	This form holds the estimated and actual project data in a convenient and readily retrievable form.
Header	Enter the following: • Your name and today's date • The program name and number • The instructor's name • The language you will use to write the program
Minutes/LOC	Prior to development • Enter the Minutes/LOC planned for this project.Use the To Date rate from the most recent previous program. After development • Divide the total development time by the actual program size to get the actual and To Date Minutes/LOC. • For example, if the project took 196 minutes and you produced 29 LOC, the Minutes/LOC would be 196/29 = 6.76.
LOC/Hour	Prior to development • Calculate the LOC per hour planned for this program by dividing 60 by the Plan Minutes/LOC. After development • For Actual and To Date LOC/Hour, divide 60 by the Actual To Date Minutes/LOC. • For Actual Minutes/LOC of 6.76, Actual LOC/Hour are 60/6.76 = 8.88.
Defects/KLOC	*Prior to development* • *Find the defects/KLOC To Date on the most recent previous program.* • *Use this as the Planned Defects/KLOC for this project.* *After development* • *Calculate the defects/KLOC actual and To Date for this program.* • *For Actual, multiply the total actual defects by 1000 and divide by the Actual Total New & Changed LOC.* • *Make a similar calculation for To Date.* • *With 17 defects to date and 153 Total New & Changed LOC, defects/KLOC To Date = 1000*17/153 = 111.11*
Program size **(LOC)**	Prior to development • Enter under plan the estimated Total, Maximum, and Minimum New & Changed LOC. After development • Count and enter the Actual New & Changed LOC. • For To Date, add Actual New & Changed LOC to the To Date New & Changed LOC for the previous program.

(Continued)

TABLE 15.4 (*Continued*)

Time in Phase Plan	For Total development time, multiply Total New & Changed LOC by Minutes/LOC. For Maximum time, multiply the Maximum size by Minutes/LOC. For Minimum time, multiply the Minimum size by Minutes/LOC. From the Project Plan Summary for the most recent program, find the To Date % values for each phase. Using the To Date % from the previous program, calculate the plan time for each phase.
Actual	At job completion, enter the actual time in minutes spent in each development phase. Get these data from the time log.
To Date	For each phase, enter the sum of actual time and To Date time from the most recent previous program.
To Date %	For each phase, enter 100 times the To Date time for that phase divided by the Total To Date time.
Defects Injected ***Plan***	*Before development, estimate the total number of defects to be injected in the program.* *The value is Plan Defects/KLOC times the Plan Total New & Changed LOC for this program divided by 1000.* *For example, with a Plan Defects/KLOC of 75.9 and a Plan New & Changed LOC of 75, Plan Total defects = 75.9*75/1000 = 5.69, so use 6.* *Before development, estimate the defects injected by phase using the estimate total defects and the To Date % defect injected distribution from the previous program.*
Actual	After development, find and enter the actual number of defects injected in each phase.
To Date	For each phase, enter the sum of the actual defects and the To Date defects from the most recent program.
To Date %	For each phase, enter 100 times the To Date defects for that phase divided by the total To Date defects.
Defects Removed ***Plan***	*In the total row, enter the estimated total defects.* *Using the To Date % values from the most recent program, calculate the plan defects removed for each phase.*
Actual	After development, find and enter the actual number of defects removed in each phase.
To Date	For each phase, enter the sum of the actual defects and the To Date defects from the most recent programs.
To Date %	For each phase, enter 100 times the To Date defects for that phase divided by the total To Date defects.

TABLE 15.5 PSP PROJECT PLAN SUMMARY EXAMPLE

Student	Student X		Date	11/18/96
Program			Program #	13
Instructor	Mr. Z		Language	Ada

Summary		Plan		Actual		To Date
Minutes/LOC	b	5.92	p	4.87	x	5.73
LOC/Hour		10.14	q	12.32	y	10.47
Defects/KLOC	i	94.79	r	106.4	z	96.90
Yield						
A/FR						

Program Size (LOC):

Total New & Changed	a	58	o	47	w	258
Maximum Size	a	72				
Minimum Size	a	41				

Time in Phase (min.)		Plan		Actual		To Date		To Date %
Planning	f	18	m	22	s	88	u	6.0
Design	f	35	m	24	s	151	u	10.2
Code	f	149	m	93	s	637	u	43.1
Code Review	f	20	m	37	s	111	u	7.5
Compile	f	24	m	4	s	92	u	6.2
Test	f	64	m	8	s	240	u	16.2
Postmortem	f	33	m	41	s	160	u	10.8
Total	c	343	m	229	s	1479	u	100
Maximum Time	d	426						
Minimum Time	d	243						

Defects Injected		*Plan*		Actual		To Date		To Date %		*Def./Hour*
Planning										
Design	l	1			t	4	u	16.0		
Code	l	5	n	5	t	21	u	84.0		
Code Review										
Compile										
Test										
Total	j	6	n	5	t	25	u	100.0		

Defects Removed		*Plan*		Actual		To Date		To Date %		*Def./Hour*
Planning										
Design										
Code										
Code Review	l	2	n	3	t	8	u	32.0		
Compile	l	3	n	2	t	12	u	48.0		
Test	l	1			t	5	u	20.0		
Total	j	6	n	5	t	25	u	100.0		

TABLE 15.6   STUDENT X's PROGRAM 12 PLAN SUMMARY

Student	Student X			Date	11/11/96
Program				Program #	12
Instructor	Mr. Z			Language	Ada

Summary	Plan	Actual		To Date
Minutes/LOC	6.30	4.93	b	5.92
LOC/Hour	9.52	12.17		10.14
Defects/KLOC			g	94.79
Yield				
A/FR				

Program Size (LOC):

	Plan	Actual		To Date
Total New & Changed	51	58	h	211
Maximum Size	65			
Minimum Size	37			

Time in Phase (min.)	Plan	Actual		To Date		To Date %
Planning	16	18	s	66	e	5.3
Design	27	44	s	127	e	10.2
Code	146	104	s	544	e	43.5
Code Review	12	38	s	74	e	5.9
Compile	26	11	s	88	e	7.0
Test	68	29	s	232	e	18.6
Postmortem	26	42	s	119	e	9.5
Total	321	286	s	1250		100.0
Maximum Time	410					
Minimum Time	233					

Defects Injected	Plan	Actual		To Date		To Date %	Def./Hour
Planning							
Design		1	t	4	k	20.0	
Code		5	t	16	k	80.0	
Code Review							
Compile							
Test							
Total		6	i	20		100.0	

Defects Removed	Plan	Actual		To Date		To Date %	Def./Hour
Planning							
Design							
Code							
Code Review		2	t	5	k	25.0	
Compile		2	t	10	k	50.0	
Test		2	t	5	k	25.0	
Total		6	t	20		100.0	

15.7   Entering the Actual Data

After developing the program, Student X then entered the actual data in the form as follows:

1. He entered the Actual values of Time in Phase from the Time Recording Log (m).

2. He entered the Actual values of Defects Injected and Defects Removed from the Defect Recording Log (n).

3. He counted 47 New & Changed LOC in the finished program and entered that number under Actual (o).

4. With these data, he calculated the Actual Minutes/LOC as the total minutes, 229 (m), divided by the New & Changed LOC of 47 (o), or 229/47 = 4.87 (p).

5. He also calculated the Actual LOC/Hour from the actual minutes/LOC (p) as 60/4.87 = 12.32 (q).

6. He calculated the Actual Defects/KLOC from the actual total defects (n) and actual LOC (o) as 1000*5/47 = 106.4 (r).

7. He next calculated the To Date values for Time in Phase by adding the phase times for this project to the To Date times for the previous project (s).

8. He also calculated the To Date values for Defects Injected and Defects Removed by adding the actual defects in each phase to the To Date defects for the previous project (t).

9. The To Date % values were also calculated as shown (u).

10. He next calculated the To Date value for Minutes/LOC by dividing the To Date Total time of 1479 minutes (s) by the To Date Total New & Changed LOC value of 258 (w). This gave 1479/258 = 5.73 (x).

11. Using this 5.73 value (x), he now calculated the To Date LOC/Hour as 60/5.73 = 10.47 (y).

12. Finally, he calculated the To Date Defects/KLOC by multiplying 1000 by the To Date Total Defects Injected (t) and dividing by the To Date Total New & Changed LOC (w). This is 1000*25/258 = 96.90 (z).

Note that the To Date and To Date % figures keep a running total of the time and defect distribution. With more experience, you may find that your productivity and defect levels change so significantly that the data on the earliest programs is no longer a useful guide for current planning. At that point, you might wish to recalculate all the To Date and To Date % values without these earliest programs.

15.8 Summary

With this chapter, you use defect data to project the number of defects you will inject and remove in each phase of a new program. As you learn to make defect projections, you will also learn to make better development plans and to better control the number of defects you inject and remove.

To make a defect projection, you need defect and size data for prior programs, and a size estimate for the new program. To calculate the expected number of defects, assume that the defects/KLOC for this program will be the same as the average of the previously developed programs. Also assume that the defect injection and removal distributions will be similar. Then use the defects/KLOC and To Date % defect numbers from the prior program to make the planning calculations.

An updated Project Plan Summary is introduced for defect estimating. Produce the Plan numbers during the planning phase for each programming project. Calculate the Planned, Actual, and To Date defects/KLOC values during the postmortem for each new program and use these data for planning the next project.

15.9 Assignment 15

For the next program you write, determine the defects/KLOC rate and estimate the defects to be injected and removed by phase. Enter these data in a Project Plan Summary like that in Table 15.3.

Submit copies of those Time Recording Log and Weekly Activity Summary sheets you have not previously submitted. Also, turn in completed copies of the Project Plan Summary form, the Defect Recording Logs, and the Code Review Checklist for every completed program. Include both planned and actual values for development times and defects injected and removed.

Reference

[Humphrey 95] Humphrey, W. S. *A Discipline for Software Engineering.* Reading, MA: Addison-Wesley, 1995.

16

The Economics of Defect Removal

This chapter discusses the economics of defect removal. Defect removal is an economic issue because many defect-removal decisions concern trade-offs between cost, schedule, and quality. While product quality must always be a high priority, most projects have schedule and cost constraints. Thus, the relative costs of removing defects during development, the impact of any remaining defects on the customer, and the resulting customer support costs are important issues in software development. For the chapter assignment, you will analyze the defect injection and removal rates for the programs you have developed so far in this semester.

16.1 The Need for Quality Work

In spite of the many technological advances in the computer field, the work of software engineers has not appreciably changed in over 30 years. Software engineers have always broken big programs into smaller parts. They then generally work by themselves to develop one or more of these parts. In the process, they spend 30–40% or more of their time trying to get these programs to run some basic tests. Once the programs run, the programmers then test and integrate them with other programs into progressively larger systems. The process of integrating and testing is almost totally devoted to finding and fixing more defects. When the resulting products are finally shipped, their quality is often so poor that the engineers must spend many more months fixing the defects the customers report. This was the common software practice 30 years ago and it is the common practice today.

There are better ways to develop software. The basic problem is that when software engineers first write their programs, they typically rush through the design and coding so they can get their programs into the compile and test phases. A principle of quality work, however, is to build the product right the first time. When you learn to do this, there won't be all these defects to remove in compile and test and you and your organization will not need to spend all that time finding and fixing defects.

The example of some engineers at Motorola shows how important this is. Their software was used to run the factory producing advanced pager products. Whenever the product or the production process was changed, the engineers had to change the software. To find the many defects in each new software release, the production line had to be stopped for testing. Even after the testing, however, production was periodically interrupted by software defects that had been missed. In the very first software update after the engineers learned the PSP, there was only one defect in test and none in the next several months of production. This not only saved testing time, but it reduced manufacturing interruptions. As a result, the plant could produce more products, and the company could earn more revenue.

16.2   The Defect-Removal Problem

Defect removal is expensive because defects are hard to find and fix. As we build larger and more complex software systems, this problem will only get worse. The size and complexity of software systems has increased about ten times every ten years. Where an early laser printer needed 20,000 LOC in its support programs, the latest version uses over 1 million LOC. Ten years ago, automobiles had no software; today the newest cars contain many thousands of lines of software. Since software size and complexity will likely continue to increase, defect removal will continue to get more expensive and more time consuming.

To understand and control defect costs, it is essential to measure defect-removal effectiveness. One such measure is the number of defects removed in an hour. Another useful measure is defect-removal yield. Yield measures the percentage of the defects found by a removal method. Thus, if a product contained 100 defects at test entry, and if 45 defects were found in test, the test yield would be 45%. When you know the yield and removal rates of each defect-removal method, you can best decide how to find and fix defects. These yield and defect-removal measures are discussed in this chapter and subsequent chapters show how these measures are used.

16.3   Defect-Removal Time

With programs of a few dozen to a few hundred LOC, you will probably inject only a few defects. While finding and fixing them will be an annoyance, it will not take very long. With larger projects, however, the time involved is much greater. For example, 250 engineers on the Microsoft NT system spent a full year in system test finding and fixing 30,000 defects [Zachary]. This averages 16 hours per defect.

On large systems, when the engineer developing a program does not remove all the injected defects, someone else must find and fix them. The more defects there are and the later they are fixed, the more this repair work costs. With larger products, these costs can grow alarmingly. As pointed out in Chapter 13, an engineer can find and fix a defect in a few minutes during a personal code review. In unit test, the costs are several times higher, but they still average only about a quarter to a half an hour each. The defects engineers miss in their personal work, however, must be found in later testing and customer use. Then each defect generally takes many hours to find and fix.

16.4   Defect-Injection and -Removal Experience

Students and engineers typically inject 1 to 3 defects per hour during design and 5 to 8 defects when writing code. They only remove about 2 to 4 defects per hour in testing but find 6 to 12 defects per hour during code review. Figure 16.1 shows the defect-injection rates for one class of 14 engineers and Figure 16.2 shows their defect-removal rates. At program 1, at the left, the students did not generally do code reviews or track yield and defect-removal rates. From program 1 to program 10, these engineers learned how to calculate yield and defect-removal rates and they became reasonably proficient at the PSP defect-removal methods.

There are several interesting points about the data in Figures 16.1 and 16.2: First, The rates shown in Figures 16.1 and 16.2 are averages for 14 engineers. They thus look reasonably regular. Rates for individual engineers, however, are more variable. Your personal rates will likely have wide variations from one program to the next. By using the PSP to track your work, however, you will ultimately see improvement.

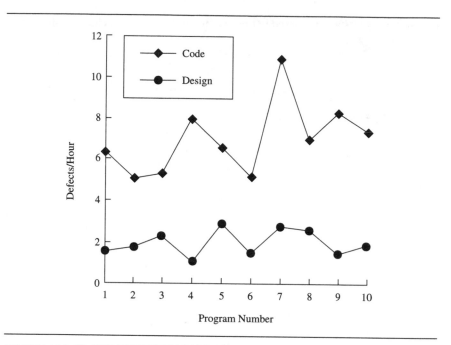

FIGURE 16.1 CLASS DEFECT-INJECTION RATES

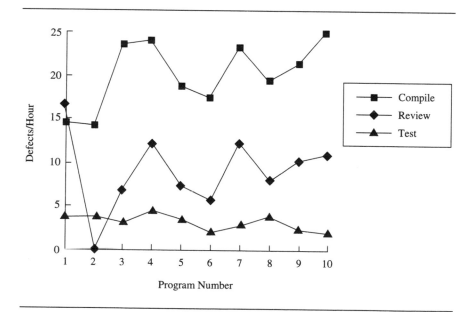

FIGURE 16.2 CLASS DEFECT-REMOVAL RATES

The defects removed per hour in test were consistently between 2 and 4. Similar rates are found with inexperienced students and with very experienced engineers.

Code reviewing is a skill. With practice, most engineers can achieve defect-removal rates of 8 to 10 defects per hour. The key is to use the methods described in Chapters 13 and 14.

Defect management is a little like climbing a down escalator. When designing and coding, you inject defects. As you find and remove these defects you will spend more time redesigning and recoding. During this time you are also injecting more defects. To gain in this race you need to reduce defect injection rates and increase removal rates. To do this, you must calculate and track these injection and removal rates.

The data gathered with the PSP are all you need to calculate personal defect-injection and defect-removal rates.

16.5   Defect-Removal Savings

An understanding of defect-removal rates is important for large projects and it can be helpful for individual software engineers. When developing a moderate-sized program, and assuming your data are similar to those of other engineers, you would inject about 100 defects/KLOC, find about 50 per KLOC in compile, and find another 40 defects/KLOC in unit test.

As shown in Table 16.1, this means that a 500 LOC program would have about 50 total defects. Of these, 25 would be found in compile and, with luck, another 20 would be found in unit test. If you did not use code reviews, you would likely take about 2 hours to get a clean compile and to find these 25 defects. Unit test would take about 10 hours to find the expected 20 defects. This is a total of 12 hours spent in defect removal.

After learning the PSP, you should only inject about 50 defects per KLOC (25 defects). With code reviews, you should also find 60% to 70% of these defects before the first compile. Now, compile only takes about 30 minutes and there are only 4 or 5 defects to find in unit test. Testing thus takes about 2 hours. Assuming you spent about 2.5 hours in the code review, the total defect removal time would be about 5 hours. This is a saving of 7 hours.

While it may not seem worth a lot of effort to cut defect-removal time by 7 hours for a job of several days, consider how these numbers scale up. If, instead of a 500 LOC program, you were developing 10,000 LOC, you would start with 1000 defects. With PSP training, this would only be 500 defects. If you spent 50 hours in code reviews, you would cut compile time from 40 to 10 hours and unit testing time from 200 to 40 hours. The 140 hours you save is several weeks' work.

TABLE 16.1 DEFECT-INJECTION AND -REMOVAL EXAMPLES

	500 LOC		10,000 LOC	
	Without PSP	*With PSP*	*Without PSP*	*With PSP*
Defects				
Total Defects	50	25	1,000	500
Found in Code Review	0	15	0	300
Defects Remaining	50	10	1,000	200
Found in Compile	25	5	500	100
Found in Unit Test	20	4	400	80
Defects Remaining	5	1	100	20
Time (hours)				
Code Review Time	0	2.5	0	50
Compile Time	2	0.5	40	10
Unit Test Time	10	2	200	40
Personal Defect-Removal Time	12	5	240	100
Integration and System Test Time			1,000	200
Total Defect-Removal Time	12	5	1,240	300

Of more significance, however, is the cost of the defects that you did not find in your process. In the 500 LOC case this was only a few defects. With the larger component, there would be about 100 of these missed defects. Finding them would typically take about 1000 hours. With the PSP process, there would only be 20 defects left, reducing testing by another 800 hours.

To see what this might mean in practice, suppose you and four other engineers were to develop a 50,000 LOC software product. You each plan to develop a 10,000 LOC component and then to jointly integrate and test the entire system. Based on typical engineering data, you and your teammates will likely inject about 100 defects/KLOC in the program. This means there will be 5000 defects to find and fix. Using typical rates, about 2500 of these defects would be found during compiling and another 2000 in personal unit testing. This leaves about 500 defects to be found in integration and system test. Assuming your product was simpler than Microsoft's NT, you might find these defects at an average cost of only about 10 hours. Removing these defects would thus take your team of five engineers about 5000 hours. If the entire team did nothing else for 40 hours a week, this work would take six months. If you had all personally reviewed and then team-inspected your programs, however, you could have saved at least five months of testing. For a two-year project, this difference in testing time could make the difference between delivering on time and being seriously late.

16.6 Calculating Defects/Hour on the PSP Project Plan Summary

Table 16.2 shows how To Date defect-removal rates are calculated on the updated Project Plan Summary form. For any phase, start with the number of defects injected To Date in that phase and the number of minutes spent To Date in that phase. Then calculate the To Date defects per hour injected as 60*(defects To Date injected in a phase)/(minutes spent To Date in that phase). Similarly, defects removed per hour are 60*(defects To Date removed in a phase)/(minutes spent To Date in that phase). In the example in Table 16.2, these calculations are shown in the farthest right column in the Defects Injected and Defects Removed sections. These calculations are done as follows.

For defects injected per hour:

To Date Defects/hour injected in design
= 60*(defects injected To Date in design)/(minutes spent To Date in design)
= 60*5/195
= 1.54.

To Date Defects/hour injected in code
= 60*(defects injected To Date in code)/(minutes spent To Date in code)
= 60*25/792
= 1.89.

While you could calculate injection rates for all the other phases, these two are the most important. For the defect-removal rates:

To Date Defects/hour removed in code review
= 60*(defects removed To Date in code review)/(minutes spent To Date in code review)
= 60*12/145
= 4.97.

TABLE 16.2 PSP PROJECT PLAN SUMMARY

Student	Student X		Date	11/28/96
Program			Program #	14
Instructor	Mr. Z		Language	Ada

Summary	Plan	Actual	To Date
Minutes/LOC	5.73	4.65	5.48
LOC/Hour	10.47	12.90	10.95
Defects/KLOC	96.90	77.9	92.53
Yield	33.3	80.0	40.0
A/FR			

Program Size (LOC):

	Plan	Actual	To Date
Total New & Changed	67	77	335
Maximum Size	85		
Minimum Size	49		

Time in Phase (min.)	Plan	Actual	To Date	To Date %
Planning	23	32	120	6.5
Design	39	44	195	10.6
Code	166	155	792	43.1
Code Review	29	34	145	7.9
Compile	24	8	100	5.5
Test	62	39	279	15.2
Postmortem	41	46	206	11.2
Total	384	358	1837	100.0
Maximum Time	487			
Minimum Time	281			

Defects Injected	Plan	Actual	To Date	To Date %	To Date % Def./Hour
Planning					
Design	1	1	5	16.1	1.54
Code	5	4	25	80.7	1.89
Code Review					
Compile		1	1	3.2	
Test					
Total	6	5	31	100.0	

Defects Removed	Plan	Actual	To Date	To Date %	Def./Hour
Planning					
Design					
Code					
Code Review	2	4	12	38.7	4.97
Compile	3	1	13	41.9	7.80
Test	1	1	6	19.4	1.29
Total	6	5	31	100.0	

To Date Defects/hour removed in compile
  = 60*(defects removed To Date in compile)/(minutes spent To Date in
    compile)
  = 60*13/100
  = 7.80.

To Date Defects/hour removed in test
  = 60*(defects removed To Date in test)/(minutes spent To Date in test)
  = 60*6/279
  = 1.29.

While these calculations are only done for the To Date values, you could calculate the defects per hour for the planned and actual data if you wished. Note that these values will change as your process changes. Also, the defect numbers are a bit lower than they should be since the defect data were not recorded for the early programs. The updated Project Plan Summary form instructions are shown in Table 16.3 on the next two pages.

TABLE 16.3 PSP PROJECT PLAN SUMMARY INSTRUCTIONS

Purpose	This form holds the estimated and actual project data in a convenient and readily retrievable form.
Header	Enter the following: • Your name and today's date • The program name and number • The instructor's name • The language you will use to write the program
Minutes/LOC	Prior to development • Enter the Minutes/LOC planned for this project. Use the To Date rate from the most recent previous program. After development • Divide the total development time by the actual program size to get the actual and To Date Minutes/LOC. • For example, if the project took 196 minutes and you produced 29 LOC, the Minutes/LOC would be 196/29 = 6.76.
LOC/Hour	Prior to development • Calculate the LOC per hour planned for this program by dividing 60 by the Plan Minutes/LOC. After development • For Actual and To Date LOC/Hour, divide 60 by the Actual To Date Minutes/LOC. • For Actual Minutes/LOC of 6.76, Actual LOC/Hour are 60/6.76 = 8.88.
Defects/KLOC	Prior to development • Find the defects/KLOC To Date on the most recent previous program. • Use this as the Planned Defects/KLOC for this project. After development • Calculate the defects/KLOC actual and To Date for this program. • For Actual, multiply the total actual defects by 1000 and divide by the Actual Total New & Changed LOC. • Make a similar calculation for To Date. • With 17 defects to date and 153 Total New & Changed LOC, defects/KLOC To Date = 1000*17/153 = 111.11
Yield	*Calculate the plan, actual, and to date yield.* *Yield = 100* (defects removed before compile) / defects injected before compile), so with 5 injected and 4 found, yield = 100*4/5 = 80.8%.*
Program Size (LOC)	Prior to development • Enter under plan the estimated Total, Maximum, and Minimum New & Changed LOC. After development • Count and enter the Actual New & Changed LOC. • For To Date, add Actual New & Changed LOC to the To Date New & Changed LOC for the previous program.

(Continued)

Time in Phase Plan	For total development time, multiply Total New & Changed LOC by Minutes/LOC. For Maximum time, multiply the Maximum size by Minutes/LOC. For Minimum time, multiply the Minimum size by Minutes/LOC. From the Project Plan Summary for the most recent program, find the To Date % values for each phase. Using the To Date % from the previous program, calculate the plan time for each phase.
Actual	At job completion, enter the actual time in minutes spent in each development phase. Get these data from the time log.
To Date	For each phase, enter the sum of actual time and To Date time from the most recent previous program.
To Date %	For each phase, enter 100 times the To Date time for that phase divided by the Total To Date time.
Defects Injected Plan	Before development, estimate the total number of defects to be injected in the program. The value is Plan Defects/KLOC times the Plan Total New & Changed LOC for this program divided by 1000. For example, with a Plan Defects/KLOC of 75.9 and a Plan New & Changed LOC of 75, Plan Total defects = 75.9*75/1000 = 5.69, so use 0. Before development, estimate the defects injected by phase using the estimated total defects and the To Date % defect injected distribution from the previous program.
Actual	After development, find and enter the actual number of defects injected in each phase.
To Date	For each phase, enter the sum of the actual defects and the To Date defects from the most recent program.
To Date %	For each phase, enter 100 times the To Date defects for that phase divided by the total To Date defects.
Defects/hour	*Calculate the defects injected per hour for design and code.* *For design, for example, multiply 60 times the design defects To Date and divide by the design time To Date = 60*5/195 = 1.54 defects/hour.*
Defects Removed Plan	In the total row, enter the estimated total defects. Using the To Date % values from the most recent program, calculate the plan defects removed for each phase.
Actual	After development, find and enter the actual number of defects removed in each phase.
To Date	For each phase, enter the sum of the actual defects and the To Date defects from the most recent programs.
To Date %	For each phase, enter 100 times the To Date defects for that phase divided by the total To Date defects.
Defects/hour	*Calculate the defects removed per hour for code review, compile, and test.* *For test, example, multiply 60 times the test defects To Date and divide by the test time To Date = 60*6/279 = 1.29 defects/hour.*

16.7   Calculating Yield on the Project Plan Summary

When removing defects during a phase, you would like to know both how many defects were found and how many were missed. While there is no way to know this at development time, historical process data can help you to get a pretty good idea. The way to do this is to calculate and track yield. For the PSP, we define *process yield* as the percentage of the defects found before the first compile and test.

The yield calculations for Plan, Actual, and To Date are shown in the summary section at the top of the Project Plan Summary form in Table 16.2. Under Plan, for example, the process yield values are calculated as follows:

The Plan defects injected before compile are $1 + 5 = 6$.
The Plan defects removed before compile are 2.

The planned value of process yield is then:

$\text{Yield}_{\text{Plan}}$
= 100*(Plan defects removed before compile)/(Plan defects injected
before compile)
= 100*2/(1 + 5)
= 100*2/6
= 33.3%.

The Actual process yield value is calculated as follows:

$\text{Yield}_{\text{Actual}}$
= 100*(Actual defects removed before compile)/(Actual defects
injected before compile)
= 100*4/(1 + 4)
= 100*4/5
= 80.0%

and for To Date:

$\text{Yield}_{\text{ToDate}}$
= 100*(ToDate defects removed before compile)/(ToDate defects
injected before compile)
= 100*12/(5 + 25)
= 100*12/30
= 40.0%.

Note that in Table 16.2, a defect was injected during compile. Since the process yield calculation concerns the percentage of defects removed before starting to compile, you should only consider the defects injected and removed before the compile phase. Any defects injected in compile or test were not in the program at code review time and are thus not included in process yield calculations.

16.8   Improving Defect-Removal Rates

You can quickly improve defect-removal rates by doing code reviews. Once you have obtained these initial benefits, however, further improvement will be more difficult. Since the challenges facing software engineers are increasing every year, you cannot afford to stop improving. Some suggestions for how to continually improve your defect-removal rates are:

- Focus on yield first. Remember, the goal is to remove all the defects. Your first objective must thus be to consistently achieve yields of 70% or more.

- Do the code reviews before the first compile. As noted in Chapter 13, to achieve the highest possible yields, use the compiler to check the quality of your code review.

- Once you consistently achieve respectable yields, use the methods described in Chapters 13 and 14 to improve review rates. Track where the checklist is finding and missing defects and make periodic adjustments. If some steps don't find or miss many defects, consider dropping them. When you consistently miss defects, however, consider adding a checklist step to specifically address this type.

- Remember that one definition of insanity is doing the same thing over and over and expecting a different result [Brown]. If you don't change the checklist, you will keep missing the same defects.

Continue gathering defect data and calculating the yield and defect-injection and defect-removal rates. Then track these data and experiment with various approaches to see what helps you to improve.

One objective of this book is to make you so conscious of the costs and consequences of defects that you become personally committed to producing high-quality programs. This, it turns out, will also save time. As you can see from Figure 16.3, students who tracked and managed their yield and defect-removal rates spent less time in compile and test. At the beginning of the course for programs 1 and 2, these 14 students spent around 30% of their time in compile and test. By the end of the course, when they consistently used the PSP, they averaged only around 10% of development time in compile and test.

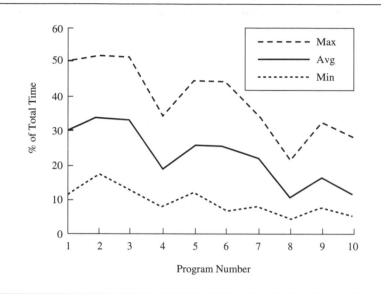

FIGURE 16.3 CLASS COMPILE AND TEST TIME

16.9   Reducing Defect-Injection Rates

Defect-injection rates are harder to reduce because you inject defects in every part of the process. You thus need to consider every software task. Some approaches to reducing injection rates are the following:

1. *Record all of your defects.* By being aware of defects, you will work more carefully and will reduce the number of defects you inject.

2. *Produce better designs.* By producing more complete and better-documented designs, you can improve program quality in two ways. First, this will actually prevent those defects that would have resulted from a confusing or incomplete design. Second, a more complete design will save coding time. Since defect-injection rates are lower during design than during coding, this will also reduce defects. This issue is discussed in Chapter 17.

3. *Use better methods.* Since defects can be injected in any phase, improvements in the way you develop requirements, specifications, designs, test cases, and source code will all help to reduce defects. Many software engineering courses teach useful methods for these activities. By using the PSP and measuring your work with these methods, you can see how well they work for you.

4. *Use better tools.* If a tool saves time, it will probably reduce the number of defects you inject. New software tools are developed every year and PSP data will permit you to measure and evaluate them. You can then see which help you and by how much.

16.10   Summary

Defects are a principal cause of software problems. They cost money to fix and they delay project schedules. Because defect fix times are unpredictable, defects also reduce planning accuracy. Defect management can thus be viewed as an economic issue. This chapter explains the economic consequences of defects and introduces measures to help you manage the defects in the programs you produce.

Even experienced engineers inject a lot of defects. The cost of finding defects increases by about 10 times with every phase after compile. Typical defect-removal rates show that testing is an inefficient way to remove defects. In unit test, engineers typically find 2–4 defects per hour. In code review, they find and fix 6–12 defects per hour. Compilers are very efficient at finding syntax defects, but they will not find all of the syntax defects in your programs. The time to find and fix each defect missed in a personal process will average several hours in subsequent integration, system test, and product use.

To improve your effectiveness at finding and fixing defects, two new measures are introduced: Defects/Hour measures phase efficiency for injecting and removing defects. In the PSP, process yield measures the percentage of defects removed before the first compile. To see where and how to improve your process, calculate the defect-injection and defect-removal rates and the process yield.

16.11   Assignment 16

For each of the programs you have written this semester, find the To Date defect-injection rates for design and code and the To Date defect-removal rates for code review, compile, and test. Also calculate the actual process yields for each of these programs. Plot and submit these values together with a paragraph that briefly describes the implications of these data for you.

Submit copies of those Time Recording Log and Weekly Activity Summary sheets you have not previously submitted. Also, turn in completed copies of the updated Project Plan Summary form, the Defect Recording Logs, and the Code

Review Checklist for every program. Include Plan, Actual, and To Date values for development times, defects injected, defects removed, and yield.

References

[Brown] Brown, Rita Mae. Private communication.

[Humphrey 89] Humphrey, W. S. *Managing the Software Process.* Reading, MA: Addison-Wesley, 1989.

[Zachary] Zachary, G. Pascal. *Showstopper!* New York: The Free Press, 1994.

17

Design Defects

This chapter discusses design defects, the design process, and design representations. It also addresses methods for reducing the number of design defects you inject. The principal issue in managing design defects is to understand when and how you inject them. For the assignment, you will analyze the design defects in your programs and determine when and why they were injected.

17.1 The Nature of Design Defects

Many of the defects you find in test were probably injected during the coding phase. This implies that the principal defect problem is with simple coding errors. In fact, for the defects they found in test, 14 students in one of my courses injected half again as many defects during coding as they did during design. Since the compiler had already removed most of the syntax errors, this seems a bit surprising. As shown in Table 17.1, however, this ratio changed as the students learned the PSP. Of the defects found in testing, the students started out injecting one and a half times as many defects during coding as they did during design. By the end of the course, they injected an average of only about 14% more. While they reduced the numbers of defects they injected in both cases, the improvement was

TABLE 17.1 TEST DEFECTS INJECTED IN DESIGN AND CODING PHASES

	Design Defects/KLOC	Code Defects/KLOC	Ratio of Code to Design Defects
Exercise 1	8.66	12.99	1.50
Exercise 10	5.05	5.77	1.14
% Reduction	41.67%	55.56%	

somewhat less for the test defects injected during design. Notice, though, that the numbers in Table 17.1 refer to the phases when the defects were injected. If, however, we look at the defect types, we get a different story. In the PSP, defect types are ordered by problem sophistication with types 10 and 20 being the simplest and types 90 and 100 the most complex. We can thus say that types 10 through 40 are the simpler or codinglike defects and types 50 through 100 are the more complex or designlike defects.

If we categorize these same test defects by type, we get Table 17.2. Here, the bulk of the test defects are of design types, but many of them were injected during coding. Even though these engineers had sharply reduced the number of defects they injected, they still made many of their design mistakes during the coding

TABLE 17.2 TEST DEFECT CATEGORIES BY PHASE INJECTED

	Design Type Defects/KLOC	Code Type Defects/KLOC	% Defects of Design Types
Exercise 1			
Design phase	7.22	1.44	83.33%
Coding phase	9.38	3.61	72.22%
Total	16.59	5.05	76.67%
Exercise 10			
Design phase	3.61	1.44	71.43%
Coding phase	3.61	2.16	62.50%
Total	7.22	3.61	66.67%
Percent Reduction			
Design phase	50.00%	0%	
Coding phase	61.54%	40.00%	
Total	56.52%	28.57%	

phase. As we saw in Chapter 16, however, the same engineers injected five to eight defects per hour during coding and only one to three defects per hour during design. This suggests that a potentially effective way to inject fewer design defects would be to stop doing design during the coding phase. This chapter deals with this problem and how to address it.

17.2   Identifying Design Defects

One might think that all the defects caught by a compiler should be classed as coding defects. This implies that the defects not caught by the compiler are design defects. Unfortunately, this is not the case. Even the best compilers do not find all the syntax defects, and some design mistakes could also produce incorrect syntax.

The reason compilers do not find all the syntax defects is that some syntax errors produce code that is valid syntax to the compiler. That is, with random keystroke errors, you will occasionally produce characters that look like valid language. This, it turns out, is generally about 10% of all the syntax defects. One example of this would be where you entered x = y when you meant to type x == y. A C++ compiler would not catch this mistake. Then, instead of logically testing whether x is equal to y, the program would set x equal to y. Similarly, in Ada or Pascal, you could get the same problem by mistakenly typing x := y when you wanted x = y. While these errors are not normally considered design errors, they do result in incorrect program logic.

There is thus no simple and objective way to define design defects. The two choices are:

- □ Define all those defects injected in the design phase to be design defects.
- □ Define those defect types that involve issues of programming function, logic, performance, and timing to be design defects.

In this book, we follow the second definition.

17.3   What Is Design?

In considering design defects, it is important to define what we mean by design. This, it turns out, is not easy to do. The reason is that everything about the structure and implementation of a program concerns its design. This includes the program flow, the structure and makeup of the language constructs, and even the source code punctuation. While these are all parts of the design, they are at very different levels of detail.

The problem is that design is a matter of perspective. You can design in detail and you can design at a high level. When developing programs, you do some design work at almost every step. When implementing the details of a case statement or a loop construct, you specify the detailed design. When defining a data structure or establishing a module interface, you are working at a somewhat higher level.

The split between designing and coding is thus an arbitrary one. Software engineers typically find it helpful to divide their activities according to the levels of detail involved in their work. This helps them focus on the right issues in the right order. For example, engineers make fewer mistakes and are more efficient when they think through designs before implementing them. This does not mean that they do all their work from the top down. It does mean that they generally start with a high-level concept before they delve deeply into detail.

The term we use for describing this high-level conceptual approach is *abstraction.* Thus when we talk about some functional abstraction like a square root, we are talking about a program procedure that calculates the square root. At this level, however, we do not worry about all the details of how this square root is calculated. By following this abstraction strategy, engineers can produce a complete high-level design before they get deeply embroiled in the details of how each abstraction or function is built.

Thus, for example, you might start designing a simple program by defining four functional abstractions or procedures: Input, File, Calculate, and Output. You could then design the program's main routine using these abstractions. While you would also have to define the principal variables and files, it is possible to complete the program's high-level design by using these functional abstractions. The next step, of course, would be to design each of these abstractions. For large programs, you might have several levels of abstractions and you might even build up a library of previously developed abstractions for use in future programs.

17.4   The Design Process

In doing what they call design, experienced engineers often move dynamically among design levels [Curtis]. The reason is that they are dealing with many functional abstractions. Before they feel comfortable using these abstractions in a high-level design, they generally need to understand how they work. If they have previously used such functions, they can defer defining the details. If they have never worked with such an abstraction before, however, they will often stop and complete its detailed design. They might even write and test a prototype before they are sufficiently satisfied to continue with the high-level design. Experienced designers do this because they have learned that seemingly simple abstractions often have subtle complications. Thus when they use an abstraction that they do not know how to build, they frequently find the job is far more difficult than expected. Occasionally, in fact, when system designs are based on seemingly simple but ill-defined abstractions, the entire design approach is later found not to be feasible.

The notion of abstraction is very useful when you deal with known and defined functions. When you use this conceptual approach to defer the hard design work, however, it is easy to get into trouble. Experienced engineers are thus reluctant to use any abstractions in a higher-level design unless they have previously worked with similar functions or have an implementation they know works.

The distinction between designing and coding is thus arbitrary. This also means that the specification of what constitutes a complete design is arbitrary. It is therefore important to distinguish between the design process and the specific design phase in your PSP. The design phase is when you produce the artifact you call the design. The design process then describes the tasks you do to produce this design product or artifact. In a sense, we are defining design as what we do in the design phase. This probably seems about as helpful as defining *thought* as what people do when they think. It is often useful, however, to define activities in terms of the products they produce. We discuss how to represent the design artifact later in this chapter.

17.5 The Causes of Design Defects

Design defects are caused by several problems. The first is a design mistake. You have thoughtfully worked through the problem and made a design decision that was wrong. Perhaps you have misunderstood a mathematical function, designed a loop that stepped under the wrong conditions, or ignored some system condition. You may have been poorly informed, tired, or inadequately trained. Regardless of the cause, you made a conscious but incorrect design decision.

A second cause would be knowing what the design should be but making a simple error. You meant to terminate a loop under certain conditions but forgot to include all the cases. This could be an oversight or a simple goof. You knew what to do and even knew how to do it, but you made a silly error. These errors are most common when you are in a hurry or overtired.

A third cause of design defects is misunderstanding what was wanted. Either you misread the high-level design or did not understand the requirements. In any event, you produced an incorrect design. Actually, your design was correct in the sense that it performed the function you intended. You just built the wrong function.

Another case is much like the last. Again you understood the local design and the system design. In fact you even understood the requirements. You just did not understand the system context. This is what I call the "literal interpretation" problem. For example, when you ask someone to explain the expression "spilled the beans," you will likely get quite different results depending on whom you ask. Someone who understands colloquial English as spoken in the United States would interpret this as "told a secret," while someone who learned English in another country might say it meant "knocked over the food."

This is a problem in software because many design decisions involve details that affect the users of the system. When designers do not have intimate knowledge of user context, they are likely to interpret the requirements literally without understanding their operational implications. Although such systems typically meet all the stated requirements, they are generally inconvenient and sometimes even impossible to use.

Surprisingly often, design errors come from overconfidence. The most common example would be a one- or two-line fix in a big program. Because such changes are small, engineers typically think they are simple and do not take the time to really understand the problem or the implications of the fix. While these errors could be classified in any of the foregoing categories, they would typically fall under the third, or fourth: misunderstandings or context mistakes.

17.6   The Impact of Design Defects

An example of a common design problem was reported to me by a software development manager in IBM. She had overheard two engineers debating how a particular program function should be implemented. Even though neither knew precisely what the customer wanted, they had different opinions. Rather than find out exactly what was wanted, they compromised on some third interpretation. When engineers make uninformed design decisions, they often produce inconvenient designs and possibly even inoperable ones.

While all these causes are real and they all contribute to the total number of design defects, by far the largest number come from simple oversights, goofs, and misunderstandings. The reason these causes outnumber all the others is that when software engineers face a challenging design problem, they generally take considerable care. They know they could easily make a mistake and are careful to check their work. Because software engineers make so many simple mistakes and because even simple mistakes can be very hard to find, these simple defects are the ones that cause the most trouble. Many such defects get through the entire development and testing process to impact the system's users. These trivial defects cause many of the problems users have with software systems.

It also turns out that many of these defects are avoidable. The engineer knew what was intended. The design was properly conceived, but it was poorly represented. Thus when the time came to produce the code, the implementer could not see what was intended. Rather than stop to find the designer, most implementers then complete the design on the fly. Since they are working at an implementation level, however, they often do not understand all the implications of the design. They are thus more likely to make a mistake. While the designer knew what was intended, the implementer did not.

You can also have such misunderstanding when you are implementing a design you yourself produced. When producing a design, you will often reach a point where the rest of the design seems obvious. If you also plan to produce the code, there seems little reason to document this part of the design. Unfortunately, later in implementation, you may not remember the once-obvious design and recreate the design during implementation. Since you will likely have forgotten the design context, you must also reconstruct all the relevant design concepts and conditions. Since this reconstruction process is error prone, you will likely make design errors. The error cause was not a poor implementation, however, but a poorly represented design.

17.7 Design Representation

A clear and complete design representation will help you to reduce the number of defects you inject. This means that once you have figured out the design, you need to represent it so that it will be clear to whoever implements it. This is a critical issue with programs of 10,000 LOC or more and it can even be a problem with 50 or 100 LOC program modules.

By completely representing the design when you create it, you will likely save time. This is because you can generally produce code much more rapidly from a clear and complete design than from a vague or incomplete one. Since less coding time implies fewer coding defects, a good design is much more likely to result in a higher quality program.

There are three common ways to represent designs: graphically, with a pseudo code, or mathematically. The next sections of this chapter discuss these representation methods. While this is a large subject and a lot more could be said about it, this brief treatment should give you some ideas about designing module-sized programs. It also provides a context for thinking about design as you use the

PSP in the future. The objective here is not to teach representation methods but to convince you of the importance of doing a design and of clearly representing that design. Then, when you are exposed to various representation methods in courses or on the job, you will see why they are important and consider trying them.

Graphical Design Representations

People generally understand pictures more readily than formulas or text. When you describe a complex design, an illustrative picture will help people understand it. Since a large part of the design problem concerns understanding, you should generally use graphical representations to augment designs.

The most common form of graphical representation is the flowchart. This is a diagram with the program functions represented by boxes and the logical program flow represented by lines connecting the boxes. Although there are many ways to draw such diagrams, we will only describe the basic flowchart symbols shown in Figure 17.1.

A simple example of these symbols is shown in Figure 17.2. At the top of the diagram, the connector symbol shows that input x comes from 8Ax and at the bottom it shows that output y goes to 3Ay and 5By. The symbols in the connectors refer to other pages of the design. In this notation, variable x comes from page 8 of the design at point Ax. Similarly, variable y goes to points Ay on page 3 and By on page 5.

The box in the middle of Figure 17.2 shows a decision function. You might implement this with an if-then-else structure or with a case statement. This choice is left to the implementer. The computation box, y = f(x), describes a calculation.

The two boxes at the left and right sides of Figure 17.2 represent defined functions. The one on the left, Error_Routine, has two vertical bars to represent a predefined function. This refers to a function that has already been implemented and is reused by this program. The box at the right, Null_Correction, has a horizontal line to represent a defined function. This is a new functional abstraction you are developing and will use with this program when it is completed.

While graphical representations are easy to understand, they are often either imprecise or voluminous. This is not an inherent problem with the method, however, but just another example of an incomplete and imprecise representation. This precision problem can be addressed by having a complete written design and using the graphical representation to help explain the program's logic. Remember, however, that the more information you put on the diagram, the more you will clutter it up and the harder it will be to understand. The best approach to this problem is to use various levels of flowcharts where each level includes abstractions that are defined on lower-level flowcharts.

Because of their advantages, you should use a graphical representation to illustrate the design of every program you produce. Often, in fact, the process of

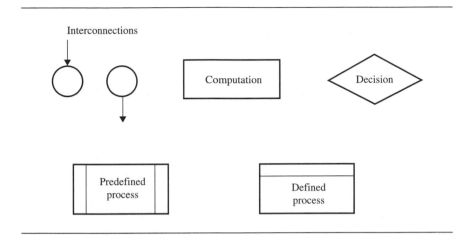

FIGURE 17.1 DIAGRAMMING SYMBOLS

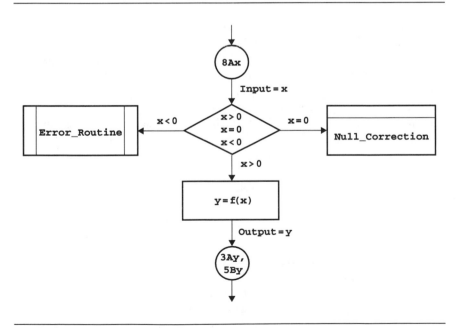

FIGURE 17.2 EXAMPLE LOGICAL DIAGRAM

drawing the flowchart will reveal relationships you had not considered. Regardless of how you produce them, such diagrams can save time and reduce confusion when you later implement, test, fix, or enhance the program.

Pseudo Code Design Representations

Pseudo code provides another way to represent program logic. Here, the approach is to write the program in a language similar to the one used for implementation but with an easily understood shorthand for complex expressions. The idea is to represent the logic but to ignore many of the syntactic requirements of the programming language. An example of a pseudo code design description is shown in Table 17.3. You could expand this description with additional statements to describe how the function f(x) is calculated. You could also add type definitions, declarations, or other details if they would likely be needed at implementation time.

A pseudo code design description is thus a mixture of human language and programming constructs. Instead of the complete logic for well-known functions, simple statements are used. Similarly, the program flow can be represented with traditional conditional statements, using written expressions to describe the logic. While there are no generally accepted pseudo code notation standards, it is a good idea to use language constructs that are similar to those in the high-level language being used. When you do, the pseudo code will look familiar at implementation time and will provide a framework for implementation.

Because pseudo code does not require the programming language details, it is generally easier and quicker to produce than a completed source program. You can also document a design in as much detail as you need. This makes it easier to capture the design when you first develop it. That is when you best understand the design and when you can most efficiently record it.

The principal advantages of pseudo code are that it can be as precise as you need and it is easy to understand. The principal disadvantage is that a pseudo code design can be so detailed as to be difficult to understand. That is why it is a good idea to provide both pseudo code and a flowchart for any but the simplest designs.

TABLE 17.3 EXAMPLE PSEUDO CODE REPRESENTATION

```
algorithm (Function f(x) calculation)

if (x < 0)
          then (Error_Routine)
          elseif (x = 0)
                        then (Null_Correction)
                        else
                              y = f(x)
end.
```

A potential problem with pseudo code is caused by the fact that it omits much of the punctuation and structure used to fully define the meaning of a source program. It is thus easy to make mistakes with common logical constructs. For example, it is a good idea to use indentation or punctuation to connect each `else` statement with the appropriate `if` or to show the extent of loops or case conditions. Variable and parameter scopes can also cause confusion and should be carefully noted where not obvious.

A common problem with pseudo code concerns the level of detail. Most engineers will write a line of pseudo code for about three to five lines of a finished source program. I have, however, seen cases where the engineers have produced one line of pseudo code for every line of the finished source. While they may call this the design, it is really the implementation in a less rigorous form. Since the simple act of copying injects defects, designing in such detail could actually inject more defects than would coding from scratch.

Because of its flexibility, a pseudo code design can be at almost any level of detail. There is thus no way to specify precisely what a pseudo code design must contain. While pseudo code representations can be very helpful, we are still left with the problem we started with: how to precisely define what is meant by design. In fact, a major advantage of pseudo code is that it allows the engineer to specify the level of design detail needed for each situation.

When using pseudo code, PSP data can help you decide on an appropriate level of detail. When reviewing defect data, for example, if you find that you are injecting design type defects during the coding phase, consider using a more precise design. Conversely, if you do not have design representation problems, you might try a less detailed pseudo code to see if it speeds up your design work without causing design mistakes in implementation.

Other Representation Methods

Various mathematical methods have also been devised to precisely define software systems. These methods have the advantage of being precise and the disadvantage of being hard to learn, at least by engineers who have not had appropriate training in mathematics. Formal methods, however, offer great promise of helping engineers produce programs with a minimum number of defects [Gries].

Because design representation is such an important problem, there will undoubtedly be many new ideas and approaches. As you consider using various representations, consider the following points:

- □ Design is a thinking process.
- □ A rich design notation can help you precisely think about and represent a complex design.
- □ Rich notations, however, are hard to learn.

☐ When using a design notation with which you are not familiar, you will probably not think in that notation.

☐ You must then think through the design in a familiar notation and then mentally translate to the unfamiliar notation.

☐ This translation process inhibits creativity, slows design work, and causes mistakes.

While you should try new design methods and notations, try to become reasonably fluent with them before you evaluate them. Also remember that the design notation is a communication medium. If the implementers are not thoroughly comfortable with it, they will have many of the problems described above.

17.8   Summary

The source of many design defects is the coding phase. One way to reduce design defects is to analyze defect types. We define design defects as PSP defect types 50 through 100. If you inject many of these types in the coding phase, consider spending more time in design. It is most efficient to produce the logical and functional design in the design phase and not during coding.

Precise design representations can save implementation time and reduce design defects. A poor representation can cause defects. Graphical representations are easy to understand but can be imprecise. Pseudo code representations can be at varying levels of detail and can use a language that is similar to the programming language used. In selecting a design representation, become familiar with the representation before you do an evaluation. Use your PSP data in making the evaluation and decision.

17.9   Assignment 17

For the assignment, review the defects you have found in all the programs for which you have defect data. Using the methods shown in Tables 17.1 and 17.2, show which of these defects likely resulted from an imprecise design representation and suggest steps to prevent them. For the homework, list the number of design defects by problem category and the representation action that could have prevented them. Also give the total repair time these improvements could have saved.

Produce a pseudo code and a flowchart design for the next program. Turn in these designs with the program and write a brief paragraph on the likely impact these design methods had on the number of design defects injected. Show the data that led to these conclusions. Note that both the defect analysis and design assignments are optional and need not be completed unless requested by the instructor.

Submit copies of those Time Recording Log and Weekly Activity Summary sheets you have not previously submitted. Also, turn in completed copies of the PSP Project Plan Summary form, the Defect Recording Logs, and the Code Review Checklist for every program. Include both Plan, Actual, and To Date values for development times, defects injected, defects removed, and yield.

References

[Curtis] Curtis, Bill, Herb Krasner, and Neil Iscoe. "A Field Study of the Software Design Process for Large Systems," *Communications of the ACM,* November 1988, vol. 31, no. 11.

[Gries] Gries, David. *The Science of Programming.* New York: Springer-Verlag, 1981.

18

Product Quality

This chapter discusses how your personal working discipline affects the quality of the products you produce. It illustrates the relationship between the number of defects you find during compiling and testing and the number that will be left in your finished products. It then describes steps you can take to improve the quality of your programs. For the assignment, you will examine the relationship between the number of compile and the number of test defects in the programs you have developed this semester.

18.1 Quality Comes First

As we have seen, testing is expensive, even for small, module-sized programs. We have also seen that you can save time by finding defects early. By reviewing programs before you compile and test them, you reduce the number of defects found in test and will therefore spend less time in test. We have also seen that by reviewing the code you will save about as much time in compiling and testing as you spent in the review. In addition to these advantages, finding defects early produces higher quality products. This chapter explains why this is the case.

Many software engineers feel that they shouldn't worry about defects until they start to compile and test their programs. They thus rush through the design and coding steps so they can start testing. With the PSP, engineers focus on producing clean and defect-free programs from the very beginning. The reason for this strategy is that, once an engineer produces a sloppy product, there is no tool that can clean it up. One way to demonstrate this is to show data on the relationship between the defects found in compile, those found in test, and the defects found by the program's users. Another approach would be for you to gather data on your work and see for yourself how this strategy works for you. This chapter addresses both of these approaches.

18.2   Testing

As products get more complex, testing becomes more time consuming and expensive. Testing also becomes less effective at finding defects. That is, with larger and more complex programs, it will cost more to find and fix each defect and you will find a lower percentage of them.

There are several reasons for this. First, defects mask or aggravate other defects. That is, when a program has many defects, their interactions complicate the defect identification and correction process. This makes some of the defects much harder to find and fix. One defect may also mask the symptoms of other defects. Making these masked defects harder to find increases the chance that they will escape detection altogether.

Another reason that even modest-sized programs are hard to test is that the number of logic paths can become very large. It is not generally practical to test all possible combinations of even small programs. The larger and more complex the programs become, the harder it is to do even a moderately comprehensive test. Consider the simple case of a program to analyze character strings. If there were only 60 possible characters, a 10-character string would have 60^{10} possible combinations. This is a 6 followed by 17 zeros. If you could test 1,000,000 combinations a second, it would take 20,000 years to test every possibility. It is thus not possible to test even this simple program for all conceivable combinations.

In this example, most of the character combinations would be logically identical, but the systems testers could not know which ones to skip and which to test. The designers, of course, could tell them which combinations to ignore. The problem with this strategy is that designers make mistakes. If they didn't, of course, there would be no need to test their programs. Testing is a problem largely because programs do not behave the way we think they will. Thus, with complex systems, when we only test the conditions we think are important, we generally miss many defects.

If you follow disciplined methods and carefully review and test your small program modules, you will be much more effective than any test group at finding the defects in your programs. This is because you know the program logic and you know what it should do. You also understand the unusual cases and odd conditions and can quickly see which will work or not work. If you do your utmost to ensure that your program modules have no defects, you can largely eliminate the cost and time required to later clean them up. While you cannot avoid an occasional mistake, you can at least ensure that your products are essentially defect-free. What is more, you are the only person who can do this. If you do not produce a defect-free program, no one else can do it for you.

18.3 The Filter View of Testing

Think of defect removal as a filter. That is, each review, compilation, and test removes some percentage of the defects that were in the product. Thus, if you put more defects into the filter, you will likely find more defects. When, for example, you test a program that contained 25 defects, you would expect to find some fraction, say 12 of them. Similarly, if you put another program into test with 50 defects, you would expect to find a similar fraction, or about 24. The more defects there are to find, the more you are likely to find.

The converse of this, however, is that every defect-removal process also misses a fraction of the defects. Thus, the more defects went into the filter, the more will likely be missed. The number of the defects getting through the filter is therefore proportional to the number that enter the filter. While the degree to which this relationship holds varies considerably with the quality and type of defect-removal process, this relationship will generally hold. Thus, the more defects enter at test, compile, or review phase, the more will likely be left in the product at the exit of that phase.

The next question, of course, concerns the quality of the filters. If we could devise filters with defect-removal yields nearing 100%, our defect-removal problems would be solved. Unfortunately, the data on compile and test yields are not reassuring. As shown in Table 18.1, code reviews and inspections have the best yields, while compiling, unit testing, and other forms of testing are less effective [Humphrey 89]. These figures are based on limited data and may not apply to your particular situation, but this is all the data we have. The best answer, of course, would be for you to gather yield data on your own defect-removal methods and draw your own conclusions. It is interesting to note that the highest yield method in Table 18.1 is for the engineers' personal code reviews. The next highest yield is for inspections where several engineers review each other's designs and code.

TABLE 18.1 DEFECT-REMOVAL YIELDS

Method	Approximate Yield (%)
Code Review	70–80
Code Inspection	50–70
Compile	50
Unit Test	40–50
Integration Test	45
Requirements Test	45
Algorithm Test	8

Both of these highest yield methods are manual and do not involve any automated tools whatever. The reason they are so much better than other methods is that the human mind is a vastly more powerful defect-detection instrument than any currently known software tool.

The logical conclusion from these data is that to produce high-quality programs, you must have the fewest possible defects at the start of testing. Entering test with the fewest number of defects, however, means exiting compile with the fewest number of defects. Finally, to exit compile with the fewest number of defects, you must remove defects before starting to compile. Of course, to produce the highest quality products, you should measure, analyze, and improve every defect-removal phase.

18.4   The Benefits of Careful Work

Another way to state the filter view of testing is: "Once a lemon, always a lemon." In essence, when engineers produce sloppy software products, more defects will enter and leave every compile and test phase. When engineers do careful work, however, the benefits show up throughout the process. This means, for example, that when you have a lot of defects in compile, you will likely have a lot of defects in test. With a lot of defects in test, you will also likely have a lot of defects in the finished program.

As the data in Figures 18.1, 18.2, and 18.3 show, there is a general relationship between the number of defects found in compile and those found in test. While the relationship is not strong in statistical terms, a high number of compile defects usually indicates likely problems in test.

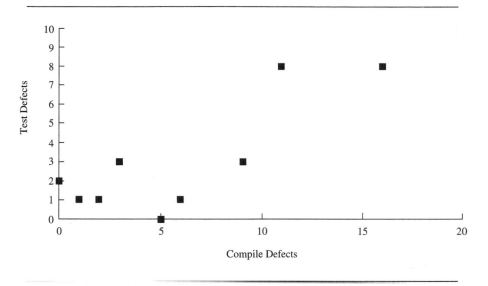

FIGURE 18.1 STUDENT 1'S COMPILE AND TEST DEFECTS

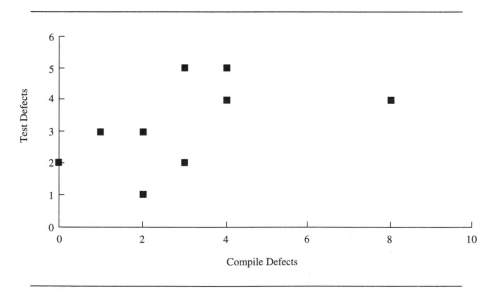

FIGURE 18.2 STUDENT 14'S COMPILE AND TEST DEFECTS

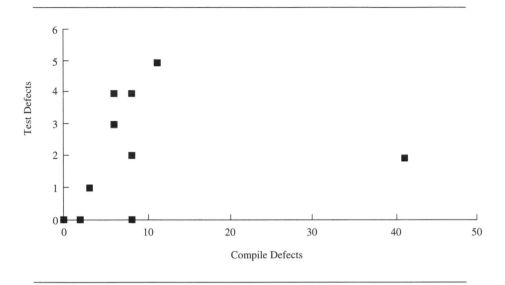

FIGURE 18.3 STUDENT 20'S COMPILE AND TEST DEFECTS

18.5   Calculating Yield Values

The process yield measure introduced in Chapter 16 concerned the percentage of defects removed before the first compile. The yield measure, however, can be applied to any defect-removal step. Thus the phase yield can be calculated as follows:

Phase yield = 100*(defects removed during phase)/(defects in product at phase entry).

An accurate yield calculation requires defect data from all the subsequent process phases. For example, if you found 5 defects in a code review, 3 in compiling, and 2 more in test, the code review would have found 5 of the 10 total defects. This would be a review yield of 50%. Although there may still be defects in the program, this is the review yield at this point.

As shown in Figure 18.4, when you subsequently find defects, the yield of all the phases that missed those defects declines. At code review exit, you had found 5 defects. Since this is all you could find, this is all you believed were there. At review exit, you therefore believed that the review yield was 100.

If in compiling you found 3 more defects, the review would now be known to have only found 5 of the total 8 defects. Thus, the review yield was really only 62.5% instead of 100%. The apparent compiler yield is 100%.

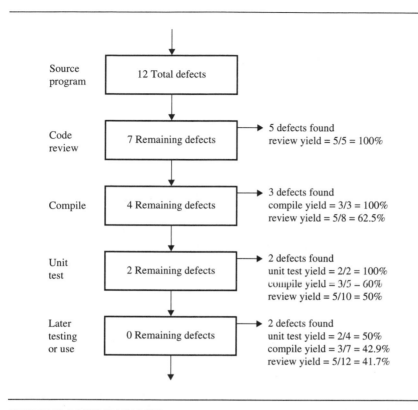

FIGURE 18.4 YIELD VALUES

If in unit test you now find 2 more defects, the review would now have apparently found only 5 of the total of 10 defects. Thus the review yield was only 50%. At this point the compiler found 3 defects but missed 2, so its yield to this point is 60%. Since unit testing is presumed to have found all the remaining defects, its apparent yield is 100%.

Suppose that in subsequent program testing, you found 2 more defects. Then the review would have only found 5 of the total 12 defects in the product. Thus the review yield at this point would be 41.7%. Similarly, the compiler would have found 3 of 7 defects, so its yield to this point would be 42.9%. Even now, however, you could not be certain of the final yield values. Once the product is shipped to the end users, more defects could still be found, further reducing the yield of all these defect-removal phases.

The yield measure can be applied to any process phase. When applied to unit testing, for example, it refers to the percentage of defects in the product at unit test entry that were removed during unit test. As described in Chapter 16, the process yield refers to the percentage of defects removed before the first compile. Thus, process yield is calculated as follows:

Process yield = 100*(defects removed before compile)/(defects injected before compile).

18.6   Estimating the Ultimate Yield

Although you can never be certain of the yield when you finish a phase, the yield measure will help you evaluate and improve the process. For example, when you find 17 defects in a code review, 2 in compile, and 1 in test, you can be reasonably sure that the review yield was near 85%. While a few more defects may later be found, you have probably found most of them. If, however, you found 17 defects in code review, another 15 in compile, and 8 more in test, the initial 42.5% review yield will probably decline in the future. When you find 23 defects in compile and test, you can be reasonably sure there are still quite a few defects left in the product.

The only way to determine how many defects remain is to track the defects found in the product during the rest of its useful life. Since even years of usage might never find all the defects, you will never know for certain. If the number of found defects declines sharply with each defect-removal phase, however, the yield numbers are probably pretty accurate. After you have gathered defect data, you can develop yield measures for every phase. Then you can calculate the likely number of defects remaining in any product you develop.

One helpful rule of thumb is to assume that the remaining defects in a product equal the number found in the last removal phase. This is the same as assuming that the yield of this last phase was 50%. Based on my data, this is a bit low for well-run inspections and code reviews, about right for compile, and a bit high for most test phases.

Consider again the case with 17 defects in code review, 2 in compile, and 1 in test, the current estimate of review yield is $17/(17 + 2 + 1) = 85\%$. The rule of thumb would then assume that one more defect will be found. This would give an ultimate yield of $17/(17 + 2 + 1 + 1) = 80.95\%$. In the other example, 17 defects were found in code review, 15 in compile, and 8 in test. Here, the current yield value is $17/(17 + 15 + 8) = 42.5\%$. The rule of thumb suggests that eight more defects will be found, giving an estimated ultimate review yield of $17/(17 + 15 + 8 + 8) = 35.4\%$.

With historical data on the actual yield for each defect-removal phase, you could make more accurate ultimate yield estimates. You would do this by using the known yield value for the final phase and calculating the number of defects that were likely missed. With enough yield data, you could even calculate statistical ranges for the number of defects remaining. While you will never actually know the true yield values, these data will help you make pretty good estimates.

18.7   The Benefits of 100% Process Yield

The code review objective should be to consistently achieve 100% process yield. If you could do this, you would find all the defects and none would be left to find in compile or test. Not only will this save compile and test time, but the big benefit will be in project cost and schedule. With defect-free program modules, your development team would not spend much time testing your programs. This would save testing costs, reduce testing time, and improve development schedules. It would also produce better products.

Reaching a 100% yield is not easy. It takes time, practice, and a lot of data gathering and analysis. High-yield software development, however, is a skill that can be learned and improved. Consider the analogy with playing a musical instrument. When you first learn to play, you will likely hit a lot of wrong notes. With practice, you will gradually hit more right notes and fewer wrong ones. After a lot of practice, you may ultimately learn to play without hitting any wrong notes. This, it turns out, is when musicians start to be real artists.

The job of producing quality software is much like playing a musical instrument. Until you can produce code that has few or no defects, you will not be an accomplished software engineer. As long as you spend most of your time finding and fixing defects, you are not performing as a professional. With disciplined quality methods, however, you will produce defect-free small programs with reasonable consistency. Then you can concentrate on the more important challenges of producing high-quality large programs. While mastering these disciplines takes time and consistent effort, you will see gradual improvement. Your personal goal, however, must be to consistently achieve a 100% process yield. Remember that you will never produce high-quality large programs until you can routinely produce high-quality small programs. This takes personal discipline and lots of practice.

18.8   Yield Experience

As difficult as it is to reach high yields, it can be done. Figures 18.5–18.7 show the yield improvements for three engineers who did it. These engineers all learned the PSP in a one-semester graduate course where they wrote a total of 10 small programs.

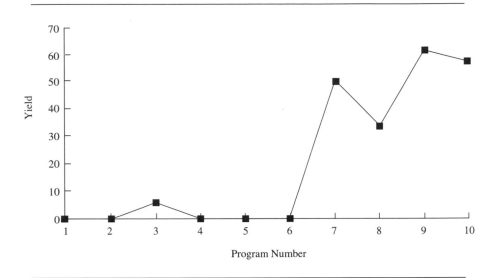

FIGURE 18.5 STUDENT 1'S YIELD IMPROVEMENT

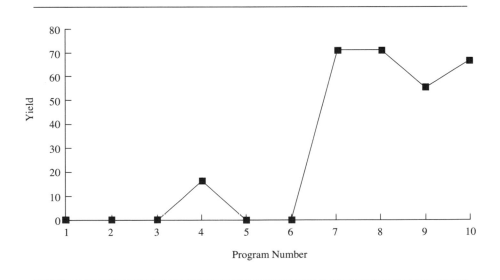

FIGURE 18.6 STUDENT 14'S YIELD IMPROVEMENT

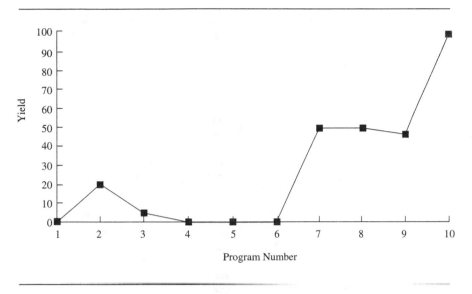

FIGURE 18.7 STUDENT 20'S YIELD IMPROVEMENT

They started with program 1 and progressively added PSP measurements and methods with each succeeding program. With program 7, code reviews were required. Here, as the figures show, all the engineers had sharp yield improvements.

Note, however, that there is no standard improvement pattern. Some engineers will make steady improvements, while others will have considerable fluctuation. Some students can naturally achieve yields of 80% or higher, while others struggle to get above 50%. During my development of the PSP, I learned to consistently achieve yields of 80%. This, however, was only after I had worked on yield improvement for three years and had written 62 PSP programs.

People have different skills. Some naturally produce quality code while others can easily visualize complex designs. Some people are born testers and others are adept at designing easy-to-use interfaces. All engineers should be able to consistently achieve yields of over 70%, but some will take longer than others.

18.9 Prototyping

Once you consistently reach yields of over 70%, continued improvement will be more difficult. While you will occasionally miss a syntax defect or two, most of the missed defects will concern design. You will encounter new system or support issues or need to use unfamiliar program functions. With large programs, interfaces, performance, memory management, and many other issues will be more important.

Every time you do something new you will likely make mistakes. Thus, to eliminate all defects, you should try writing small prototype programs. Experiment with every unfamiliar function or procedure before you use it in a program. Test out new ideas and build simple prototypes of any structures or constructs that you have not previously used. This will prevent many of the defects that would normally escape your personal reviews.

You will also find that certain defect types are harder to find or prevent than others. As you devise ways to find the defects you most frequently miss, many will involve applications, systems support, and development environment issues. Every source of confusion is a source of defects. The key is to recognize the difference between really knowing something and just thinking you understand it. Occasionally you will make a mistake with something you really know, but most of the time your mistakes will involve assumptions that were not entirely correct. Learn to recognize these assumptions. Then build a prototype to test them before you build the assumptions into the product.

18.10 Summary

As programs get larger, it becomes more expensive to find and fix defects. The defect-removal process is also less effective. The strategy for producing high-quality large programs is to first remove all the defects from the modules that make up these large programs.

Defect removal is a filtering process: View every defect removal phase as a filter. The more defects are put into the filter, the more will be found. Also, the more defects are put into the filter, the more will be missed. The yield of most test phases is less than 50%. Thus, to get a high-quality product out of test, you must put a high-quality product into test.

Careful work will pay off in every step of your process and will save time. If you produce a sloppy program, more defects will be found in compile and in every subsequent test phase.

Yield measures the quality of defect removal. Process yield refers to the percentage of defects in the product that are removed before the first compile. Yield can also measure the percentage of defects in a product that are removed by a defect-removal phase. Your objective should be to achieve 100% process yield. Remember, you will not be able to produce high-quality large programs until you can consistently produce high-quality small programs. This takes a consistent dedication to quality, personal discipline, and lots of practice.

To achieve the highest program quality, build small prototypes to test every assumption before you use it in a product. Learn to recognize the difference between thinking you know something and really knowing. Every time you make an assumption, you are likely to inject a defect.

18.11   Assignment 18

For the assignment, show the relationship between the compile and test defects for all the programs you have written this semester. Show it on a plot like those in Figures 18.1, 18.2, and 18.3. Also calculate the process yield for each program and estimate the likely ultimate yield once all the remaining defects in the program are found. Note that this defect analysis is an optional assignment and it need not be completed unless requested by your instructor.

Submit copies of those Time Recording Log and Weekly Activity Summary sheets that you have not previously submitted. Also, turn in completed copies of the PSP Project Plan Summary form, the Defect Recording Logs, and the Code Review Checklist for every program. Include both Plan, Actual, and To Date values for development times, defects injected, defects removed, and yield.

Reference

[Humphrey 89] Humphrey, W. S. *Managing the Software Process.* Reading, MA: Addison-Wesley, 1989.

19

Process Quality

This chapter describes process quality and some measures you can use to evaluate the quality of your software work. It also shows how to calculate and track these measures. For the exercise, you will calculate one of these measures for the programs you have developed in this semester and plot a graph to show how this measure has changed.

19.1 Process Measures

The quality of your programs is determined by the quality of your process. The quality of your process, in turn, is determined by the way you work. Thus, to develop better programs, you need to change the way you work. To do this most efficiently, you need to know how good your process is. To know this, you need to measure the quality of your process.

The most fundamental process measures concern the volume of products produced, their quality, and the time and resources required to do the work. From these, you can determine your current performance and how you can change to produce better results in the future. In Chapters 3–11, we introduced various cost and size measures. Starting with Chapter 12, we tracked defects and introduced measures of defect removal and the number of defects removed per hour. Chapters 16–18 introduced yield and other measures of the effectiveness of the process in finding and fixing defects. Now, we address process quality measures.

It is important to remember that in this book we only address quality from the perspective of defect injection and removal. After you have learned and practiced the PSP methods described in this book, you should consider how to enhance the process you use in other important areas. For example, do you really understand the requirements? Some process steps to address requirements misunderstandings could include developing an early prototype to review with your instructor or customer. Other important topics concern usability or performance testing, compatibility standards, interface reviews, and so forth. For each of these, you can devise various steps to improve product quality. Quality is a large subject and there are many potentially useful process actions you could take to help ensure that you deliver quality products to your customers.

19.2   The Defect-Removal Paradox

One phenomenon you may have noticed is that defect-removal rates decline as product quality improves. This is why, for example, the average removal rate for test defects in Figure 16.2 (page 212) declined from around 4 to about 2 per hour over a span of 10 programs. Over this same period, the defects these students found in test decreased about 10 times: from around 40 to around 4 defects/KLOC.

This decline seems natural when you consider extreme cases. When there are a lot of defects to be found, you will generally find many very quickly. Although an occasional defect may take much longer, the average time will be relatively short. At the other extreme, with only one defect in a very large program, all the time spent in reviewing and testing will be allocated to this one defect. Depending on the nature of the defect and the order of the tests and reviews, this could take a very long time.

Thus, with fewer defects, it will take longer to find them, regardless of the methods you use. This is clearly true for reviewing and testing, but somewhat less true of compile. While there is a slight downward trend for the compile defect-removal rate, the automatic nature of compilers makes them less sensitive to defect density. The downward trend for reviews and testing may not be apparent for short sequences of data, but the rate for any given method will generally decline as the number of defects declines.

Thus, as you put progressively higher quality programs through several successive phases of integration and system test, their residual defects will be progressively harder to find and to fix. This suggests that the more defects you find, the more important it is to find and fix them all.

19.3   A Defect-Removal Strategy

One could argue that many of the defects in large programs are in the system and not in the modules. This, however, is not true. With few exceptions, the defects in large systems are in the modules that make them up. These defects can be divided into two classes: those that involve only one module and those that involve interactions among the modules.

When you achieve a high PSP yield, you will remove almost all of the first kind of defect. The second kind, however is much more difficult. The reason is that large and complex systems involve so many interactions that it is hard for the designers to visualize them all. A good way to address this problem is to follow a strategy like the following:

- □ Strive to develop modules of the highest possible quality.
- □ Do thorough inspections of all the module interfaces and interactions. (Note that an inspection is when a team of engineers reviews a product. Inspections are briefly discussed in Section 13.11.)
- □ Inspect the requirements to ensure that all of the important capabilities are properly understood, designed, and implemented.
- □ Inspect the system and program design against the requirements to ensure that it properly addresses all the key requirements.
- □ Do exhaustive unit testing after the code has been inspected.
- □ Do comprehensive integration testing.
- □ Do thorough system testing.

All but the first of these steps are beyond the scope of your personal process. The first step is up to you, however. If your modules are not of the highest quality, the rest of the steps will be much less effective. Then the development process must concentrate on finding and fixing the defects you and your associates left in your modules. This also means that the job these remaining steps were supposed to accomplish will not likely get done. Instead of ensuring that the system properly performs the intended user functions, system and integration test will be largely devoted to finding and fixing the remaining module defects.

With initially high-quality modules, however, you can follow the previously mentioned strategy. You will then have a reasonable chance of producing a high-quality system. Rather than waste time trying to find and fix the module defects, integration test can then focus on testing the interfaces among modules. System test could now address such critical system issues as performance, usability, recovery, and security. Until the engineers consistently achieve high personal yields, however, such testing will not generally be done.

19.4   Cost of Quality

While you could spend any amount of time looking for defects, you can never be certain to have found them all. Thus, if your only objective was to produce defect-free programs, you could continue reviewing and testing indefinitely. While you would likely stop after having found no defects for a while, you might still not have found them all. As a software engineer, however, you will need to thoughtfully balance the time spent and the quality of the products produced. The cost of quality (COQ) provides a way to deal with these questions. COQ has three principal elements: failure costs, appraisal costs, and prevention costs.

Failure costs include all the costs of fixing product defects. While you are fixing a defect, you are incurring failure costs. Similarly, while you are running the debugger to find the defective statement, you are also incurring failure costs. Anything done as a normal part of repairing a defect counts as failure cost. This even includes redesigning, recompiling, or retesting.

Appraisal costs include all the work to assess the product to see if it has defects, excluding the time spent on fixing defects. This includes code reviewing and the time to compile and test a defect-free program. Thus, appraisal costs do not include repair costs. The appraisal cost is the insurance paid to assure that the program is defect free.

Prevention costs are incurred when you modify the process to avoid injecting defects. This includes, for example, the analyses done to understand defects. It also includes the process development work to improve the requirements, design, or implementation processes. The time spent in the redesign and test of a new process is also prevention cost.

Another important defect-prevention activity is building prototypes to test design or implementation ideas. When using an unfamiliar library function, you might be tempted to just use it. You know, however, that this often leads to design mistakes and program defects. The cost of writing a small prototype program to check the way this function works is prevention cost.

19.5   Calculating the Cost of Quality

The PSP measures COQ in a simplified way. While the time spent compiling includes some defect-free compile time, the PSP counts all compile time as failure costs. Similarly, testing includes some time that would be spent testing a defect-free program. Again, the PSP counts all testing time as failure costs. Finally, all review time is counted as appraisal cost. Review time includes some repair costs, but the PSP counts all review time as appraisal cost. You could calculate the exact

COQ values with the methods described in Section 19.8, but this involves a lot of work and does not appreciably change the effectiveness of the measures. I thus recommend that you use the simplified PSP definitions.

The cost of quality is calculated as a percentage of total development time. For the PSP, the appraisal and failure costs are calculated as follows:

- □ Appraisal COQ is the sum of all review time as a percentage of total development time.
- □ Failure COQ is the sum of all compile and test time as a percentage of total development time.

For example, suppose you had the process data shown in the Project Plan Summary in Table 19.1. You would calculate the appraisal COQ as follows:

- □ Actual total development time = 262 minutes
- □ Actual code review time = 29 minutes
- □ Appraisal COQ = 100*29/262 = 11.07%

For the failure costs:

- □ Actual compile time = 5 minutes
- □ Actual test time = 10 minutes
- □ Failure COQ = 100*(5 + 10)/262 = 100*15/262 = 5.73%

19.6   The Appraisal/Failure Ratio

A useful PSP measure is the Appraisal/Failure Ratio, or A/FR. It is calculated by dividing the appraisal COQ by the failure COQ. In the example in Section 19.5, with an appraisal COQ of 11.07% and a failure COQ of 5.73%, A/FR = 11.07/5.73 = 1.93.

It is simpler to calculate the A/FR as the code review time divided by the sum of the compile and test time. Using this approach, A/FR = 29/(5 + 10) = 1.93, which is the same as the answer found in the preceding paragraph. These calculations are also described in the Project Plan Summary Instructions in Table 19.2.

A/FR measures the relative amount of time spent finding defects before the first compile. Student data show that the A/FR is a good indicator of the likelihood of finding defects in test. In Figure 19.1, the A/FR values for 14 PSP students are plotted against the number of defects/KLOC they found in test. These data were for a total of 140 programs.

When A/FR is less than 1, program testing generally finds many defects. Although this is not guaranteed, most programs in this range will have a fairly high number of test defects/KLOC. Also, from Figure 19.1, it is clear that processes with A/FRs above 2 have few if any test defects/KLOC. This suggests that processes with A/FRs above 2 are much more likely to produce defect-free products than are processes with A/FRs below 1. You should thus attempt to achieve A/FRs of 2 or more.

TABLE 19.1   PSP PROJECT PLAN SUMMARY

Student	Student X		Date	12/9/96
Program			Program #	15
Instructor	Mr. Z		Language	Ada

Summary	Plan	Actual	To Date
Minutes/LOC	5.48	4.60	5.35
LOC/Hour	10.95	13.04	11.21
Defects/KLOC	92.53	52.6	86.7
Yield	40.0	100.0%	45.5
A/FR	0.375	1.93	0.44

Program Size (LOC):			
Total New & Changed	49	57	392
Maximum Size	62		
Minimum Size	36		

Time in Phase (min.)	Plan	Actual	To Date	To Date %
Planning	17	20	140	6.7
Design	29	38	233	11.1
Code	116	119	911	43.4
Code Review	21	29	174	8.3
Compile	15	5	105	5.0
Test	41	10	289	13.8
Postmortem	30	41	247	11.7
Total	269	262	2099	100.0
Maximum Time	340			
Minimum Time	197			

Defects Injected	Plan	Actual	To Date	To Date %	Def./Hour
Planning					
Design	1		5	14.7	1.29
Code	4	3	28	82.4	1.84
Code Review					
Compile			1	2.9	
Test					
Total	5	3	34	100.0	

Defects Removed	Plan	Actual	To Date	To Date %	Def./Hour
Planning					
Design					
Code					
Code Review	2	5	15	44.1	5.17
Compile	2		13	38.2	7.43
Test	1		6	17.1	1.25
Total	5	3	34	100.0	

TABLE 19.2 PSP PROJECT PLAN SUMMARY INSTRUCTIONS

Purpose	This form holds the estimated and actual project data in a convenient and readily retrievable form.
Header	Enter the following: • Your name and today's date • The program name and number • The instructor's name • The language you will use to write the program
Minutes/LOC	Prior to development • Enter the Minutes/LOC planned for this project. Use the To Date rate from the most recent previous program. After development • Divide the total development time by the actual program size to get the actual and To Date Minutes/LOC. • For example, if the project took 196 minutes and you produced 29 LOC, the Minutes/LOC would be 196/29 = 6.76.
LOC/Hour	Prior to development • Calculate the LOC per hour planned for this program by dividing 60 by the Plan Minutes/LOC. After development • For Actual and To Date LOC/Hour, divide 60 by the Actual To Date Minutes/LOC. • For Actual Minutes/LOC of 6.76, Actual LOC/Hour are 60/6.76 = 8.88.
Defects/KLOC	Prior to development • Find the defects/KLOC To Date on the most recent previous program. • Use this as the Planned Defects/KLOC for this project. After development • Calculate the defects/KLOC actual and To Date for this program. • For Actual, multiply the total actual defects by 1000 and divide by the Actual Total New & Changed LOC. • Make a similar calculation for To Date. • With 17 defects to date and 153 Total New & Changed LOC, defects/KLOC To Date = 1000*17/153 = 111.11
Yield	Calculate the plan, actual, and to date yield. Yield = 100* (defects removed before compile) / (defects injected before compile), so with 5 injected and 4 found, yield = 100*4/5 = 80.0%.
A/FR	*Calculate the plan, actual, and To Date A/FR* *For actual, for example, take the ratio of the actual code review time and divide by the sum of the actual compile and test times.* *For review time of 29 minutes, compile time of 5 minutes, and test time of 10 minutes, A/FR = 29/(5 + 10) = 1.93.*

(Continued)

TABLE 19.2 (*Continued*)

Program size (LOC)	Prior to development • Enter under plan the estimated Total, Maximum, and Minimum New & Changed LOC. After development • Count and enter the Actual New & Changed LOC. • For To Date, add Actual New & Changed LOC to the To Date New & Changed LOC for the previous program.
Time in Phase Plan	For Total development time, multiply Total New & Changed LOC by Minutes/LOC. For Maximum time, multiply the Maximum size by Minutes/LOC. For Minimum time, multiply the Minimum size by Minutes/LOC. From the Project Plan Summary for the most recent program, find the To Date % values for each phase. Using the To Date % from the previous program, calculate the plan time for each phase.
Actual	At job completion, enter the actual time in minutes spent in each development phase. Get these data from the time log.
To Date	For each phase, enter the sum of actual time and the To Date time from the most recent previous program.
To Date %	For each phase, enter 100 times the To Date time for that phase divided by the Total To Date time.
Defects Injected Plan	Before development, estimate the total number of defects to be injected in the program. The value is Plan Defects/KLOC times the Plan Total New & Changed LOC for this program divided by 1000. For example, with a Plan Defects/KLOC of 75.9 and a Plan New & Changed LOC of 75, Plan Total defects = 75.9*75/1000 = 5.69, so use 6. Before development, estimate the defects injected by phase using the estimate total defects and the To Date % defect injected distribution from the previous program.
Actual	After development, find and enter the actual number of defects injected in each phase.
To Date	For each phase, enter the sum of the actual defects and the To Date defects from the most recent program.
To Date %	For each phase, enter 100 times the To Date defects for that phase divided by the total To Date defects.
Defects/hour	Calculate the defects injected per hour for design and code. For design, for example, multiply 60 times the design defects To Date and divide by the design time To Date = 60*5/95 = 1.54 defects/hour.

(*Continued*)

TABLE 19.2 (*Continued*)

Defects Removed Plan	In the total row, enter the estimated total defects. Using the To Date % values from the most recent program, calculate the plan defects removed for each phase.
Actual	After development, find and enter the actual number of defects removed in each phase.
To Date	For each phase, enter the sum of the actual defects and the To Date defects from the most recent programs.
To Date %	For each phase, enter 100 times the To Date defects for that phase divided by the total To Date defects.
Defects/hour	Calculate the defects removed per hour for code review, compile, and test. For test, example, multiply 60 times the test defects To Date and divide by the test time To Date = 60*6/279 = 1.29 defects/hour.

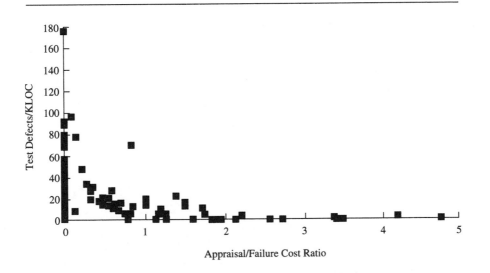

FIGURE 19.1 TEST DEFECTS VS. A/FR

Data from one company show how effective A/FR can be in judging product quality. Figure 19.2 shows a plot of the number of defects found in the unit test of six product components versus A/FR. Figure 19.3 shows the numbers of defects found during integration, system test, and customer use of these same components. Notice that one of the low A/FR components had relatively few defects in unit test but a lot were found later. Obviously, the unit testing had not been very thorough. Figure 19.4 plots the defects found in compile versus the number of defects found after compile. Clearly, when more defects were found in compile, more were also found in subsequent testing and use. The message is clear: If you want to reduce test defects, you must clean up your programs before starting to compile. The component with the highest number of compile defects had the most defects in every subsequent process phase. It also had the most defects in the product delivered to the customer.

To show the impact of early defect removal on development time, Figure 19.5 shows test hours plotted against A/FR. Here, the two components with the lowest A/FRs took 140 and 245 hours in test, while all the others took from 10 to 40 hours. Figure 19.6 shows the test hours per KLOC. With a low-quality process, testing took 80 to 100 hours per KLOC; with a higher quality process, testing took about 20 hours. This difference of 60 to 80 test hours per KLOC can be very significant when you work on products of 100,000 LOC or more. The added cost of a poor-quality PSP would then be 6,000 to 8,000 additional hours of testing, or 3

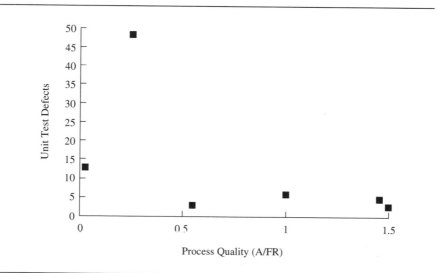

FIGURE 19.2 UNIT TEST DEFECTS VS. PROCESS QUALITY

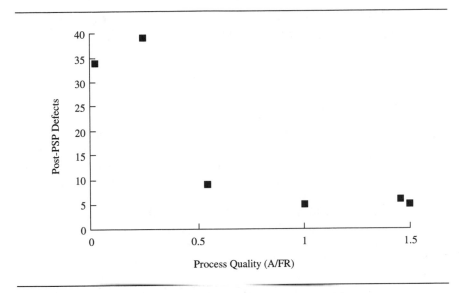

FIGURE 19.3 POST-PSP DEFECTS VS. PROCESS QUALITY

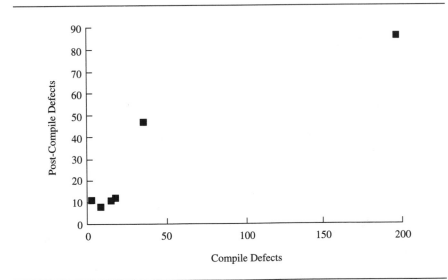

FIGURE 19.4 COMPILE DEFECTS VS. POST-COMPILE DEFECTS

to 4 wasted years of programmer time. On the multi-million LOC products that will soon be common, this could be the difference between an on-time successful product and a total failure.

Using the Appraisal/Failure Ratio

To achieve A/FRs above 2.0, review historical compile and test times and plan to spend at least twice that amount of time in the next code review. You can increase A/FR by merely spending more time reviewing the code. Unless you find defects, however, this will not improve program quality. It is thus important to productively use review time in finding defects.

As long as your yield has not reached the 80% to 100% range, continue to increase A/FR. You must not do this, however, by merely putting in more time. Review the defect data for your recently developed programs and devise ways to find all the defects you most frequently miss. If you are not sure how to do this, reread the material in Chapter 14.

After determining how to find these frequently missed defects, insert appropriate steps in the code review checklist. Finally, follow these review steps when you do the code review. If you do all of this, you will take more review time, find more defects, and increase A/FR. You will also almost certainly reduce the num-

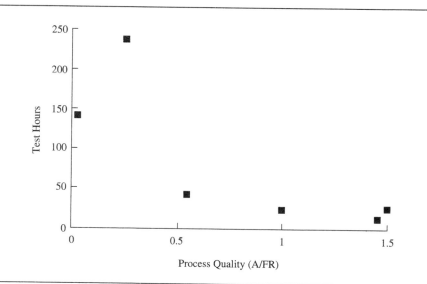

FIGURE 19.5 TEST HOURS VS. PROCESS QUALITY

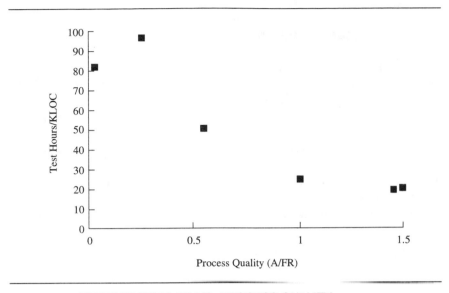

FIGURE 19.6 TEST HOURS/KLOC VS. PROCESS QUALITY

ber of defects you find in compile and test. This will save a lot of testing time, reduce failure costs, and produce higher quality products.

19.7   Improving Review Rates

Don't worry about defect/hour code review rates until you consistently find almost all defects before compile and test. Continue checking the defect data to see what review steps should have found the defects that were found in compile and test. Also, continue to update your personal code review checklist to find these defects.

Once you find most of the defects in code review, however, think about improving the code review rates. To do this, identify any review steps that neither find nor miss defects. Next, reexamine your reasons for including these steps in the first place. If these issues are no longer a problem, skip the steps. On the other hand, if you feel these checks are still important, combine several of them so you can do them more quickly. With each program, continue to monitor the defect data and reinstate any review steps that would have caught defects you later missed. When steps are not effective, however, do not hesitate to drop them.

19.8   Calculating the True Cost of Quality

For the PSP, the simplified COQ calculations are adequate. When you work on larger development projects, however, you may want to use more precise COQ measures.

To calculate the true failure and appraisal costs, you must break the review, compile, and test times into their respective appraisal and failure components. For example, we can label the compile time when no defects were found as compile (appraisal) or C_A and the defect fix time during compile as compile (failure) or C_F. Thus, $C_F + C_A = C$, the total compile time. For the review and test times, $R_F + R_A = R$, the total review time and $T_F + T_A = T$, the total test time.

Using these parameters, you can now calculate the precise appraisal and failure COQ as follows:

Appraisal COQ = 100*($R_A + C_A + T_A$)/(total development time)
Failure COQ   = 100*($R_F + C_F + T_F$)/(total development time)

The following example uses the data in the Project Plan Summary in Table 19.1 and the Defect Recording Log in Table 19.3. First, calculate the values for R_A, C_A, T_A, R_F, C_F, and T_F as follows:

- To find R_A, first calculate R_F from the Defect Recording Log as the sum of the fix times for the defects removed in code review: $R_F = 2 + 8 + 1 = 11$.

- Next, find R_A as $R - R_F = 29 - 11 = 18$.

- Since no defects were found in compile, all compile time is appraisal time. Thus $C_A = 5$ and $C_F = 0$.

- Since no defects were found in test, all test time is also appraisal time; so T_A, $= 10$ and $F_F = 0$.

Now, with these values, we calculate the appraisal and failure costs as follows:

Appraisal COQ = 100*($R_A + C_A + T_A$)/(total development time)
                    = 100*(18 + 5 + 10) / 262 = 100*33/262 = 12.60%

Failure COQ   = 100*($R_F + C_F + T_F$)/(total development time)
                    = 100*(11 + 0 + 0)/262 = 100*11/262 = 4.20%

These values are somewhat different from those calculated before. They also give a significantly higher A/FR of 3.0 instead of 1.93. Since these more accurate A/FR and COQ values are quite sensitive to the defect repair times, you should not use this method unless you are measuring defect fix times with a stopwatch. You will also want to set a higher A/FR target since an A/FR of 2.0 will now likely result in too many test defects.

```
Defect Types
10  Documentation    60   Checking
20  Syntax           70   Data
30  Build, Package   80   Function
40  Assignment       90   System
50  Interface       100   Environment
```

TABLE 19.3 EXAMPLE DEFECT RECORDING LOG

Student ___Student X_____ Date ___12/9/96___

Instructor___Mr. Z_____ Program # ____15___

Date	Number	Type	Inject	Remove	Fix Time	Fix Defect
12/9	1	40	Code	CR	2	

Description: ___Missing declaration of Set_X_____

Date	Number	Type	Inject	Remove	Fix Time	Fix Defect
	2	80	Design	CR	8	

Description: ___Forgot to step while-loop only on uneven_____

Date	Number	Type	Inject	Remove	Fix Time	Fix Defect
	3	20	Code	CR	1	

Description: ___Left off;_____

Date	Number	Type	Inject	Remove	Fix Time	Fix Defect

Description: _____

Date	Number	Type	Inject	Remove	Fix Time	Fix Defect

Description: _____

Date	Number	Type	Inject	Remove	Fix Time	Fix Defect

Description: _____

Date	Number	Type	Inject	Remove	Fix Time	Fix Defect

Description: _____

Date	Number	Type	Inject	Remove	Fix Time	Fix Defect

Description: _____

19.9   Summary

The cost of quality (COQ) measures the quality of a software process in terms of three components: appraisal, failure, and prevention costs. The PSP uses simplified COQ calculations. Appraisal cost is calculated by dividing the code review time by total development time and multiplying by 100. This calculation ignores fix times during code review. Failure cost is calculated by dividing the sum of compile and test time by the total development time and multiplying by 100. This calculation ignores defect-free compile and test times.

The appraisal/failure ratio (A/FR) measures process quality. It is calculated by dividing the appraisal COQ by the failure COQ. The A/FR indicates the relative amount of time spent finding and fixing defects before the first compile. The value of A/FR also indicates the likelihood that the program will have defects found in test. A/FR values below 1 generally indicate that many defects will be found in test, while values above 2 generally indicate that few if any defects will be found in test. When few defects are found in test, this generally indicates that the program has few remaining defects.

While the simplified COQ calculations will be adequate for now, you may want to use more accurate COQ calculations when you work on larger projects.

19.10   Assignment 19

For the assignment, determine the value of A/FR for all the programs you have written this semester. Also find the number of test defects/KLOC for these programs and show the A/FR and test defects/KLOC on a plot like that shown in Figure 19.1.

Submit copies of those Time Recording Log and Weekly Activity Summary sheets you have not previously submitted. Also, turn in completed copies of the PSP Project Plan Summary form, the Defect Recording Logs, and the Code Review Checklist for every program. Include Plan, Actual, and To Date values for development times, defects injected, defects removed, yield, and A/FR.

20

A Personal Commitment
to Quality

Quality work is important to your employers, your customers, and to you. This chapter discusses why you should establish quality as your highest personal priority.

20.1   The Importance of Quality

As a software engineer, the quality of the programs you produce will be critically important to your employers and to your customers. Software is used in many demanding applications, and software defects can cause economic damage and even physical harm. When the programs you write are used to do financial work or word processing, their defects can be annoying and even costly, but nobody is likely to be killed or maimed. When your software is part of a system that flies airplanes, drives automobiles, manages air traffic, runs factories, or controls power plants, your defects could have untold and possibly dangerous consequences.

People have been killed by software defects [Leveson]. While there have not been many fatalities so far, the numbers will almost certainly increase. This is because, in spite of all the problems, software does not wear out or deteriorate. It is thus ideally suited for critical applications involving safety. In one example, when today's nuclear power plants were originally constructed, the control instruments were electromechanical. That was the most reliable technology known at the time. Over the years, however, these early instruments have gradually deteriorated and had to be replaced. Today, the most reliable control systems are computerized. While the first generation of nuclear controls was simple and used relatively little software, the more sophisticated controls of the future will involve increasing amounts of code. This means that software quality will be progressively more important to those who build and manage nuclear power plants. It will also be important to anyone who lives nearby.

The same trend applies in just about every field. Computerized control systems are so versatile, economical, and reliable that we will see them in almost every aspect of our lives. It is thus important that all software engineers recognize that their work could have serious impacts on the health, safety, and welfare of many people.

20.2   The Increasing Risks of Poor Quality

Any defect in a small part of a large program could potentially cause serious problems. It may seem unlikely that a silly error in a remote part of a large system could be potentially disastrous, but in fact these are the most frequent sources of trouble. The reason is that software systems are unlike mechanical systems, where engineers can build in mechanical safeguards. By suitably designing mechanical safety systems, engineers can make many kinds of accidents or failures practically impossible. Common examples here are the safety harnesses worn by punch press operators. The press is mechanically coupled to the harness so that, as the machine stamps, for example, the operators cannot hold their hands inside.

With software systems, however, the safety systems are *also* generally made of software. Software protections, however, are only effective when the software obeys the system rules and conventions. This means that software defects that cause these conventions to be breached could have unpredictable consequences. While system safety should be addressed at the system level and it should use both hardware and software protections, this is not always practical. Therefore, for truly safe systems, we must strive for defect-free software.

The design of large multiuser real-time systems can be enormously complex. These complex design issues, however, get a lot of attention. While the difficult design issues are usually studied, reviewed, and tested with great care, the simpler design problems get much less focus. As a result, the most common cause of problems with large-scale software systems is simple oversights and goofs. These are typically silly mistakes that were made by individual software engineers. While most of these silly mistakes will get caught in integration and system test, some number get all the way through the testing process and into operational use.

The problem is that software engineers often confuse simple with easy. They feel that their frequent simple mistakes will be simple to find. They are often surprised to learn that such trivial errors as omitting a punctuation mark, misnaming a parameter, incorrectly setting a condition, or misterminating a loop could escape testing and cause serious problems in actual use. These, however, are the kinds of things that cause almost all the problems software suppliers spend millions of dollars finding and fixing.

The quality of large programs depends on the quality of the smaller programs of which they are built. Thus, to produce high-quality large programs, every software engineer who develops one or more of its module parts must do high-quality work. This means that all these engineers must be personally committed to quality. When they are so committed, they will track and manage their defects with such care that few if any defects will later be found in integration, system testing, or by the customers.

When engineers are personally committed to quality, they are proud of their achievements. They know how much code they have produced and how many defects others have found in their products. Engineers have told me how long it had been since anyone found a defect in any program they had produced. When software engineers are not personally committed to quality, they treat it as unimportant. They will tell you that testing will find most of the defects and that the few that remain will be easily found and fixed. Not surprisingly, when engineers feel this way, they are unlikely to produce quality products.

20.3   Making a Commitment to Quality

Many software engineers view software defects as bugs. They treat them as something that crawled in from somewhere, not as something they are responsible for. This is wrong. Defects are injected by engineers and, when a program has a defect, it is defective! The engineer who produced that program produced a defective product. When engineers are committed to quality, they care. And when they care, they are more careful in their work. When they are more careful, they produce better products.

The first step in producing quality software is thus to decide that quality is important. The second step is to establish the goal of producing defect-free programs. To have any chance of meeting this goal, you must measure the quality of your programs and take steps to improve that quality.

As humans, we all inject occasional defects. The challenge is to manage our fallibility. This, however, is a never-ending struggle. You can't just learn a few quality tricks and relax. The software products of the future will be progressively more sophisticated and complex. The problems you face will thus constantly change. The question is not whether you can do defect-free work but whether you care enough to continue doing it. Not only will this make you and your organization more productive, but also you will get more satisfaction from your work.

20.4 Your Personal Objectives

What do you want from your life? This is a big question that many people have trouble answering. A few points are worth considering as you think about the answer.

One way to get satisfaction from a job is to have status or power. People can get this by being a boss or being put in charge of an important service. Power and status can also be indirect like making a lot of money, working for an important company, or driving a fancy car. These are all parts of "being" someone.

While there is nothing wrong with status, it is temporary. You may hold an important job for a while but, sooner or later, your next step will be down. Losing status can be a crisis. Some people are devastated when they first lose an important job. It is easy to confuse the importance of a job with personal importance.

I have known managers who were crushed by a demotion. They had built an image of themselves as important people. As long as they held a big job, everybody treated them as important. The minute they lost that job, however, they were just like everyone else. Nobody cared what they said and they stopped getting special treatment. They had lost the corner office and no longer had a secretary. This can be such a severe shock that some people have nervous breakdowns, heart attacks, or family crises. Their reward was status and it is gone.

20.5 The Rewards of Accomplishment

The need is to decide what it is that you want. Think ahead. When you ultimately retire, what would a satisfying life look like? I suggest that what you have done will be far more rewarding than what you have been. If, for example, you plan to do engineering work, you probably have the instincts of a builder. Maybe you will build systems or components. You could end up building methods or processes. Or you might have a scientific bent and build theories or do research to build fundamental knowledge.

Whatever you build, however, quality will be key. You will get little satisfaction from sloppy work. Somehow, even if no one else finds out, you will know you did a sloppy job. This will destroy your pride in the work and it will limit your satisfaction with life. You cannot honestly say to yourself that you really believe in quality but you will just get by this one time. There are always lots of excuses. You might even satisfy others with an expedient answer, but you will never satisfy yourself.

When you do quality work, you will be proud. Even if no one else knows, you know you did a first-class job and you are satisfied that you did your best. The surprising thing is that quality work gets known. It may take a long time, but sooner or later quality work is recognized. Whether you know it, you will get credit for the quality of your work.

So ask yourself this question: "Do I want to feel proud of what I do?" Most people would answer yes. But if you really mean it, you need to set personal standards and strive to meet them. When you meet these standards, raise them and strive again. Challenge yourself to do superior work and you will be surprised at what you can accomplish.

Reference

[Leveson] Leveson, Nancy G. *Safeware, System Safety and Computers.* Reading, MA: Addison-Wesley, 1995.

Index

Supplements Page

In *Introduction to the Personal Software Process*, Watts S. Humphrey provides a sequence of exercises to demonstrate the personal software process (PSP) and its use.

Support Material on the World Wide Web is available for students and individual readers to help in doing these exercises and in producing the required analyses and reports. The material contains kits for doing the assignments called for in the text, including copies of the forms illustrated in the book, and data analysis spreadsheets for the exercises. Readers will find the material a practical addition to the book itself. It can be accessed at the Addison-Wesley web site at the following address:

http://www.awl.com/cseng/authors/humphrey/intropsp

An **Instructor's Guide Package**, containing a hardcopy guide and a diskette, is available free of charge for use by instructors where *An Introduction to the Personal Software Process* has been adopted as a required text. The Instructor's Guide includes suggested classroom quizzes and answers, lectures, and copies of the course assignment kits. The Instructor's Guide diskette contains electronic copies of the lecture overheads and spreadsheets to review and analyze student data.

Requirements:	The Instructor's Diskette requires an IBM PC or PC-compatible that can use files from Microsoft Windows 3.1 versions of Word 6.0, Excel 4.0, and PowerPoint 3.0 and has 5.0 MB of available disk space. No Macintosh version is available.
Ordering Information:	Instructors should contact their local Addison-Wesley representative to request the Instructor's Guide Package, or call Addison-Wesley's Computer Science Marketing Department at 1-617-944-3700 ext. 2310.
More Information:	To obtain up-to-date information about this book, its supplements, and other works of interest to software engineering educators and practitioners, access the latest information about Addison-Wesley books from our World Wide Web page: http://www.awl.com/cseng/authors

Books by Watts S. Humphrey

Introduction to the Personal Software Process[SM]
This workbook provides a hands-on introduction to the basic disciplines of software engineering. Designed as a programming-course supplement to integrate the PSP into a university curriculum, the book may also be adapted for use by industrial groups or for self-improvement. Applying the book's exercises you learn to manage your time effectively and to monitor the quality of your work.

      0-201-54809-7   1997   Paperback   278 pages

Managing Technical People: Innovation, Teamwork, and the Software Process
This insightful book, drawing on the author's extensive experience as a senior manager of software development at IBM, describes proven techniques for managing technical professionals. He shows specifically how to identify, motivate, and organize innovative people, while tying leadership practices to improvements in the software process.

      0-201-54597-7   1997   Paperback   326 pages

A Discipline for Software Engineering
This book scales down to a personal level successful methods developed by the author for managers and organizations to evaluate and improve their software capabilities. His concern here is to help individual software practitioners develop the skills and habits they need to plan, track, and analyze large and complex projects and to develop high-quality products.

      0-201-54610-8   1995   Hardcover   789 pages

Managing the Software Process
This landmark book introduces the author's methods, now commonly practiced in industry, for improving software development and maintenance processes. Emphasizing the basic principles and priorities of the software process, the book's sections are organized in a natural way to guide organizations through needed improvement activities.

      0-201-18095-2   1989   Hardcover   494 pages

These books are available where technical books are sold or directly from Addison-Wesley at 1-800-822-6339. Check out Addison-Wesley's web site: http://www.awl.com/cseng